T0203230

Metaheuristics for Vehicle Routing Problems

Metaheuristics Set

coordinated by
Nicolas Monmarché and Patrick Siarry

Volume 3

Metaheuristics for Vehicle Routing Problems

Nacima Labadie
Christian Prins
Caroline Prodhon

WILEY

First published 2016 in Great Britain and the United States by ISTE Ltd and John Wiley & Sons, Inc.

ISTE Ltd
27-37 St George's Road
London SW19 4EU
UK

www.iste.co.uk

John Wiley & Sons, Inc.
111 River Street
Hoboken, NJ 07030
USA

www.wiley.com

Library of Congress Control Number: 2015959666

British Library Cataloguing-in-Publication Data
A CIP record for this book is available from the British Library
ISBN 978-1-84821-811-6

Contents

Notations and Abbreviations   ix

Introduction xiii

Chapter 1. General Presentation of Vehicle Routing Problems . . .   1

1.1. Logistics management and combinatorial optimization   1
   1.1.1. History of logistics   2
   1.1.2. Logistics as a science   5
   1.1.3. Combinatorial optimization   5
1.2. Vehicle routing problems   6
   1.2.1. Problems in transportation optimization   6
   1.2.2. Vehicle routing problems in other contexts   7
   1.2.3. Characteristics of vehicle routing problems   7
   1.2.4. The capacitated vehicle routing problem 11
1.3. Conclusion 13

Chapter 2. Simple Heuristics and Local Search Procedures 15

2.1. Simple heuristics 16
   2.1.1. Constructive heuristics 16
   2.1.2. Two-phase methods 19
   2.1.3. Best-of approach and randomization 22
2.2. Local search 23
   2.2.1. Principle 23
   2.2.2. Classical moves 24
   2.2.3. Feasibility tests 25
   2.2.4. General approach from Vidal *et al.* 28
   2.2.5. Multiple neighborhoods 30
   2.2.6. Very constrained problems 33

2.2.7. Acceleration techniques   33
2.2.8. Complex moves   36
2.3. Conclusion   37

**Chapter 3. Metaheuristics Generating a Sequence
of Solutions**   39

3.1. Simulated annealing (SA)   39
  3.1.1. Principle   39
  3.1.2. Simulated annealing in vehicle routing problems   40
3.2. Greedy randomized adaptive search procedure: GRASP   41
  3.2.1. Principle   41
  3.2.2. GRASP in vehicle routing problems   43
3.3. Tabu search   44
  3.3.1. Principle   44
  3.3.2. Tabu search in vehicle routing problems   45
3.4. Variable neighborhood search   47
  3.4.1. Principle   47
  3.4.2. Variable neighborhood search in vehicle routing problems   49
3.5. Iterated local search   50
  3.5.1. Principle   50
  3.5.2. Iterated local search in vehicle routing problems   52
3.6. Guided local search   54
  3.6.1. Principle   54
  3.6.2. Guided local search in vehicle routing problems   55
3.7. Large neighborhood search   56
  3.7.1. Principle   56
  3.7.2. Large neighborhood search in vehicle routing problems   58
3.8. Transitional forms   59
  3.8.1. Evolutionary local search principle   59
  3.8.2. Application to vehicle routing problems   60
3.9. Selected examples   61
  3.9.1. GRASP for the location-routing problem   61
  3.9.2. Granular tabu search for the CVRP   65
  3.9.3. Adaptive large neighborhood search for the pickup and delivery
  problem with time windows   69
3.10. Conclusion   74

Chapter 4. Metaheuristics Based on a Set of Solutions   77

4.1. Genetic algorithm and its variants   77
  4.1.1. Genetic algorithm   77
  4.1.2. Memetic algorithm   79
  4.1.3. Memetic algorithm with population management   79
  4.1.4. Genetic algorithm and its variants in vehicle routing problems . . .   80

4.2. Scatter search   82
  4.2.1. Scatter search principle   82
  4.2.2. Scatter search in vehicle routing problems   83
4.3. Path relinking   83
  4.3.1. Principle   84
  4.3.2. Path relinking in vehicle routing problems   85
4.4. Ant colony optimization   86
  4.4.1. Principle   86
  4.4.2. ACO in vehicle routing problems   89
4.5. Particle swarm optimization   89
  4.5.1. Principle   89
  4.5.2. PSO in vehicle routing problems   90
4.6. Other approaches and their use in vehicle routing problems   91
4.7. Selected examples   92
  4.7.1. Scatter search for the periodic capacitated arc routing problem . . .   92
  4.7.2. PR for the muti-depot periodic VRP   97
  4.7.3. Unified genetic algorithm for a wide class of vehicle
  routing problems   101
4.8. Conclusion   106

Chapter 5. Metaheuristics Hybridizing Various Components   109

5.1. Hybridizing metaheuristics   109
  5.1.1. Principle   110
  5.1.2. Application to vehicle routing problems   111
  5.1.3. Selected examples   112
5.2. Matheuristics   122
  5.2.1. Principle   123
  5.2.2. Application to vehicle routing problems   124
  5.2.3. Selected examples   128
5.3. Conclusion   144

Conclusion   145

Bibliography   149

Index   167

Notations and Abbreviations

Here is a non-exhaustive list of the most common notations and abbreviations used in the book.

Notations

A :   set of arcs.

c_{ij} :   traveling cost between nodes i and j.

d_i :   demand of customer i.

E :   set of edges.

$f(S)$:   cost of solution S.

G :   a complete graph.

K :   set of identical vehicles.

n :   number of customers.

$N(S)$:   subset of solutions close to S in term of structure (neighborhood).

Q :   vehicles capacity.

R_i :   route i.

S :   a solution.

T :   tour or sequence of customers.

V :   set of nodes.

Abbreviations related to problems

CARP :   capacitated arc routing problem.

CCVRP :   cumulative capacitated vehicle routing problem.

CVRP :   capacitated vehicle routing problem.

DARP :   dial-a-ride problem.

HFVRP :   heterogeneous fleet vehicle routing problem.

IRP :   inventory routing problem.

LRP :   location-routing problem.

LRP-2E : two-echelon location-routing problem.

MDVRP :   multi-depot vehicle routing problem.

OVRP :   open vehicle routing problem.

PCARP :   periodic capacitated arc routing problem.

PDPTW :   pick up and delivery vehicle routing problem with time windows.

PVRP :   periodic vehicle routing problem.

RCPSP :   resource-constrained project scheduling problem.

SCP :   set covering problem.

SPP :   set partitioning problem.

SDVRP :   vehicle routing problem with split deliveries.

TOP :   team orienteering problem.

TSP :   traveling salesman problem.

TTRP :   truck and trailer routing problem.

VRP-2E : two-echelon vehicle routing problem.

VRPs :   family of vehicle routing problems.

VRPTW :   vehicle routing problem with time windows.

Abbreviations related to methods

ACO :   ant colony optimization.

ALNS :   adaptive large neighborhood search.

ELS :   evolutionary local search.

GA :   genetic algorithm.

GLS :   guided local search.

GRASP :   greedy randomized adaptive search procedure

GTS :   granular tabu search (also guided tabu search).

HGSADC :   hybrid genetic search with adaptive diversity control.

ILS :   iterated local search.

LNS :   large neighborhood search

LS :   local search.

MA :   memetic algorithm.

MA|PM :   memetic algorithm with population management.

PSO :   particle swarm optimization.

PR :   path relinking.

RVNS :   reduced variable neighborhood search.

SA :   simulated annealing.

SS :   scatter search.

TS :   tabu search.

VND :   variable neighborhood descent.

VNS :   variable neighborhood search.

VLSN :   very large scale neighborhood search.

Introduction

Unlike heuristics, which are problem-dependent techniques which try to take full advantage of the features of the problem at hand but which usually get trapped in a local optimum when followed by a local search, metaheuristics can be defined as solution methods that control the exploration of a solution space by problem-independent techniques with higher level strategies. This allows them to explore the solution space more extensively with the aim of escaping from local optima and thus a hopefully obtain a better solution. These approaches include any scheme that resorts, for example, to one or more neighborhood structures, building or destroying procedures or combining components of several solutions. Notwithstanding their general structure, it is necessary to adapt the techniques according to the problem to solve by some fine-tuning of their intrinsic parameters. Metaheuristic methods have proved to be particularly effective for solving many types of complex problems.

This book is dedicated to these methods developed to one of the most important and studied categories of combinatorial optimization problems: the family of vehicle routing problems (VRPs). The aim of the basic version also called capacitated VRP (CVRP) is to determine the optimal set of routes to be performed by a fleet of capacitated vehicles to serve the demand of a given customer set.

More than 15 years have elapsed since Dantzig and Ramser introduced the problem in 1959 [DAN 59], and the number of models and solution methods has experienced a strong growth as exposed in [LAP 09]. Although the CVRP still attracts researchers, many variants are now investigated. This interest is motivated by two main concerns:

– this class of problems has a high practical relevance;

– it is challenging to solve given its considerable difficulty.

Despite the abundant activity on VRPs, the current exact methods are limited to problems of about 100 customers [BAL 08a], while real cases can reach 1,000 clients.

Therefore, a large number of metaheuristics have been proposed to solve very different problems of vehicle routing, as stated by the surveys periodically published on the subject. From procedures with tabu to hybrid approaches combining heuristic and exact methods, metaheuristics remain the favorite methods for dealing with realistic cases.

Several books are available on either metaheuristics [DRÉ 03, SIA 14] or VRPs [TOT 02] but, to the best of our knowledge, the only books addressing these two topics simultaneously are published PhD dissertations [EUC 12] or books with contributed chapters [GOL 08]. The aim here is more to provide a book for people wishing to discover and quickly master metaheuristics dedicated to VRPs. The particularity is to combine a tutorial with algorithms, examples, and a quick overview of the state-of-the art for such methods developed in the last decades for the CVRP and some of its main variants.

The key points are to present:

– a progressive approach, from the basics to several recent and efficient methods;

– different metaheuristics for the same VRP and, conversely, the way of adapting the same metaheuristic template to several problems;

– algorithms allowing the readers to implement the methods on a computer;

– an up-to-date bibliography focusing on the references which have a real interest.

The book consists of five chapters. After this introduction, the first chapter gives a general presentation that intends to make the readers more familiar with the related fields of logistics and combinatorial optimization.

This preamble is followed, in Chapter 2, with a description of significant heuristic methods classically applied to provide feasible solutions quickly, and local improvement moves widely used to search for enhanced solutions. The overview of these fundamentals allows appreciating the core of the work devoted to an analysis of metaheuristic methods for VRPs. Those methods are exposed according to their feature of working either on a sequence of single solutions, or on a set of solutions, or even by hybridizing metaheuristic approaches with other kinds of methods (mixed integer programs, mathematical decompositions, etc.).

Thus, Chapter 3 begins with the class that works on a single solution at a time, making it evolve through a particular iterative process. This kind of exploration requires us to define at least one neighborhood to jump from an incumbent solution to another area of the solution space. Eight approaches are presented in this chapter, namely simulated annealing, greedy adaptive search procedure, tabu search, variable neighborhood search, iterated local search, guided local search, adaptive large neighborhood search and transitional forms such as evolutionary local search.

Chapter 4 exposes methods operating on a set of solutions. Their feature is to generate new solutions by either combining existing ones or by making agents cooperate through a learning process. Two main variants are put forward: those that combine solutions selected from a population such as genetic algorithms, memetic algorithms, scatter search and path relinking; the ones that make cooperate homogenous agents in their environment such as particle swarm optimization and ant colony optimization.

Chapter 5 is devoted to two main classes of hybrid methods: either by combining components from several stand alone metaheuristics, or by crossing exact algorithms with metaheuristics (leading to the so called matheuristics). The main motivation of this trend is to take advantage of the complementarity of different optimization strategies and cooperate in synergy.

Finally, the Conclusion closes the book and draws up some perspectives of the research on VRPs. In the three chapters detailing the different class of metaheuristics, several selected implementations of methods dedicated to typical VRPs are given as illustrative examples.

General Presentation of Vehicle Routing Problems

Vehicle routing problems (VRPs) represent an important family of problems encountered in the fields of logistics, as well as in many other applications. In general, a number of customers have to be served with a fleet of vehicles. They can be modeled as an integer programming problem, solved by combinatorial optimization tools. However, exact methods cannot solve instances that consider a large set of customers, as encountered in most real cases. It is, therefore, often necessary to resort to approximate paradigms generally carried out through metaheuristics.

This first chapter introduces what the logistics management and the combinatorial optimization are, before giving a formal definition of the CVRP, with notations useful throughout the remainder of the book.

1.1. Logistics management and combinatorial optimization

In the last few decades, a great interest has grown up in the area of logistics among both industry and academia, for different reasons [BRA 98]. First, companies are facing fierce competition in today's global markets. They need to innovate to keep their position, and they realize the savings that can be achieved by a better planning and management of their logistic systems.

Furthermore, the evolution of lifestyles is significant. Modes of consumption are changing and expectations of consumers switch to products with short lifecycles, and the advancement in communications and transportation technologies, such as mobile communication and overnight delivery, motivates continuous development of the management of logistic systems.

These changes attract attention of the academic community, whose approach consists of determining characteristics of the problems and developing solution methodologies, as well as providing specific guarantees of effectiveness.

1.1.1. *History of logistics*

Logistics is not a recent trend in managing the flow of goods from an origin to a destination, with the aim to meet some requirements. Logistics made an important stride during the construction of the pyramids in ancient Egypt, for example. It played a key role in global sea trade with the invention of rowing vessels around 300 B.C. Logistics was also one of the main factors for the victory of most wars throughout history.

In military context, logistics is responsible for supplying the troops. It deals with the inventory management and transportation. However, this type of requirement also predominates in carriers and wholesalers activities. Thus, it is natural that modern logistics appears in industry.

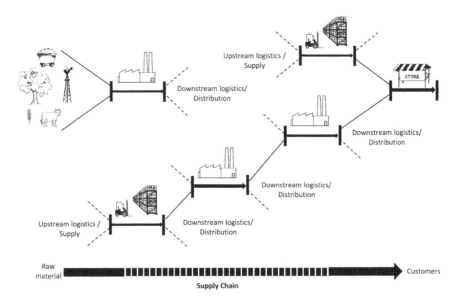

Figure 1.1. *Example of a supply chain*

Nowadays, the function extends from production to distribution, leading to the supply chain (Figure 1.1). In this chain, upstream activities take place prior to a particular link, when the latter orders for material to suppliers in the aim to bring its added value. On the contrary, downstream activities involve the sale of a material to other businesses, governments or private individuals. The extreme link in the upstream part usually concerns raw materials, while the extreme downstream link is related to the final customer. However, each other link in the midstream is both customer of predecessor actors and supplier of successors. Midstream can be a manufacturer, a cooperative warehouse, a regional consolidation center, a city hub, local depot, etc.

Most of the freight transport in the chain is carried in containers, although bulk transport is used more for large volumes of durable goods. The reason is that this option is often the most efficient and cost-effective way to supply the products. However, for the smaller quantities generally required at the final destination, the supply chain is often less efficient. This characteristic is known as the "last mile problem", which can represent up to 28% of the total cost to move goods. In addition, if transport plays an important role in economic growth and globalization, it causes air pollution and a large amount of traffic. Hence, a good transport planning is essential to control the costs, as well as the flow and limit nuisances.

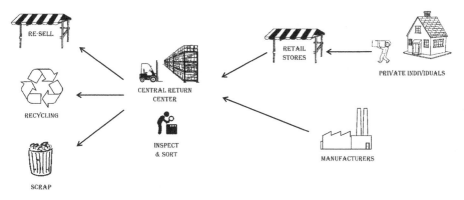

Figure 1.2. *Possible outline of a reverse logistics chain*

In an even more global view, the network also integrates reverse flows. These cover all operations related to the recycling of products and materials thrown away by the public or by industries (obsolete products, mixed waste and even hazardous). The so-called *reverse logistics* brings together the movements of products from consumers to producers through a distribution chain (Figure 1.2). The growing concern for integrating environmental requirements into green supply chain management concepts and practices makes it even more relevant. The reverse logistics process refers to activities undertaken to reduce, manage and dispose of waste from industrial activities. It meets the need to decommission the products after use and treat the destruction, by transforming or recycling in order to reduce costs, and valuing the recovered products. Several related activities, therefore, involve: collecting waste, the location of recycling points/storage, inventory management and integration of products from the collection at the related industries. It also includes the optimization of the Ecodesign to facilitate future recycling.

Other issues have arisen recently about *city logistics* which are obviously related to the last mile problem described before. In fact, the freight distribution in urban area has to deal with several aspects. First, traffic may be difficult because of congestion at some rush hours, which makes the travel time dependent on the time of the day. Another particularity is the accessibility constraint. It might be quite complicated to deliver the goods in some areas because of the lack of parking for example, or because of city restrictions on the use of trucks in favor to smaller vehicles. In the same vein, economic and environmental problem concerns might lead to choose alternative types of transport for urban freight distribution (such as electric vehicles), as well as to adopt new commercialization behaviors. For example, the growth of e-commerce brings new questions and some retail companies have studied the use of drones to deliver online purchased goods to consumers.

Hence, many activities are involved in the supply chain, from the network design, to logistics of transportation, passing through warehouse management, international commerce or information systems. Transportation is one of the main parts of logistics. It can be made through several modes such as air, rail, road, water, cable, pipeline and space and may require particular infrastructures (Figure 1.3). These include links in the network (roads, railways, canals or pipelines, for instance) and terminals such as airports, railway stations, warehouses and depots. A wide range of issues emerges in this context, sweeping topics as diverse as the routing, inventory, cross-docking or network structure.

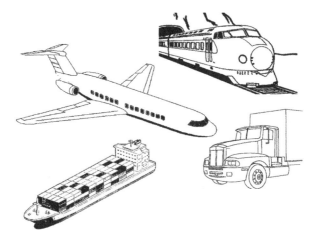

Figure 1.3. *Example of transportation modes*

1.1.2. *Logistics as a science*

The logistics function has risen to such an important place that it is now a profession in itself, and even a science. The goal in logistics management is to be efficient and cost-effective across the entire system [BRA 98]. Therefore, the objective is not simply to minimize locally transportation cost or reducing inventories. Every facility that has an impact on system effectiveness must be taken into consideration, from suppliers to retailers through manufacturing facilities, warehouses and distribution centers.

In fact, logistics management encompasses many of the firm's activities, from the strategic level through the tactical to the operational level:

– the strategic level deals with decisions that have usually a long-term effect. Concerning logistics, this includes, for instance, decisions regarding the number, location and capacities of warehouses and manufacturing plants;

– the tactical level typically includes decisions that are updated anywhere between once every quarter and once every year. This includes purchasing and production decisions, inventory policies and transportation strategies including the frequency with which customers are visited;

– the operational level refers to day-to-day decisions such as scheduling, routing and loading trucks.

Therefore, logistics activities obviously deserve to be recognized as a science, and this has begun to be true from the middle of the 20th Century [TAY 07].

1.1.3. *Combinatorial optimization*

The science of logistics can be seen as the study of the physical flow of products and services through the supply chain. Therefore, the chain can be seen as a network, or a graph, in which a flow has to go through, with some constraints that need to be encounter and an objective, often relative to a cost function, to optimize. Thus, most of the decision-making to manage the logistics can be taken by modeling the problem in terms of a mathematical program to optimize.

Optimization is a branch of mathematics particularly applied in operations research and management science. It consists of finding one or more best (optimal) solutions from all feasible solutions. Optimization problems can be divided into two categories depending on whether the variables are continuous or discrete. The latter case is known as a combinatorial optimization problem. Solving such problems can be a difficult task. The difficulty arises from the fact that feasible solutions belong to a finite but high cardinality set. In fact, finding a global optimum to the problem requires proving that a particular solution dominates all feasible points by arguments other than the calculus based on derivative approaches of convex programming. Therefore, different approaches exist. The simplest one relies on the enumerative techniques, but an exhaustive search is often not possible due to the time required. Other options are, for example, relaxation and decomposition techniques, and cutting planes approaches based on polyhedral combinatorics. An algorithm is usually required to search the solution space, and most often, it cannot find and prove the optimality in polynomial time. In such a case, the problems are said to be "NP-hard" (non-deterministic polynomial-time hard).

In fact, in many cases, combinatorial optimization problems are NP-hard. Consequently, metaheuristics are mainly developed for real-world problems, which often attain notably high levels of complexity, although they are not able to certify the optimality of the solutions they find.

1.2. Vehicle routing problems

Vehicle routing problems are well-spread combinatorial optimization problems. They can be encountered in various areas, even if their main application stands on logistics of transportation.

1.2.1. *Problems in transportation optimization*

Truckload transportation from sources to destinations represents a first family of transportation problems, where the amount of goods fully fills a vehicle (or a vehicle carries goods directly from the source to the destination, without any other service on the way). The shortest paths between these sources and destinations are computed, mainly through a graph where vertices correspond to intersections and the edges correspond to road segments, each weighted by the length of its road segment, for instance. Then, a typical transportation problem deals with sources, where a supply of some commodity is available, and destinations where the commodity is demanded. The first studies on this subject appeared in the 1930s. An example is Tolstoi who published an article called *Methods of finding the minimal total kilometrage in cargo-transportation planning in space*, for the freight between sources and destinations along the railway network of the Soviet Union [TOL 30].

In this book, transportation is considered as *less-than-truckload*: vehicle capacity is large enough to allow servicing several customers without returning to the depot. This leads to interesting combinatorial optimization problems which need to handle routing aspects. In fact, the classical vehicle routing problem (capacitated VRP – CVRP) is an important problem in the fields of logistics and transportation. It consists of the determination of the optimal set of routes to be performed by a vehicle fleet to serve the demand of a given set of customers. With the traveling salesman problem (TSP), it is one of the most important and studied combinatorial optimization problems. Theoretical research on vehicle routing started in 1959 by Dantzig and Ramser with the truck dispatching problem, and it was the beginning of a proliferation of work in this field.

1.2.2. *Vehicle routing problems in other contexts*

In fact, VRPs belong to a family of problems outreaching the field of transportation optimization, with applications in additional areas, particularly services. In such contexts, a vehicle is more a generic term to represent a mobile that visits a number of sites in order to complete certain tasks. The latter can be pick up or delivery tasks, as well repairs, meter reading or any other activity.

Therefore, a problem can be seen as a VRP when allowed movements describe a graph, and the result must be to visit some arcs or nodes by one or several circuits in this graph, especially with the same start and end point, while respecting a set of constraints. Nowadays, many more examples arise, from helicopters sent to evacuate the casualties after a disaster, to a laser beam that engraves transistors making up the integrated circuits, including inspection of three-dimensional (3D) structures (such as bridge girders) by a robot.

With these numerous applications, utilization of optimization software, based on operations research and mathematical programming techniques, extends to efficiently manage the supply of goods and services. Technological innovations such as geographic information systems, radio frequency identification and parallel computing entail new challenges.

1.2.3. *Characteristics of vehicle routing problems*

Vehicle routing problems cover a wide variety of problems. Let us describe the typical characteristics of these problems by considering their main components, constraints and possible objectives to be optimized.

1.2.3.1. *Components*

Four components constitute a vehicle routing problem. Without limiting the generality, the terminologies mainly used for these components are:

– the network, which is generally described through a *graph*;

– the sites to be visited (customers to serve, tasks to process, etc.), denoted as *customers* which have a specific request often called a *demand*;

– the *fleet of vehicles* that represents the mobiles performing the task;

– the *depot(s)*, usually from where the vehicles start and come back.

The network is made up of vertices and arcs/edges representing the links between vertices. In a logistics context, it is characterized by the transport infrastructure. It consists of the fixed installations including the road junctions, and nodes which are terminals (such as seaports, stations, warehouses and depots). Nonetheless, in other applications, the network is not always materialized by a physical structure, and arcs are used to describe the allowed movements. The original graph (which is often very sparse) is generally transformed into a complete graph by removing the links between nodes that do not need to be visited (such as keeping only vertices corresponding to the customers and the depots). The links then represent the shortest path between vertices. They can be directed (particularly when they can be traversed in only one direction because of the presence of one-way streets, for instance) or undirected. Each link is weighted by a cost, which generally represents its length and/or travel time, possibly dependent on the vehicle type or on the period during which the arc is traversed.

Demand can be of many types from a product to be supplied to a service to be given. The latter case includes passenger transport that may be public (where operators provide scheduled services) or private. Much of the recent research in logistics is related to this type of transport, where the demand stands for getting people from an origin to their destination by an alternative mode to their private vehicles, either because of traffic congestion, or their concern about environmental issues for instance. Solutions include the use of feeder buses, car sharing programs and even pod cars. Other types of services also arise in vehicle routing problems, and can be related to health care (such as home health care and aid supplies during humanitarian relief), maintenance (repairs or inspection) or production (setting fastener materials on airplane cabin), among others.

A depot represents the location where mainly the vehicles are parked, reset, unloaded or recharged. It is generally the starting and/or ending node for the vehicles.

Vehicles traveling on the network embody service providers. They can be of various types, and may include trucks, aircraft, boats and trains, as well as bicycles, buses, helicopters and even pedestrian, drones, laser beams or robot arms. Depending on the demand, the task can be performed by the vehicle itself or, most often, by the operator in the vehicle (a caregiver in health service, a technician for a maintenance task, etc.). However, in the latter case, the vehicle and the operator are considered as a whole. Routes performed by vehicles are often classified as less-than-truckload. This means that the capacity enables the vehicle to perform several tasks without returning to the depot. Procedures may impose some constraints including financing, legalities and policies. In the transport industry, operations and ownership of infrastructure can be either public or private, depending on the country and transportation mode.

Then, from a general point of view, each customer has a demand, often represented like an amount of goods, which must be delivered or collected and there may be a service time, possibly dependent on the service provider. In some variants of the problem, it is not possible to fully satisfy the demand. Thus, the amounts to be delivered or collected can be reduced, or a subset of customers can be left unserved (*VRP with profit* or *orienteering problems – OP*), which often affects the objective function (penalization of non-visited customers or maximization of profits associated with visits). If the visit can be made only on specific periods of the day, these periods are called *time-windows* (*VRPTW*). Finally, some customers may have accessibility constraints (e.g. access limitations or loading and unloading requirements) and in these cases, only a subset of the available vehicles that can be used to serve these customers, as in the *truck and trailer routing problem* (*TTRP*). In this problem, some customers cannot be visited by the complete vehicle and the trailer must be detached and parked to reach them.

The routes performed to serve customers start and end at one or several depots (*multi-depot VRP - MDVRP*). If the vehicles do not return to their home depot, routes can end at the last visited customer (*open VRP*). Sometimes, vehicles may stop at intermediate depots. Other variants consider several levels of the supply chain (*two-echelon VRP - VRP-2E*).

Each depot may be characterized by a limited capacity. Their locations are usually fixed but it may be a decision variable as in the *location-routing problem –* (LRP). In this case, each depot can have a set-up cost if at least one route is assigned to it.

A homogenous or heterogeneous fleet of vehicles (*HFVRP*) can be associated with each depot. A type of vehicle is identified by (1) its capacity, (2) fixed and variable costs associated with its utilization, (3) possible subdivision into compartments, each one having a specific capacity and particular types of goods they can contain *multi-compartiment VRP* (MC-VRP), (4) and the subset of arcs they can traverse (accessibility constraints).

1.2.3.2. *Constraints*

The characteristics of the VRPs components, the nature of the demand and additional regulations (such as working periods during the day, number and duration of breaks, maximum duration of driving periods, etc.) impose to comply with a number of operational and regulatory constraints.

Examples of constraints are given here:

– depots and vehicles may have limited capacities, which require the current load to not exceed the related limit;

– when several depots are available, possibly with limited capacity, and/or the fleet of vehicles is limited, routes are assigned accordingly and in particular, no more vehicle can be used. However, in some applications, each vehicle can operate more than one route during the considered time period as in the *multi-trip VRP* (VRPMT);

– the customer demand must be satisfied, and in case of transportation, this can require either only the delivery or the collection task, or both possibilities. The demand is sometimes allowed to be split to be served by several vehicles during the time period as it occurs in the *Split-Delivery VRP* (SDVRP). In other cases, if the time horizon is composed of several time periods, the customers may have to be visited several times over this horizon (for example in the *periodic* VRP (PVRP));

– usually, a route beginning at a given depot must finish at this depot, but sometimes it can last for more than one period;

– customers have to be served within both their time windows and the working periods of the drivers associated with the vehicle routes in which they are scheduled;

– precedence and synchronization constraints can affect the visit order of the customers. For instance, in the VRP variant called *dial-a-ride problems* (DARP), a demand task is made up of a number of people to be transported from an origin to a destination by one vehicle, implying that the origin point must be visited before the destination node. Collection and delivery of goods are also performed in routes of the *VRP with Backhauls*, but constraints associated with the loading and unloading operations mean that all deliveries must be performed before the collections. *Synchronization* occurs when a customer needs at least two simultaneous visits (e.g. by technician with different skills) to be served.

Generally, data are supposed to be perfectly known in advance. However, this is not always the case and only partial knowledge of the customer demands or the costs (and travel times) associated with arcs of the graph may be available. In these situations, it is necessary to consider stochastic or time-dependent dynamic versions of the problem.

Different optimization problems can be combined with the CVRP. The LRP quoted before encompasses a facility location problem with routing decisions. Inventory decisions can be added to the problem so that vehicles can supply customers according to their stock level *inventory routing problem* (IRP). Loading constraints may also be part of the problem as in the *VRP with two/three-dimensional loading constraints* (2L-VRP and 3L-VRP).

Several other constraints can be considered, so the list cannot be exhaustive. The resulting problems can be called *rich vehicle routing problems* [HAR 06, HAS 07].

1.2.3.3. *Objectives*

The classical objective in the CVRP is the minimization of the total cost, which is dependent on the global traveled distance (or on the global travel time) and on the fixed costs, associated with the use of vehicles. Further variants also include the fixed costs of using depots (LRP) or inventory costs (IRP). If the constraints are partially satisfied, penalties are generally applied but must be minimized (as when a partial service of the customers is delivered). In some cases, the minimization of the number of vehicles required to serve all the customers can be added. Balancing of the routes, in terms of travel time and/or vehicle load, can be interesting to obtain fair timetabling between drivers. Some contexts require unusual criteria to optimize. This is the case in humanitarian logistics, when the objective relies on the time required to bring aid to victims. Instead of minimizing the total time, the *cumulative CVRP* (CCVRP) aims at minimizing the sum of the arrival time, that is equivalent to the mean arrival time at each customer.

In this manner, any weighted combination of these objectives can be considered for the vehicle routing problems. However, particularly when they are conflicting, multi-objective optimization may be more appropriate.

In summary, a large class of problems is hiding behind the VRPs. Next section provides a formal definition of the basic version.

1.2.4. *The capacitated vehicle routing problem*

The basic version of the VRP, the *Capacitated VRP* (*CVRP*), is a routing problem in which each customer has a known and deterministic demand that must be satisfied by a single visit. A fleet of identical capacitated vehicles starts and ends at a single central depot and the load in each vehicle does not exceed the related limit. The objective is to minimize the total cost to serve all the customers, which includes the global traveled distance and, when the fleet size is a decision variable, the fixed costs of vehicles. Figure 1.4 illustrates an instance of possible solution.

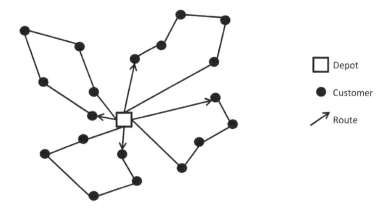

□ Depot

● Customer

↗ Route

Figure 1.4. *Example of a CVRP solution*

1.2.4.1. *Mathematical model*

The CVRP belongs to the class of *node routing problems*, in which tasks are associated with nodes of the network, by contrast to *arc routing problems* where the demands are associated with edges or arcs. It can be formally defined on a graph. Let $G = (V, E)$ be a complete undirected graph. The node set V is made of a depot (node 0) from where a set K of a homogeneous fleet of vehicles of capacity Q can start, and n customers with a given demand q_i, $i = 1, 2, \ldots, n$ for a good. Each edge $[i, j]$ from E represents on shortest path between nodes i and j in a real road network. Its associated cost c_{ij} is known. Depending on the authors, the number of available vehicles can be fixed or not, a service time s_i can be added for each customer i, and each route cost can de-limited by L (corresponding to a limited working time, for instance).

Various integer linear programs exist to model the CVRP [TOT 02, GOL 08]. The main difficulty stands on the way to eliminate subtours, i.e. cycles that do not go through the depot. Hereafter, a simple mathematical formulation is given in which two nodes represent the depot (nodes 0 and $n+1$, respectively, the starting and ending point of the routes) and each edge $[i, j]$ is replaced by two arcs (i, j) and (j, i) belonging to set A. The binary variables x_{ij}^k are equal to 1 if vehicle k goes through arc (i, j).

$$\min \sum_{k \in K} \sum_{(i,j) \in A} c_{ij} \cdot x_{ij}^k \tag{1.1}$$

$$\sum_{j \in V \setminus \{i\}} \sum_{k \in K} x_{ij}^k = 1 \qquad \forall i \in V \setminus \{0, n+1\} \tag{1.2}$$

$$\sum_{j \in V \setminus \{i\}} x_{ji}^k = \sum_{j \in V \setminus \{i\}} x_{ij}^k \qquad \forall i \in V \setminus \{0, n+1\} \quad \forall k \in K \tag{1.3}$$

$$\sum_{i \in V \setminus \{0, n+1\}} \sum_{j \in V \setminus \{i\}} q_i \cdot x_{ij}^k \leq Q \qquad \forall k \in K \tag{1.4}$$

$$t_i^k + s_i + c_{ij} \leq t_j^k + M(1 - x_{ij}^k) \qquad \forall i \in V \tag{1.5}$$

$$x_{ij}^k \in \{0, 1\} \qquad \forall (i, j) \in A \quad \forall k \in K \tag{1.6}$$

$$t_i^k \geq 0 \qquad \forall i \in V \quad \forall k \in K \tag{1.7}$$

The objective-function [1.1] sums the total cost of the routes. Constraints [1.2] and [1.3] are the continuity constraints: a single vehicle visits customer i and this vehicle leaves it. Vehicle capacities hold due to constraints [1.4]. Variables t_i^k give the arrival time of vehicle k at customer i. Equations [1.5] remove subtours: if vehicle k goes from i to j ($x_{ij}^k = 1$), the right-hand side with the big positive constant M turns to t_j^k, so vehicle k can go to j only after having served i and traveled from i to j; otherwise (if $x_{ij}^k = 1$), the constraint is trivially true.

1.2.4.2. *Solution methods*

This basic version, already NP-hard [LEN 81], was introduced in 1959 by Dantzig and Ramser [DAN 59] under the name of the *truck dispatching problem*. Since then, the number of publications on the subject has exploded as exposed in [LAP 09].

Several surveys are dedicated to vehicle routing problems. Laporte [LAP 09] provided in 2009 a paper drawing a picture on the state of the researches made on the vehicle routing problem, 50 years after its introduction by Dantzing and Ramser [DAN 59]. Other overview papers focusing either on exact resolution methods and/or heuristic ones are published [BAL 07, LAP 02]. The text book, edited by Toth [TOT 02], covers entirely the subject through a selection of six contributed chapters. A second edition updates the first book, and including emerging applications, such as disaster relief and green vehicle routing [TOT 14].

Some recent surveys dealing with VRP variants have also appeared in the literature. For instance, [BAL 12] and [BAL 08b] provide overviews dealing with the VRPTW in the first paper and the heterogeneous fleet VRP in the second paper. Vidal *et al.* [VID 12b, VID 13a] present surveys on multi-attribute vehicle routing problems. Gendreau *et al.* [GEN 15] offer a review for time-dependent routing problems. Montoya-Torres *et al.* [MON 15] contributed with a state-of-the-art on multi-depot vehicle routing problems. The two-echelon VRP is the subject considered in the recent survey from Cuda *et al.* [CUD 15], and the location routing literature is summarized in the article from Prodhon and Prins [PRO 14]. Labadie and Prins [LAB 12a] also present a paper including the most important results on a large variety of vehicle routing variants, with an emphasis on problems occurring in developing countries. Labadie and Prodhon [LAB 14] give an overview of vehicle routing problems dealing with more than one objective function.

The book coordinated by Golden *et al.* [GOL 08] offers an overview of different vehicle routing extensions, summarizing the new trends in terms of methods and models since the early 2000.

Despite this rich and diverse amount of research, exact methods are still limited to problems involving up to 100 clients [BAL 08a], when real cases can achieve more than 1,000 customers. Hence, metaheuristics are the most appropriate way to deal with these problems.

1.3. Conclusion

This chapter gives a general presentation of vehicle routing problems (VRPs) and the main related fields, which are logistics and combinatorial optimization. Good transport planning is essential to controlling the costs, as well as the flow and other side constraints (regulations, nuisances, etc.). For instance, the last mile problem often behind VRPs includes the challenge of delivering goods in urban areas where congestion and safety problems are often encountered.

In addition to its great interest in today's global markets, and the savings that can be achieved by a better planning and management of logistic systems, and beyond its attractiveness as a benchmark problem in combinatorial optimization, the family of VRPs also draws attention of both the academic and economic communities for the variety of its applications.

In addition to classical supply of goods, VRPs can model a large range of problems on various scales. At a microscopic level, how to engrave transistors on an integrated circuit with a laser beam is a question that can be handled as a VRP. In production sites, several issues arise such as the optimization of robot trajectories to perform welds. Warehouse management brings its topics like the pick up of goods in shelving. From a macroscopic point of view, subjects can be related to the collection of satellite images.

In real contexts, VRP models include a large number of customers to be served and the related integer program cannot be solved in acceptable time by combinatorial optimization tools. Therefore, in this case, heuristic approaches are more suitable. Chapter 2 introduces significant constructive heuristic methods and local improvement moves classically applied in VRPs to provide feasible solutions quickly to metaheuristics.

2

Simple Heuristics and Local Search Procedures

Simple heuristics and local search procedures are important components of metaheuristics for vehicle routing problems, this is why they deserve a dedicated chapter.

Simple heuristics are necessary for providing initial solutions. While some metaheuristics like simulated annealing can be applied to an initial set of routes with a completely random order of customers, others like iterated local search require good initial solutions. In addition to cost considerations, feasibility and diversity are important concerns. Building a feasible solution can already be hard when the problem is very constrained, e.g. in the vehicle routing problem (VRP) with time windows and a limited fleet of vehicles. Randomizing a simple heuristic and calling it several times is a useful technique to increase both solution quality and the probability of getting a feasible solution. It is also possible to work with infeasible solutions, by adding constraint violation penalties to the objective function. Diversity is essential for avoiding premature convergence, for instance when preparing the initial population of a genetic algorithm: the solutions must be well spread in solution space, instead of being clustered in a small region.

Local search procedures constitute a key-ingredient in bringing intensification to metaheuristics. While genetic algorithms or ant methods in their basic version (i.e. without local search) may work well in applications such as classification and pattern recognition, they are superseded on vehicle routing problems by metaheuristics which include an improvement procedure. In fact, it is fair to say that the best current metaheuristics for vehicle routing include at least one improvement procedure.

This chapter presents a few classical heuristics before explaining the principles of local search, taking the capacitated vehicle routing problem (CVRP) as the main example. In the following, n, c_{ij}, d_i and Q, respectively, denote the number of customers, the cost of edge (i, j), the demand of customer i and the capacity of identical vehicles.

2.1. Simple heuristics

Simple heuristics are designed to build a single solution, while local search procedures and metaheuristics examine several solutions, either by generating a sequence of solutions or working on a population. Apart from the construction of initial solutions in metaheuristics, they are also widely used in commercial VRP software to quickly find feasible solutions of good quality. Two reasons for their popularity are their simplicity and the fact that they can be easily extended to cope with various constraints. A good review can be found in Laporte and Semet, who distinguish between constructive and two-phase methods [LAP 02].

2.1.1. *Constructive heuristics*

Many constructive methods for the CVRP are obtained by modifying a traveling salesman problem (TSP) heuristic to build several routes. The simplest example is probably *nearest neighbor*: starting from the depot, a route is progressively extended by adding the nearest unrouted customer, among those compatible with the vehicle residual capacity. When no customer can be added, the vehicle returns to the depot and a new route is initialized. In this policy, called *sequential route building*, the routes are constructed one by one. It is difficult to predict the number of routes at the end and the last one has often a small load compared to the others. To get more balanced routes or use a fixed number K of vehicles, some dispatchers prefer the *parallel route building* policy, where K routes are extended in parallel: starting from the depot, each emerging route $1, 2, \ldots K$ serves the closest unrouted customer, which yields K routes with one customer. The K routes are browsed again to receive their second customer, and so on. Note that this does not guarantee K routes at the end: if at some iteration no customer can be added, extra routes must be added like in the sequential policy.

The two policies are shown in Figure 2.1, assuming a fleet of three vehicles with capacity $Q = 10$. The number close to each customer is its demand. In the sequential mode (a), route R_1 is completed (no customer can be added) and a second route is built. In the parallel mode (b), three routes are constructed in parallel (one for each vehicle) and the first two customers have been determined for each of them.

Nearest neighbor heuristics can be implemented in $O(n^2)$ for n customers but they often give poor results, especially on vehicle routing problems with additional constraints such as time windows. For instance, if the closest customer added at an iteration has the latest time window, the incumbent route can no longer be extended, which leads to a final solution with an excessive number of vehicles. In such situations, *insertion heuristics* work better. They consist of initializing routes as empty loops on the depot, in which customers are inserted one by one. These routes can be constructed sequentially or in parallel, like in the nearest neighbor algorithm, and the goal of each insertion is to minimize the increase in length (cheapest insertion).

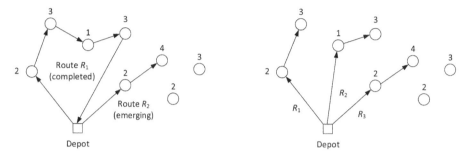

Figure 2.1. *Sequential a) and parallel b) route building*

Consider an emerging route $R = (r_1 = 0, r_2, \ldots, r_{|R|} = n + 1)$, 0 and $n + 1$ denoting the depot, and a set U of unrouted customers. For one customer $j \in U$, the insertion cost after $r_i, i = 1, 2, \ldots, |R| - 1$, is $\Delta_{ji} = c_{r_i,j} + c_{j,r_{i+1}} - c_{r_i,r_{i+1}}$. The cheapest insertion of j is defined by its cost $\Delta_j^* = \min\{\Delta_{ji} \mid i = 1, 2, \ldots, |R| - 1\}$ and the node after which j is inserted, $P_j = \arg\min\{\Delta_{ji} \mid i = 1, 2, \ldots, |R| - 1\}$. The customer finally inserted at each iteration is $k = \arg\min\{\Delta_j^* \mid j \in U\}$, after node P_k. A basic implementation runs in $O(n^3)$ but it is possible to reach $O(n^2)$. More elaborated insertion algorithms exist, for instance Mole and Jameson [MOL 76] build several solutions using different edge cost weights in the calculation of the Δ_{ji}.

In the previous two heuristics, customers are added progressively to emerging routes and a complete solution is obtained only at the end. In the *Clarke and Wright heuristic* [CLA 64], the initial solution is complete but very expensive, with n routes reduced to one customer. Then, each iteration evaluates the possible mergers (concatenations) of two routes and executes the one with the largest positive saving (smallest negative cost variation). Two routes $R = (r_1 = 0, r_2, \ldots, r_{|R|} = n + 1)$ and $S = (s_1 = 0, s_2, \ldots, s_{|S|} = n + 1)$ can be merged if their total load fits one vehicle. The merging process stops when a single route (TSP tour) is obtained, after $n - 1$ mergers, or when merging any two remaining routes violates vehicle capacity.

For instance, the vehicle doing route R can proceed with route S after customer r_p, instead of returning to the depot. The cost variation is then $c_{r_p,s_1} - c_{r_p,0} - c_{0,s_1}$ and it is negative if the triangle inequality holds. For undirected networks with symmetric costs, four concatenations are possible because each route can be inverted or not in the merger, as shown in Figure 2.2. For instance, the vehicle can follow route R in its given order and then move to s_q to perform route S in reverse order. Note that concatenating R and S without inverting them gives the same cost as concatenating the inverse of S and the inverse of R, thus the second option is not considered. This is not the case for directed networks with asymmetric costs, where eight mergers must be evaluated for each pair of routes $\{R, S\}$.

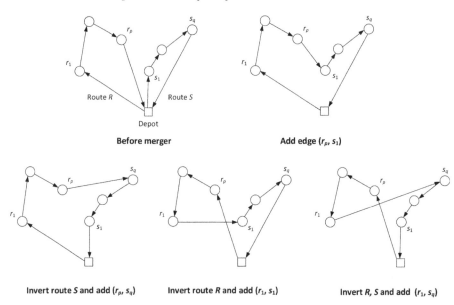

Figure 2.2. *Possible mergers in Clarke and Wright heuristic (undirected network)*

The Clarke and Wright heuristic gives good results in practice and outperforms nearest neighbor and insertion methods on average. As one vehicle is saved by each merger, the algorithm tends to minimize both the total cost and the number of vehicles. A naive evaluation of all possible mergers at each iteration leads to an $O(n^3)$ algorithm. To do better, note that each merger can be defined by the edge added to link the two routes, e.g. (r_p, s_1). So, the $n(n - 1)/2$ edges of the network can be sorted at the beginning in a list L, in increasing order of cost variation. Using a fast sorting algorithm like heapsort, L can be computed in $O(n^2 \log_2 n)$. Then, the algorithm tests each edge (i, j) of L, starting from the first. If customers i and j are still extremities of two distinct routes and the total load of these routes fits a single vehicle, the merger is executed. Using *ad hoc* data structures, each edge of L can be checked in constant time and the overall complexity is dominated by the sorting phase, in $O(n^2 \log_2 n)$.

2.1.2. *Two-phase methods*

The idea of two-phase methods is to return to the TSP. *Cluster-first, route-second* methods begin by creating groups of customers (clusters) whose total demand fits vehicle capacity and then solve a TSP for each cluster. Each cluster can be viewed as a subset of customers assigned to the same vehicle. The sweep heuristic by Gillett and Miller [GIL 74] is a good example where clusters are defined as angular sectors centered on the depot. The process is shown in Figure 2.3.

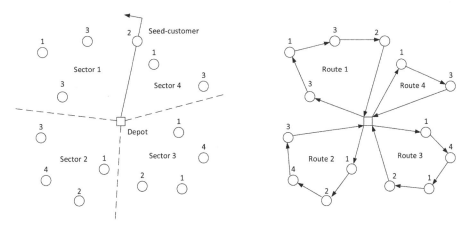

Figure 2.3. *Sweep heuristic for a vehicle capacity $Q = 10$*

The numbers close to the customers are their demands. In the clustering phase, one seed-customer is arbitrarily selected and the other customers are swept (here anticlockwise) from this seed to get the sectors on the left. Each sector is finished if adding another customer violates vehicle capacity, here $Q = 10$. Any exact or heuristic algorithm can then be used in the routing phase. Here, the nearest neighbor heuristic gives the routes on the right. Algorithmically, the sectors are simply built by computing the polar angle of each customer, using the depot as origin. If coordinates (x_i, y_i) are provided for each node i, its angle is $\alpha_i = \arctan(y_i - y_0)/(x_i - x_0)$. Then, the nodes can be sorted in ascending order of quadrants and polar angles, giving a list which is browsed and split into successive sectors. To improve the result, it is recommended to run the sweep heuristic using different seed-customers, and to apply a local search to each pair of adjacent sectors. In Figure 2.3 for instance, if travel costs are proportional to the Euclidean distances, the first customer in route 4 can be relocated between the last customer of route 1 and the depot.

The sweep heuristic builds its clusters one by one and the last one is often too small. Moreover, the algorithm does not work well when the depot is excentered, for instance in a port at the extremity of a peninsula. More sophisticated methods can be used to remedy these drawbacks. Fisher and Jaikumar [FIS 81] solve a generalized assignment problem (GAP) *via* Lagrangian relaxation to get more compact and balanced clusters. The objective function of the GAP is an approximation of the total length of the routes. Novães and Graciolli [NOV 99] divide a large city into angular sectors and each sector into nested rings and districts, to achieve a quasi-homogeneous distribution effort in each resulting zone (similar number of vehicles). Petal heuristics [BAL 64, FOS 76] build a large number of routes and then solve a set partitioning problem to extract a subset of routes visiting each customer exactly once.

Contrary to cluster-first route-second methods, *route-first, cluster-second* heuristics relax vehicle capacity to solve a TSP in a first step. The resulting giant tour visits all customers. In a second step, a splitting procedure *Split* cuts the giant tour into CVRP routes. In 1983, Beasley proposed an optimal splitting procedure, subject to the sequence defined by the giant tour [BEA 83]. Given a giant tour with customers $T_1, T_2, \ldots, T_n$ visited in this order, an auxiliary directed graph $H = (V, A, Z)$ is built first to model all the feasible routes which can be extracted from the tour. More precisely, the vertex-set V contains one dummy node 0 and customer-nodes 1 to n. The arc-set A includes one arc $(i - 1, j)$ for each subsequence of customers $(T_i, T_{i+1}, \ldots, T_j)$ which can lead to a feasible CVRP route, i.e. if $\sum_{k=i}^{j} d(T_k) \leq Q$. The cost $z_{i-1,j}$ is nothing but the cost of the associated route, i.e. $z_{i-1,j} = c(0, T_i) + \sum_{k=i}^{j-1} c(T_i, T_{i+1}) + c(T_j, 0)$. Note that the resulting graph is a directed acyclic graph (DAG). The optimal splitting corresponds to a shortest path from node 0 to node n, which can be computed in $O(|A|)$ using Bellman's algorithm for DAGs.

An example is given in Figure 2.4. The giant tour with five customers is shown with demands (in brackets), edge costs and possible returns to the depot (dashed lines). The auxiliary graph is built assuming $Q = 10$. For instance, arc $(0, 2)$ models a route visiting customers 1 and 2, with a cost equal to 55 as can be checked on the giant tour. Arc $(0, 3)$ is not included because the total demand of customers 1, 2, 3 (13) exceeds vehicle capacity. Above each node i is written the label V_i computed by Bellman's algorithm (cost of the shortest path from node 0 to node i in the auxiliary graph). The resulting path is shown in boldface. It corresponds to the solution plotted in the upper right corner, with a total cost equal to 205.

In Beasley's article, this approach is presented as a way of recycling any exact or heuristic algorithm for the TSP to solve the CVRP, but without numerical results. This explains why route-first cluster-second heuristics have been considered as a curiosity for a long time. In 2004, Prins had the good idea of using Split in a memetic algorithm for the CVRP, to evaluate chromosomes encoded as giant tours [PRI 04a]. This led to the first evolutionary algorithm able to compete with the state-of-the-art tabu search algorithms of that time.

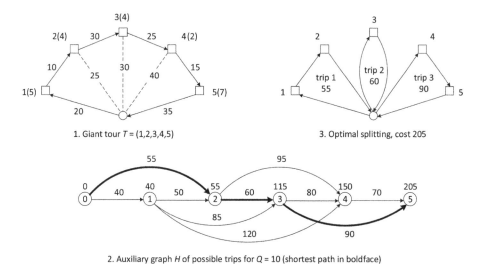

Figure 2.4. *Splitting procedure*

Prins also gave a compact version of Split in which the auxiliary graph is not explicitly generated, see algorithm 2.1. The *for* and *repeat* loops inspect each feasible route $(T_i, T_{i+1}, \ldots, T_j)$ and compute its cost C and load L. When j is incremented, L and C are updated in $O(1)$ instead of rescanning the whole subsequence (lines 6-9). If the route, modeled by arc $(i - 1, j)$, satisfies the vehicle capacity constraint (line 10) and if the path obtained by adding arc $(i - 1, j)$ to the shortest path ending at node $i - 1$ improves the provisional shortest path to node j (line 11), label V_j is updated and the predecessor of j along the path is recorded in P_j. The predecessors are required to deduce the successive routes once the shortest path is determined.

The complexity of this algorithm can be easily established. The two nested loops inspect $O(n^2)$ feasible subsequences, all checked in constant time, so the algorithm runs in $O(n^2)$. More precisely, let b be the average number of customers per feasible subsequence. Since b is also the average number of outgoing arcs for each node of the auxiliary graph, H contains nb arcs and Split runs in $O(nb)$.

The use of Split in simple heuristics was evaluated later, in 2009 [PRI 09b]. For instance, 20 giant tours can be constructed using a randomized version of the nearest neighbor heuristic, and then split to return the best solution. Such randomized route-first cluster second heuristics are surprisingly good on the CVRP and the capacitated arc routing problem (CARP). Nowadays, metaheuristics working on giant tours and calling a splitting procedure are widespread in vehicle routing: a recent survey covers more than 70 publications [PRI 14]. This success can be explained by two strong points: the metaheuristics explore a smaller search space (the set of giant tours) and various additional constraints can be handled in the Split procedure.

Algorithm 2.1: Compact version of Split for a given giant tour T

---

1   $V_0 = 0$; initialize the other labels $V_1, V_2, \ldots, V_n$ to $+\infty$

2   **for** $i := 1$ **to** n **do**

3     $L := 0; C := 0; j := i$

4   **repeat**

5       $L := L + d(T_j)$

6   **if** $i = j$ **then**

7         $C := c(0, T_j) + c(T_j, 0)$

8   **else**

9         $C := C - c(T_{j-1}, 0) + c(T_{j-1}, T_j) + c(T_j, 0)$

10   **if** $L \leq Q$ **then**

11   **if** $V_{i-1} + C < V_j$ **then**

12          $V_j := V_{i-1} + C$

13          $P_j := i - 1$

14        $j := j + 1$

15   **until** $j > n$ **or** $L > Q$

2.1.3. *Best-of approach and randomization*

Two fruitful techniques can improve solution quality of simple heuristics, before resorting to local search. The first one is the "*best of*" method. If you already have several simple heuristics, write a procedure which calls them one by one and returns the best solution found at the end. Due to a compensation effect, the results are on average much better than the ones obtained by each initial heuristic. Indeed, heuristics rarely achieve their worst case on the same instances. For example, constructive heuristics give poor results on three-dimensional container loading problems (e.g. load the most compact boxes first, or the ones with the largest volume, or build successive walls of boxes using two-dimensional (2D) algorithms, etc.) but commercial software packages obtain interesting results by grouping several algorithms in a kind of black box.

The second technique is *randomization*. This idea is to introduce some randomness into the decisions of the original deterministic heuristic. To do so in the sequential nearest neighbor heuristic, for instance, we can determine at each iteration the M closest customers in the set U of unrouted customers, M being a given integer, and randomly select one of them to extend the route. As $M = 1$ corresponds to the deterministic version and $M = |U|$ corresponds to completely random routes, a small value like $M = 2$ or 3 is chosen as a trade-off between solution quality and diversity. If the randomized version is called only once, it is inferior to the deterministic version on average but the best result of, say, 20 calls without resetting the random number generator can yield impressive results. The results can be improved by doing a large number of calls but the running time increases quickly and it is more profitable to switch to local search.

Adding randomization is sometimes even simpler. The $O(n^2 \log_2 n)$ implementation of the Clarke and Wright heuristic that we already described browses the list L of all edges of the network, sorted in increasing order of cost variation, to determine if the merger defined by the incumbent edge should be executed. The simplest way to randomize this implementation is to select an acceptance threshold α, e.g $\alpha = 0.9$, and to execute the merger with probability α, provided that it is still feasible. Otherwise, the incumbent edge is discarded and the heuristic repeats the same process on the next edge of L.

2.2. Local search

This section gives the general structure of a local search, presents classical moves and discusses important issues such as feasibility tests, genericity, multiple neighborhoods, very constrained problems, complex moves and acceleration techniques.

2.2.1. *Principle*

An *improvement procedure* or *local search* starts from one initial solution S, often obtained by a simple heuristic, and considers a subset $N(S)$ of solutions close to S in terms of structure, called *neighborhood of S*. In practice, $N(S)$ is implicitly defined by a modification $S \to S'$ called *move*, instead of being generated in extenso. This neighborhood is inspected to find a better solution S'. If S' exists, it becomes the incumbent solution and the process is repeated. In this way, the input solution is progressively improved until reaching a local optimum for the considered neighborhood.

Algorithm 2.2 works on a given solution S with cost $f(S)$. The *repeat* loop performs successive neighborhood explorations. The *for each* loop tests each solution S' in $N(S)$ (each move $S \to S'$), to find the best cost variation Δ^*. If $\Delta^* = 0$ in line 8, S cannot be improved and the procedure stops, otherwise the move is applied and the process is repeated. The *attributes* of the move are the required data to do it later. For instance, for a relocation of node i after node j, these attributes are the node i^* corresponding to the best relocation and the node j^* after which it must be reinserted.

Algorithm 2.2: General structure of a local search to improve a given solution S

---

1 **repeat**
2 | $\Delta^* := 0$
3 | **for each** $S' \in N(S)$ (i.e. for each move $S \to S'$) **do**
4 | **if** $f(S') - f(S) < \Delta^*$ **then**
5 | $\Delta^* := f(S') - f(S)$
6 | record the attributes of the move
7 | **break**
8 | **if** $\Delta^* < 0$ **then**
9 | execute the move: $S := S'$
10 **until** $\Delta^* = 0$

The *break* statement leaves the *for each* loop as soon as an improving move is detected, which gives a *first-improvement local search*. It can be deleted to get a *best-improvement local search*. Depending on the problem at hand, the structure of instances and the percentage of feasible moves, one of the two strategies can dominate the other: it is recommended to test both in practice.

2.2.2. *Classical moves*

The simplest moves have been defined for the TSP and can be applied to each route in the CVRP. For instance, one customer can be removed to be reinserted at a different position (*node relocation*) or two customers can be swapped (*node exchange*). The neighborhoods for these two moves can be browsed in $O(n^2)$. The k-opt moves [LIN 73], more efficient, remove k edges from a route and reconnect the obtained subsequences with k other edges. As all possible k-opt moves are tested in $O(n^k)$ for n customers, the 2-opt and 3-opt moves are often used to keep a low complexity.

The Or-opt move introduced by Or [OR 76] relocates a string of 1 to λ customers, while Osman's λ-*interchange* [OSM 93] exchanges two strings having at most λ customers each (the two strings may have different lengths). As these two neighborhoods can be searched, respectively, in $O(\lambda n^2)$ and $O(\lambda^2 n^2)$, $\lambda = 3$ is often selected to limit running times. λ-interchanges are particularly interesting: if one of the strings can be empty and if each string can be reversed during the reinsertion, these moves include node relocations, node exchanges, 2-opt and Or-opt moves as particular cases.

Figure 2.5 shows the 2-opt and λ-interchange moves (the 2-opt* move is presented in the sequel). The key-point is to evaluate the cost variation in constant time for each move. For instance, the 2-opt move on one route which replaces arcs (u, x) and (v, y) by (u, v) and (x, y) has a cost variation $\Delta = c_{uv} + c_{xy} - c_{ux} - c_{vy}$.

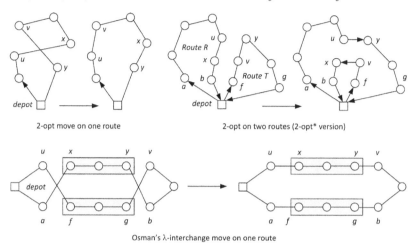

2-opt move on one route   2-opt on two routes (2-opt* version)

Osman's λ-interchange move on one route

Figure 2.5. *Examples of 2-opt and λ-interchange moves*

Algorithm 2.3 is a detailed version of algorithm 2, to apply 2-opt moves to each route $R = (r_1 = 0, r_2, \ldots, r_{|R|} = n + 1)$ in a given solution S. The replacement of arcs (u, x) and (v, y) by (u, v) and (x, y) is equivalent to reversing the string from x to v included, see Figure 2.5. This string must have two customers at least because for one customer the cost does not change. Our implementation uses the best-improvement strategy and two *for* loops to browse the strings. The customers x^* and v^* delimiting the best string are memorized and reversed in lines 10–12.

2.2.3. *Feasibility tests*

All the moves described previously can be generalized to two routes, but it becomes more difficult to evaluate their feasibility or cost variation in $O(1)$. We are going to analyze the 2-opt move applied to two routes R and T in Figure 2.5. In this version, called 2-opt*, arcs (u, x) and (v, y) are replaced by (u, y) and (v, x). There also exists a variant where the arcs are replaced by (u, v) and (x, y), the neighborhood sizes are in $O(n^2)$ for both versions. Let $C(R, i, j)$ and $L(R, i, j)$ be, respectively, the cost and load of route R between two nodes i and j (included), and $cost(R)$ and $load(R)$ the total cost and the total load of the route. After the move, the capacity constraints must still hold for each route:

$$L(R, 0, u) + load(T) - L(T, 0, v) \leq Q \qquad\qquad [2.1]$$

$$L(T, 0, v) + load(R) - L(R, 0, u) \leq Q \qquad\qquad [2.2]$$

Algorithm 2.3: Detailed local search with 2-opt moves on each route

---

1 **repeat**
2     $\Delta^* := 0$
3   **for each** route $R \in S$ **do**
4   **for** $x := 2$ **to** $|R| - 2$ **do**
5   **for** $v := x + 1$ **to** $|R| - 1$ **do**
6              $\Delta := c(r_{x-1}, r_v) + c(r_x, r_{v+1}) - c(r_{x-1}, r_x) - c(r_v, r_{v+1})$
7   **if** $\Delta < \Delta^*$ **then**
8                 $\Delta^* := \Delta; x^* := x; v^* := v$

9   **if** $\Delta^* < 0$ **then**
10        $i := x^*; j := v^*$
11   **while** $i < j$ **do**
12   swap r_i and r_j; $i := i + 1; j := j - 1$

13 **until** $\Delta^* = 0$

Note that $load(T) - L(T, 0, v)$ is the total amount delivered by route T after node v (customers y to g in Figure 2.5). An additional constraint like the maximum length D of a route (driver's maximum working time, for example) can be checked as follows, where $cost(T) - C(T, 0, y)$ is the total cost of route T from node y onward:

$$C(R, 0, u) + c_{uy} + cost(T) - C(T, 0, y) \leq D \qquad [2.3]$$

$$C(T, 0, v) + c_{vx} + cost(R) - C(R, 0, x) \leq D \qquad [2.4]$$

Note that $load(R)$, $load(T)$, $cost(R)$ and $cost(T)$ are usually route attributes which are stored with the solution. But if the other useful quantities like $L(R, 0, u)$ are determined for each move by browsing the routes, using $O(n)$ loops, the whole neighborhood is searched in $O(n^3)$ instead of $O(n^2)$. To evaluate each move in $O(1)$, the useful quantities must be either precomputed or calculated incrementally.

Algorithm 2.4 provides a version with incremental computations. For each pair of distinct routes $\{R, T\}$, indices u and v are used to test each pair of nodes (r_u, t_v) in constant time. Q_R and Q_T are the cumulated loads from the beginning of routes R and T, respectively. They correspond to $L(R, 0, u)$ and $L(T, 0, v)$ in equations [2.1]. For each pair (u, v), the cumulated loads are updated, vehicle capacity is verified, the cost variation Δ is computed and the best move is updated. Note that r_u and t_v can be the depot, assuming that $d_0 = 0$. In particular, if r_u is the last customer of R and t_v is the depot at the beginning of T, the two routes are merged by the 2-opt* move.

Time windows constitute another frequent complication factor. For instance, in the VRP with time windows (VRPTW), inserting a customer in a route delays the subsequent visits, which may violate time windows. Once again, it is possible to check feasibility with a loop in $O(n)$, but can we reach $O(1)$? Kindervater and Savelsbergh [KIN 97] have proposed precomputing the maximum delay (*push forward*) that is allowed at each node without violating time windows.

Algorithm 2.4: 2-opt* local search on a given solution S

1 **repeat**
2 $\quad \Delta^* := 0$
3 $\quad$ **for each** pair of distinct routes $\{R, T\}$ in S **do**
4 $\quad\quad Q_R := 0; Q_T := 0$
5 $\quad\quad$ **for** $u := 1$ **to** $|R|$ **do**
6 $\quad\quad\quad Q_R := Q_R + d(r_u)$
7 $\quad\quad\quad$ **for** $v := 1$ **to** $|T|$ **do**
8 $\quad\quad\quad\quad Q_T := Q_T + d(t_v)$
9 $\quad\quad\quad\quad$ **if** $Q_R + load(T) - Q_T \leq Q$ **and** $Q_T + load(R) - Q_R \leq Q$ **then**
10 $\quad\quad\quad\quad\quad \Delta := c(r_u, t_{v+1}) + c(t_v, r_{u+1}) - c(r_u, r_{u+1}) - c(t_v, t_{v+1})$
11 $\quad\quad\quad\quad\quad$ **if** $\Delta < \Delta^*$ **then**
12 $\quad\quad\quad\quad\quad\quad \Delta^* := \Delta; u^* := u; v^* := v$

13 $\quad$ **if** $\Delta^* < 0$ **then**
14 $\quad\quad R := (r_1, \ldots, r_u^*, t_{v^*+1}, \ldots, t_{|T|})$
15 $\quad\quad T := (t_1, \ldots, t_v^*, r_{u^*+1}, \ldots, r_{|R|})$
16 **until** $\Delta^* = 0$

To do so, consider a feasible route R with p customers. If $[e_k, l_k]$ denotes the time window (opening hours) of the k-th customer, t_k is the arrival time at this customer and s_k is its service time, the service must be finished by the end of the time window ($t_k + s_k \leq l_k$) but it is possible to arrive before the opening ($t_k < e_k$) and wait. Assuming that the depot is always open, the maximum delay for the last customer is $S_p = l_p - s_p - t_p$, and, for $k = p - 1, p - 2, \ldots, 1, S_k = \min(S_{k+1}, l_k - s_k - t_k)$. So, all delays for a given solution can be computed in $O(n)$ at the beginning of the local search, which allows feasibility tests in $O(1)$ for various moves. For instance, inserting one customer i between nodes r_{k-1} and r_k delays the start of service at r_k by $\theta = c(r_{k-1}, r_i) + s_i + c(r_i, r_k) - c(r_{k-1}, r_k)$, which is allowed only if $\theta \leq S_k$. After a move, the S_k must be recomputed only for the routes modified (one or two). Figure 2.6 gives an example with four customers where each small rectangle represents a service with its duration. For instance, we obtain $S_1 = 2$ for the first customer.

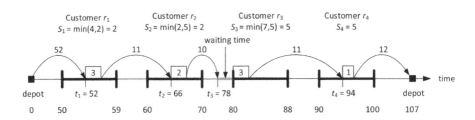

Figure 2.6. *Computation of maximum delays in the VRPTW*

2.2.4. *General approach from Vidal et al.*

Vidal *et al.* [VID 15] proposed a general approach for solving *timing problems*: given a list of tasks, a set of constraints satisfy and an optimization criterion, how do we determine the optimal starting times of the tasks, and how do we reoptimize quickly in case of sequence modifications? Such problems are widespread in scheduling and vehicle routing. In particular, a timing problem must be solved when a route is modified by a move in a local search procedure.

Vidal *et al.* noticed that most moves can be expressed as concatenations of node sequences. For each useful quantity Z used during the local search, they proposed to precalculate $Z(\sigma)$ for any sequence of nodes σ contained in the routes of the input solution, using two main operators:

– one to initialize $Z(\sigma)$ when σ contains a single node;

– one deriving Z from $Z(\sigma)$ and $Z(\tau)$ when σ and τ are concatenated ($Z(\sigma \oplus \tau)$).

In practice, a matrix Z is prepared, in which Z_{ij} gives the value associated with the sequence delimited by nodes i and j (included), if it exists in a route. Like in our previous examples, a route is coded by a list of nodes, beginning and finishing at the depot (nodes 0 and $n + 1$). Each node i is examined and, for a given i, each node j is located after i. The initialization operator allows us to evaluate Z_{ii}, then the second operator is called to provide the value of Z_{ij} for each node j, until the end of the route. In most cases, the two operators can be implemented in $O(1)$, so the matrix Z can be precalculated in $O(n^2)$.

We are going to illustrate Vidal *et al.*'s approach on a simple case, the CVRP, and then on a more involved example, the cumulative CVRP (CCVRP). A detailed algorithm is also provided in the next section devoted to multiple neighborhoods. In the following, the length (number of nodes) of a sequence σ is denoted as $|\sigma|$, σ_i is the node at the ith position and $\sigma_{i,j}$ represents the sequence from nodes σ_i to σ_j (included).

In the CVRP, many move evaluations require the total demand $Q(\sigma)$ and the cost $C(\sigma)$ for each sequence σ within the routes. These sequences may include the depot at the beginning and/or at the end, so the rows and columns of matrices Q and C are indexed from 0 to $n + 1$. If σ contains a single node i, the initialization operators are $Q(\sigma) = d_i$ (setting $d_0 = d_{n+1} = 0$) and $C(\sigma) = 0$. For two sequences σ and τ, the concatenation operators are $Q(\sigma \oplus \tau) = Q(\sigma) + Q(\tau)$ and $C(\sigma \oplus \tau) = C(\sigma) + c(\sigma_{|\sigma|}, \tau_1) + C(\tau)$. Using this information, it becomes easy to check the capacity and maximum duration constraints for any move. Consider, for instance, the 2-opt* move of Figure 2.5. Using precomputations, the capacity tests in line 9 of algorithm 2.4 can be rewritten in a simpler way: $Q_{0,u} + Q_{y,n+1} \leq Q$ and $Q_{0,v} + Q_{x,n+1} \leq Q$. Moreover, when a move is really applied, $Q(\sigma)$ must be updated only for each sequence σ in the two affected routes: the precomputations for the other routes are still valid.

The 2-opt move on one route depicted in Figure 2.5 is equivalent to a reversal of the subsequence from x to v. In the academic CVRP, it is assumed that the cost of an edge does not depend on its traversal direction. Hence, the costs of a subsequence σ and its reversal $\bar{\sigma}$ are equal. This is no longer true in directed networks, and even in undirected networks when the objective function is the total duration of the routes and waiting times are induced by adding time windows. The technique described before can be easily adapted for the moves which imply reversal operations, by precomputing both $Z(\sigma)$ and $Z(\bar{\sigma})$ for each subsequence σ in the current routes.

Consider now the CCVRP. In this problem raised by disaster logistics, the cost of a route is the sum of arrival times at the affected sites, see Figure 2.7, and the return cost to the depot is ignored. Computing the cost variations of the moves is more complicated than in the CVRP. For instance, the insertion of a customer affects all arrival times after the insertion point and, contrary to the CVRP, the inversion of a route can improve its cost although the network is undirected [NGU 10b].

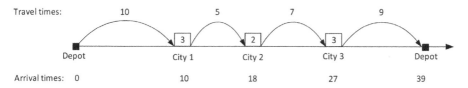

Figure 2.7. *CCVRP route – the sum of arrival times is* $10 + 18 + 27 = 55$

Silva *et al.* [SIL 12] studied the single-route case, called *cumulative TSP* or *minimum latency problem*. They showed that the *ad-hoc* quantities to precalculate are:

– $D(\sigma)$, the total duration to visit the nodes of σ, starting from σ_1;

– $C(\sigma)$, the cost (sum of arrival times) assuming a departure at time 0;

– $W(\sigma)$, the extra cost if the departure is delayed by one unit of time.

From these quantities, the total duration and the cost of any sequence generated by a move can be deduced as follows and these formulas are also valid for the CCVRP:

– if $|\sigma| = 1$, $D(\sigma) = C(\sigma) = 0$, $W(\sigma) = 1$ for a customer and 0 for the depot;

– $D(\sigma \oplus \tau) = D(\sigma) + c(\sigma_{|\sigma|}, \tau_1) + D(\tau)$;

– $C(\sigma \oplus \tau) = C(\sigma) + W(\tau) \times [D(\sigma) + c(\sigma_{|\sigma|}, \tau_1)] + C(\tau)$;

– $W(\sigma \oplus \tau) = W(\sigma) + W(\tau)$.

To conclude with Vidal *et al.*'s approach, some readers can object that a classical implementation like algorithm 2.4 has the same algorithmic complexity with less lines of code, since there is no precomputation. However, three drawbacks must be underlined. First, the code becomes quickly unreadable if other constraints must be handled, e.g. time windows, because the computations of interesting quantities such as Q_R and Q_S are interleaved with the neighborhood search, instead of being clearly separated. Second, adding other moves requires new variables, while the precomputed values in Vidal's approach can be used for any move, for instance 3-opt moves. Third, the apparently simpler code relies on the specific order in which the routes are scanned. It is incompatible with the neighborhood reduction techniques presented in the sequel, such as the random sampling of a subset of moves and the lists of neighbors, which examine the pairs (r_u, t_v) in any order. The interested readers will find similar formulas for many other vehicle routing problems in [VID 14] and [VID 15].

2.2.5. *Multiple neighborhoods*

Efficient improvement procedures involve several neighborhoods $N_1, N_2, \ldots, N_p$, which is equivalent to browse a combined neighborhood $N_1 \cup N_2 \cup \ldots \cup N_p$. A simple example is to evaluate the 2-opt moves on one route and the 2-opt* moves on two routes. Algorithms 3 and 2.4 can be easily merged for this purpose. For instance, we can examine each pair of routes (R, T) and evaluate the 2-opt moves on one route if $R = T$, and the 2-opt* moves otherwise.

When several intraroute (or interroute) moves are considered, it is in general possible to examine several moves at a time instead of rescanning the same routes for each kind of move. For instance, the 2-opt local search of algorithm 3 uses two indices x and v to evaluate the reversal of the node sequence from x to v. We can take this opportunity to check at the same time the relocation of x after v, the relocation of v after x and the exchange of these two nodes. When recording the attributes of the best move, a move code must be added to remember the kind of move to be executed.

To illustrate the approach on a non-trivial example, we consider a local search combining the two kinds of 2-opt moves on two routes depicted in Figure 2.8. The version in the middle is the 2-opt* move already described. In the version on the right, the node sequences from 0 to v in route T and from x to $n+1$ in route R are inverted. To complicate this, we assume that the network is directed, so $c_{ij} \neq c_{ji}$ in general. Algorithm 2.5 gives an implementation based on Vidal *et al.*'s approach, using the notations already introduced.

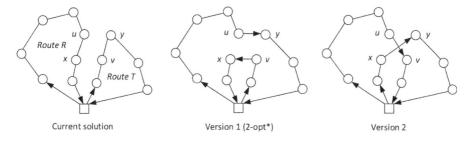

Figure 2.8. *Two kinds of interroute 2-opt moves*

In first-improvement local searches, the order in which the different neighborhoods are browsed can have a strong influence on the results. Deroussi [DER 02] defines the *depth of a neighborhood $N(S)$* as the average cost variation:

$$Depth(S) = \frac{\sum_{S' \in N(S)} (f(S') - f(S))}{|N(S)|} \qquad [2.5]$$

He recommends exploring the neighborhoods in decreasing depth order and reports computational results on small TSP where the set of local optima can be determined by complete enumeration. In large instances, the depth can be statistically approximated by testing a given number of random moves for each neighborhood.

Other techniques are possible. Some authors randomly change the neighborhood ordering at each local search iteration [SUB 12]. The local search can be made reactive by reordering dynamically the neighborhoods according to a score such as the depth and the average percentage of feasible moves. Another idea is to explore one neighborhood at a time, in a given order, and to proceed with the next one only when the incumbent neighborhood yields no improvement. The *Variable Neighborhood Descent* metaheuristic presented in Chapter 3 is based on this principle: in general, its neighborhoods are ordered in increasing order of cardinality, to speed up.

Algorithm 2.5: Local search with the two kinds of 2-opt move on two routes

---

1 //Pre-computations
2 **for each** route R in solution S **do**
3   **for** $i := 1$ **to** $|R|$ **do**
4        $u := r_i; Q_{u,u} := d_u; C_{u,u} := 0; \overline{C}_{u,u} := 0$
5   **for** $j := i+1$ **to** $|R|$ **do**
6            $v := r_{j-1}; w := r_j$
7            $Q_{u,w} := Q_{u,v} + d_w$
8            $C_{u,w} := C_{u,v} + c_{v,w}$
9            $\overline{C}_{u,w} := \overline{C}_{u,v} + c_{w,v}$

10 //Local search main loop
11 **repeat**
12     $\Delta^* := 0$
13   //Search for the best improving move
14   **for each** pair of distinct routes $\{R,T\}$ in solution S **do**
15   **for** $i := 1$ **to** $|R|$ **do**
16            $u := r_i; x := r_{i+1}$
17   **for** $j := 1$ **to** $|T|$ **do**
18                $v := t_j; y := t_{j+1}$
19   //First kind of move (2-opt*)
20   **if** $(Q_{0,u} + Q_{y,n+1} \leq Q)$ **and** $(Q_{0,v} + Q_{x,n+1} \leq Q)$ **then**
21                    $\Delta := c_{u,y} + c_{v,x} - c_{u,x} - c_{v,y}$
22   **if** $\Delta < \Delta^*$ **then**
23                        $\Delta^* := \Delta; i^* := i; j^* := j; kind := 1$

24   //Second kind of move (*newcost* is the resulting solution cost)
25   **if** $(Q_{0,u} + Q_{0,v} \leq Q)$ **and** $(Q_{x,n+1} + Q_{y,n+1} \leq Q)$ **then**
26                    $newcost := C_{0,u} + c_{u,v} + \overline{C}_{0,v} + \overline{C}_{x,n+1} + c_{x,y} + C_{y,n+1}$
27                    $\Delta := newcost - cost(S)$
28   **if** $\Delta < \Delta^*$ **then**
29                      $\Delta^* := \Delta; i^* := i; j^* := j; kind := 2$

30   //Execute the best improving move if it exists
31   **if** $\Delta^* < 0$ **then**
32   **if** $kind = 1$ **then**
33            $R := (r_1, r_2, \ldots, r_{i^*}, t_{j^*+1}, t_{j^*+2}, \ldots, t_{|T|})$
34            $T := (t_1, t_2, \ldots, t_{j^*}, r_{i^*+1}, r_{i^*+2}, \ldots, r_{|R|})$
35   **else**
36            $R := (r_1, r_2, \ldots, r_{i^*}, t_{j^*}, t_{j^*-1}, \ldots, t_1)$
37            $T := (r_{|R|}, r_{|R|-1}, \ldots, r_{i^*+1}, t_{j^*+1}, t_{j^*+2}, \ldots, t_{|T|})$
38   update the $Q_{u,w}, C_{u,w}$ and $\overline{C}_{u,w}$ for routes R and T
39 **until** $\Delta^* = 0$

2.2.6. *Very constrained problems*

Very constrained problems raise difficulties: the initial heuristics can fail to find a feasible solution and the local search may waste time in testing infeasible moves. In the first case, a randomized constructive heuristic can be called several times until a feasible solution is returned. The second case can be improved by choosing *ad-hoc* moves. Among the interroute moves for the CVRP, exchanges are less likely to fail than relocations when vehicles are nearly full. In the VRPTW, a 2-opt move on one route reverses a subsequence of customers and has a high probability of violating time windows, in contrast to node relocations or exchange moves.

Another trick [COR 01a] consists of relaxing complicating constraints and adding a penalization for their violation in the objective-function. By doing so, new paths between feasible solutions are created in the solution space, but searching this extended space may require more time.

Consider, for instance, a VRPTW solution S with p routes $R_1, R_2, \ldots, R_p$, a vehicle of capacity Q, a time-window $[e_i, l_i]$ (opening hours) and a service time s_i for each customer i. The arrival time at customer i is t_i, and the load of route R_k is L_k. A possible penalized objective function $CP(S)$ consists of adding the violations of vehicle capacity and time windows to the true solution cost $C(S)$ (total cost of traversed arcs):

$$CP(S) = C(S) + \sum_{i=1}^{n} \alpha \cdot \max(0, t_i + s_i - l_i)^2 + \sum_{k=1}^{p} \beta \cdot \max(0, L_k - Q)^2$$

[2.6]

The interest for using squared expressions is to accept small violations more easily than large ones, while coefficients α and β are used to tune the relative weights of the two types of violation. At the end of the local search, a solution with $CP(S) = C(S)$ is fully feasible. In reality, a solution can be acceptable even if there are still small violations. For instance, in waste collection, the trucks are often equipped with a compactor and vehicle capacity can be slightly exceeded, while in distribution many customers tolerate small delays (*soft time windows*) if they are not too frequent. However, to be fair, local search, even with penalization, is not ideal for very constrained problems: constraint programming is often a more effective option.

2.2.7. *Acceleration techniques*

For large-scale problems, even a neighborhood search in $O(n^2)$ can be too time-consuming. Several techniques are available to reduce running times.

The simplest consists of testing first the constraints which are more likely to be violated. Consider, for example, a VRPTW with tight time windows but enough vehicles: the relocation of one customer in a different route is more likely to violate time windows than vehicle capacity. A local search for this problem will be faster on average if time windows are tested first, which can be done in $O(1)$ by precomputing the maximum delays, as explained in section 2.2.3. By doing so, the capacity test and the computation of cost variation will be more rarely performed. This explains why local search procedures become much faster when time windows are added to a CVRP: most moves are dropped before their complete evaluation.

One difficulty is that the ordering of the different feasibility tests depends on the data. For instance, the previous order must be inverted for a VRPTW characterized by wide time windows, a fixed fleet of vehicles and a total demand close to fleet capacity. A possible solution is to compute the elimination rate of each feasibility test in the first calls to the local search, and to perform the tests in decreasing rate order. The reordering can be definitive or dynamically adjusted.

Another simple approach consists of evaluating *a restricted number M of randomly selected moves*, which constitutes a kind of neighborhood sampling. M can be fixed or proportional to the neighborhood cardinality, e.g. $M = \sqrt{|N(s)|}$.

Lists of neighbors are also frequently used. For a given node i, its list of neighbors $LN(i)$ contains the $n-1$ nodes $j \neq i$, sorted in increasing order of costs c_{ij}. The lists of neighbors for all nodes can be precomputed in $O(n^2 \log_2 n)$ at the beginning of the local search. A threshold θ is selected, for instance $n/10$ or $\sqrt{n}$, then the only moves evaluated for each node i are the ones which add one arc (i, j) such that j belongs to the first θ nodes of $LN(i)$.

To illustrate the concept, consider the 2-opt move on one route in Figure 2.5, which replaces arcs (u, x) and (v, y) by (u, v) and (x, y). In a fast implementation, a main loop inspects each node u while an inner loop tests each node v among the first θ nodes of $LN(u)$. The choice of these two nodes is enough to define the move, since x and y are, respectively, the successors of u and v in the route. The idea behind the restricted list of neighbors is that expensive arcs are unlikely in good solutions. Nevertheless, counter-examples can easily be found. Therefore, it is prudent to vary θ dynamically and even to try $\theta = n - 1$ from time to time, to browse the neighborhood completely.

Vertex marking was introduced under the name of *don't look bits* by Bentley in 2-opt moves for the TSP [BEN 92]. Here is the principle: if none of the moves involving one given node are able to improve the incumbent solution, this node can be ignored in the next iterations. Each node can be marked or unmarked. At the beginning, they are all marked and stored in an active list L. Then, each marked node x is inspected in the order of the list, to evaluate all moves involving edges incident to x. If these moves are unfruitful, x is unmarked and removed from L. Otherwise, all nodes concerned by the move (extremities of inserted and removed edges) are marked and appended to L, unless they are already in the list. The local search ends when the list is empty.

Compared to a traditional local search, which scans the whole neighborhood at each iteration, the vertex marking version is faster since L contains only the nodes involved in recent successful moves. The other nodes are forgotten until an improving move involving incident edges is discovered. Muyldermans described in detail an efficient implementation of a local search procedure for the CARP, which combines edge marking and lists of neighbors [MUY 03].

Lin and Kernighan introduced in 1973 an approach called *sequential search* for the TSP [LIN 73]. The main idea relies on the decomposition of each move into partial moves, most of them being pruned by computing bounds on partial gains. Irnich *et al.* [IRN 06] studied such decompositions for most moves used in local search procedures for the CVRP.

Algorithm 6 shows how to find the best 2-opt* move for a given solution S, using the sequential search approach. As can be seen in Figure 2.5, a natural decomposition for the 2-opt* move is to select arc (u, x) and then arc (v, y). The algorithm exploits the following property [IRN 06]: if we select arc (u, x) and have already found an improving move with gain G^*, only the arcs (v, y) such that $c_{ux} - c_{vx} > G^*/2$ need to be tested to try to find a better move. $LN(x)$ is the list of neighbors of node x, $trip(u)$ denotes the index of the route serving u, G is the gain obtained by the examined move (positive for an improving move) and $next(v)$ is the successor of node v in its route. It is assumed that two quantities are precomputed for each node u: the cumulated load Q_u^{to} from the beginning of $trip(u)$ up to u (included) and the cumulated load Q_u^{from} from u (included) up to the end of $trip(u)$.

Algorithm 2.6: Sequential search of 2-opt* neighborhood for a solution S

1 $G^* := 0$
2 **for each** arc (u, x) in the routes of S **do**
3      $B = c_{ux} - G^*/2$
4   **for each** $v \in LN(x)$ such that $trip(v) \neq trip(u)$ **while** $c_{vx} < B$ **do**
5          $y := next(v)$
6   **if** $Q_u^{to} + Q_y^{from} \leq Q$ **and** $Q_v^{to} + Q_x^{from} \leq Q$ **then**
7              $G = c_{ux} + c_{vy} - c_{vx} - c_{uy}$
8   **if** $G > G^*$ **then**
9                  $G^* := G$
10   record the attributes $u^* = u$ and $v^* = v$ of the new best move

---

Compared to algorithm 2.4, this sequential version examines less moves and in a completely different order. Irnich *et al.* [IRN 06] describe decompositions for various moves, with search times divided by 10 to 50 compared with classical implementations. Hence, this approach is very powerful but its implementation is not trivial since an *ad-hoc* decomposition must be found for each move. Moreover, the method becomes complicated when other constraints are added.

2.2.8. *Complex moves*

The literature contains local searches based on very elaborated moves, such as the GENIUS method [GEN 92], cyclic transfers [THO 93] and ejection chains [REG 96, REG 98]. An example of ejection chain is to try to move a customer to another route. If the capacity of the target route is violated, one of its customer can be ejected in a third route, etc. Obviously, the number of successive ejections must be limited to avoid excessive running times.

Very large scale neighborhood (VLSN) search considers neighborhoods with exponential cardinalities, in which an improving move (if any) can be determined in polynomial time. In general, such neighborhoods are defined by sequences of classical moves, such as relocations and swaps, and an improving sequence is determined by computing a least-cost path in an auxiliary graph [ERG 06]. In section 2.1.2, we saw an optimal procedure to split a TSP tour into CVRP routes. This procedure called Split can be used as a VLSN operator, for instance at the end of a classical local search. To do so, the successive routes are concatenated to form a giant tour, which is then submitted to Split. An improvement is often obtained because Split can shift several trip limits simultaneously. Although there is an exponential number of ways to cut the giant tour into successive CVRP routes (i.e. an exponential number of paths in the auxiliary graph), the best splitting can be determined in $O(n^2)$.

Another approach called *large neighborhood search* (LNS) [SCH 00] consists of destroying partially the solution and then to repair it. To avoid a complete enumeration of such *ruin and recreate moves*, the destruction is often based on a randomized heuristic while the repair is done using a greedy heuristic or an exact method. In the CVRP for instance, a given number k of customers can be removed randomly and reintroduced in the routes *via* a cheapest insertion heuristic.

In the adaptive LNS metaheuristic (ALNS) presented in Chapter 3, several heuristics can be employed. In each iteration, the algorithm selects randomly one destroy operator and one repair operator and computes statistics on the efficiency of each pair, for instance the average cost variation. The selection probabilities are then biased in favor of the best combinations [PIS 07].

Funke *et al.* [FUN 05] realized a state-of-the-art on most local search operators for vehicle routing problems and proposed a unified representation that can handle many complex constraints, including resource constraints.

2.3. Conclusion

The computation of initial solutions and the improvement of new solutions are essential in metaheuristics. The running time to reach a given cost objective can be strongly reduced when the metaheuristic is launched from high-quality initial solutions. Although some metaheuristics in their primary form do not include a local search (pure genetic algorithms, ant colony optimization and particle swarm optimization), it is a pity to continue a long sequence of crossover operators to find the optimum, when the first crossover has already find a solution in the attraction basin of this optimum. A single call to a local search procedure can be enough to finish the job.

This chapter has shown that these two components can already be very sophisticated, involving a rich variety of algorithmic techniques. The principles are often simple, but the codes grow quickly when speed and result quality are critical issues, e.g. by using *ad-hoc* data structures to reduce the algorithmic complexity or by combining several neighborhoods. These improvements can have a tremendous impact on the whole metaheuristic since the local search component is often called thousands of times.

A lot of researchers are fascinated by some metaheuristic templates such as genetic algorithms and ant colony optimization, without speaking about other methods inspired by various animals (cuckoos, bats, bees, glowing worms, etc.), varyingly fancy and nasty, and physical principles such as electromagnetism. They focus too much on the general structure but, according to our own experience, being an afficionado of one metaheuristic in particular brings little if the initial solutions and the local search are not elaborated enough.

3

Metaheuristics Generating a Sequence of Solutions

A metaheuristic is a higher level procedure than the basic heuristics described in Chapter 2. It intends to escape from locally optimal solutions. This chapter focuses on a class that works on a single solution at a time, making it evolve through a particular iterative process. This kind of exploration requires us to define at least one neighborhood to jump from an incumbent solution to a close one in the solution space. Eight metaheuristics generating a sequence of solutions are presented in this chapter, beginning with perhaps the first one historically, which is the simulated annealing. Some selected applications on vehicle routing problems (VRP) will be detailed afterward.

3.1. Simulated annealing (SA)

The *simulated annealing* (SA) algorithm for combinatorial optimization was introduced by Kirkpatrick *et al.* in 1983 [KIR 83] and is inspired by a physics phenomenon concerning the behavior of atoms under temperature changes. The principle is detailed hereafter.

3.1.1. *Principle*

The principle of *SA* is inspired by a physics phenomenon related to the behavior of atoms (energy E) according to changes in temperature (T), and based on the following formula: $e^{-E/kT}$, with k the Boltzmann energy constant. In physics, cooling metal too fast induces imperfections which the authors compare to local optima. On the other hand, cooling more slowly, the atoms have time to settle into a perfect crystalline lattice, which can be seen as the global optimum. An annealing treatment aims to achieve the perfect structure. In a combinatorial problem, the exponential function tends to rule the search for optimal solutions. The value E/k is represented by the variation of the objective function after the execution of a move in a neighborhood at a certain "temperature" T, the latter being a real number. More concretely, a random transformation is evaluated on the current solution. If it causes a variation Δf in favor of the optimized objective (i.e. an improvement of the solution, evaluated as a negative variation), it is then accepted and executed. Otherwise, processing is accepted with a probability $e^{-\Delta f/T}$. Thus, at a specified "temperature", a move inducing a smaller degradation has more chance of being performed. The cooling is simulated by decreasing the T value gradually throughout the iterations (e.g. by a factor α such as 0.999), reducing the probability of accepting a non-improving move. The method stops when T has reached a certain value close to 0, or after a given number of iterations. The best solution found is returned. Obviously, the acceptance rule does not require us to be driven by an exponential function as in physics applications, even if most of the authors choose this option. A pseudo-code of the general principle is presented in algorithm 3.1. $U \sim (0,1)$ is a random number generator applying a uniform distribution.

Algorithm 3.1: Simulated annealing principle

1   build an initial solution S
2   $S^* := S$
3   $T := T_{max}$
4   **while** *the stopping criterion is not met* **do**
5 | $S' := \text{RandomTransformation}(S)$
6 | evaluate Δf
7 | **if** $\Delta f < 0$ *or* $e^{-\Delta f/T} < U \sim (0,1)$ **then**
8 | $\lfloor\; S := S'$
9 | **if** S' improves S^* **then**
10 | $\lfloor\; S^* := S'$
11 | $\lfloor\; T := \alpha.T$
12 return(S^*)

Contrarily to most of the metaheuristics, SA does not require us to build a good initial solution (line 1) since the high temperatures used at the beginning of the algorithm would unmake it. Details on the methodology can be found in [VAN 87].

3.1.2. *Simulated annealing in vehicle routing problems*

A key-point of this method is to define the kind of random transformation to perform on the incumbent solution to jump in the solution space. It generally implicitly defines a particular neighborhood. In the vehicle routing context, moves are often classical, such as relocate, exchange and two-opt moves. One of the first attempts for vehicle routing was presented in 1993 by Osman. In his paper, he put forward at the same time the "λ-interchange" moves [OSM 93], explained in Chapter 2.

A few other implementations can be found, in particular those of Lin, Yu and others, with works on the truck and trailer routing problem with time windows [LIN 09, LIN 11], the team orienteering problems (TOPs) [LIN 12, LIN 13], and the location routing problems (LRPs) [YU 10, YU 14, YU 15]. The authors define a neighborhood structure that includes classical moves (such as relocate and exchange), and possibly others depending on the problem at hand (e.g. a change of service vehicle type to solve the the Truck and Trailer Routing Problem (TTRP)).

However, on the Capacitated VRP (CVRP), deterministic variants have been more successful. A good example is the *record-to-record travel* (RRT) method from Li *et al.* [LI 05] for very large-scale instances (1,200 customers). The differences between SA and RRT lie in their acceptance rules for worse intermediate solutions. In SA, it is grounded on the parameter T. If T is large, worse solutions are accepted with a higher probability. The key-point is to choose a successful *annealing schedule*, i.e. a good rule for lowering the T value during the algorithm. The quality of the results is very sensitive on this rule. RRT, for its part, has only one parameter: the deviation allowed. A solution is accepted if it improves the best value obtained so far (record) or if it is not worse than the deviation allowed from the best record.

Finally, SA is well suited for parallel implementations: Groër *et al.* have implemented a version for the CVRP [GRO 11], while Wang *et al.* have dealt with the VRP with simultaneous pickups and deliveries and time windows [WAN 15].

3.2. Greedy randomized adaptive search procedure: GRASP

The GRASP was initiated by Feo and Resende in 1989 [FEO 89]. It is built on independent iterations performing a two-stage process.

3.2.1. *Principle*

The GRASP principle is to create a new solution at each iteration, independent of the following. For this purpose, two stages are necessary:

1) first, a solution is built using a randomized greedy algorithm;

2) second, the obtained solution undergoes a local search.

The best solution found through the iterations is returned as the result.

For a particular instance, a deterministic heuristic always provides the same solution. Thus, in an iterative procedure such as GRASP, it is therefore necessary to introduce some randomness to diversify the search. On the other hand, providing completely random solutions to the local search would produce quite bad results. The goal is more to try to obtain solutions of both varied and good quality. This leads to the adaptive qualifying of the method: randomization is controlled with a shortlist *Restricted Candidate List* (RCL) of possible choices at each step of the construction of the solution. This list may change at each stage. Two policies are possible (see Figure 3.1):

– the first policy is to complete the list with possible decisions selected at random, and then choose the best one according to the greedy criterion;

– the second policy is to keep a list of the better decisions found by the greedy algorithm and pick one at random.

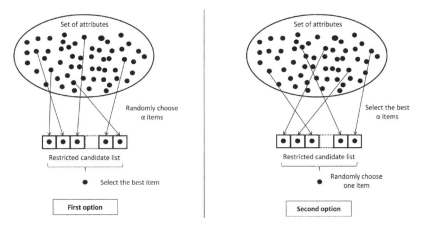

Figure 3.1. *Possible policies for the restricted candidate list*

Once the selected element is incorporated into the partial solution, the RCL is updated. This strategy is similar to the semi-greedy heuristic suggested by Hart and Shogan [HAR 87], another multi-start approach built on greedy randomized constructions, but without local search.

The really tricky part is to randomize the greedy algorithm while ensuring solution quality. In particular, it is necessary to determine the size α of the RCL. The latter can be sized at a fixed cardinality or according to the quality of its elements. In the first option provided in Figure 3.1, the filling of the list is simply achieved by introducing α decision-items. In the second option depicted in Figure 3.1, a decision can only be inserted if its associated cost is below a certain threshold determined as follows. Let e be an element and $c(e)$ be its associated cost. In minimization, if c_{min} and c_{max} are, respectively, the smallest and highest possible added costs, then e is inserted if and only if $c(e) \leq c_{min} + \beta(c_{max} - c_{min})$, with $\beta \in [0; 1]$. $\beta = 1$ results in a completely random construction, while $\beta = 0$ corresponds to a greedy deterministic algorithm. Tuning the value of β value is sometimes critical.

Anyway, one shortcoming of the method is the independence of its iterations. In fact, GRASP may be viewed as a repetitive sampling technique, which does not learn from the history of solutions found in previous iterations. However, information gathered from good solutions can be involved to implement memory-based procedures. During the construction phase, the selection probabilities associated with each element of the RCL can be influenced. For example, Prais and Ribeiro pitched for changing the size of the RCL through a learning process [PRA 00]. In fact, α is selected from a range of possible values, each associated with a probability which is updated at each iteration, to encourage those providing the best results. They named their method *Reactive GRASP*.

More elaborate techniques may be introduced in order to improve performance of the basic version [FEO 94, RES 03, RES 05]. A pseudo-code of a GRASP for a VRP is given in section 3.9.1, it includes a learning process on critical decision of the optimized problem.

3.2.2. *GRASP in vehicle routing problems*

As with the previous metaheuristics (SA), even if it can produce good quality solutions, GRASP is hardly ever among the most efficient methods on vehicle routing problems. The reason for this undoubtedly comes from its independent iterations. Marinakis proposed a multiple phase neighborhood search-GRASP for the CVRP [MAR 12], in which the stopping criterion is inspired by Lagrangian relaxation and subgradient optimization. Another way to enhance the method is, for instance, to add the path relinking technique (PR). This option has been applied to the GRASP for the LRP [PRI 06], the two-echelon LRP [NGU 12b] and the capacitated arc routing problem (CARP) [USB 13]. Examples can also be found with the version called reactive GRASP for the combined production-distribution problem [BOU 07] and the CARP [PRI 05]. The idea of coupling GRASP and PR, suggested by Laguna and Martí [LAG 95], provides the missing link between solutions. The PR principle is explained in Chapter 4. Roughly, a path from a solution U to a guide solution V is explored by gradually introducing into U attributes present in V. To do so, it could be more convenient to work on a permutation of customers as in the split algorithm described in section 2.1.2.

To better understand the GRASP principle and the use of the RCL on routing context, a detailed implementation is presented in section 3.9.1 for the location-routing problem.

3.3. Tabu search

The *Tabu Search* (TS) comes from Glover [GLO 86, GLO 89, GLO 90], and can be applied to various combinatorial problems. Unlike GRASP and SA, TS is a fully deterministic method. In several cases, TS provides very good solutions, making this method among the most effective to tackle difficult combinatorial problems. These successes have made the method very popular, although nowadays, other approaches seem to be more efficient, such as evolutionary methods and iterated local search algorithms.

3.3.1. *Principle*

The basic principle of TS is to continue the local search, even when it reaches a local optimum. Thus, the idea is to fully scan a neighborhood of the current solution and make the best possible move, even if it deteriorates the objective function. Returning to a solution previously visited is prevented by the use of memories, called *tabu lists*, which record the recent history of the search. The best solution encountered during the algorithm is stored to be returned at the end, when a stopping criterion is reached. Tabus also help the search to move away from previously visited areas of the search space and thus perform more extensive exploration.

Storage of complete solutions in a tabu list often consumes lots of memory. One option is to keep only some attributes, such as moves that allowed us to go from one solution to another, or even, more simply, the value of the objective function. Moreover, the tabu list implements a short-term memory, the *tabu tenure*. In general, it is sufficient to avoid cycling. Standard tabu lists are usually implemented as circular lists of fixed length but we can choose to vary the tabu list length during the search or to randomly generate the tabu tenure of each move within some specified interval. A long-term memory may be added to diversify the search. Adaptive memory is proposed by Glover [GLO 97a].

The *aspiration criteria* constitute another typical feature of TS. In fact, sometimes qualifying some attributes as tabus prohibits attractive moves. A simple and commonly used aspiration criterion is to allow a move, even if it is tabu, when it ends at a solution that outperforms the current best-known solution. The general structure of a TS is sketched in algorithm 3.2.

It is possible to accelerate the process by removing solutions that belong to a neighborhood involving attributes with little chance of belonging to the optimal solution. This reduction technique of space suggested by Toth and Vigo gives the granular tabu search (GTS) [TOT 03], as described in section 3.9.2. Details on the methodology can be found in [GLO 97b].

Algorithm 3.2: Tabu search principle

---

1 build an initial solution S
2 $S^* := S$
3 **while** *the stopping criterion is not met* **do**
4 | select the best move in the neighborhood
5 | **if** *the move is allowed* **then**
6 | | *//it is allowed by the aspiration criteria or it is non tabu*
7 | |_ perform the move on S
8 | **if** S improves S^* **then**
9 |_ |_ $S^* := S$

10 return(S^*)

3.3.2. *Tabu search in vehicle routing problems*

Attributes stored in the tabu list are the distinctive elements used to prevent cycling when moving away from local optima through non-improving moves. In the CVRP, for instance, if the neighborhood is defined by relocate moves, a customer i that has just been moved from route A to route B should not go back in A. Thus, moving i back from B to A is prohibited for a given number of iterations (the *tabu tenure*) by declaring tabu the triplet (i, A, B). In fact, a cycle may occur if the customer i is moved to another route C and then from C to A. To avoid this case, a stronger tabu could be implemented by storing as tabu only the pair (i, A), or even by not allowing i to be moved to another route during all the tabu tenure.

A *mid-term memory* (or a *long-term memory*) can also be applied to record the number of consecutive iterations (or respectively, the total number of iterations since the beginning of the algorithm) in which some components have not changed in the current solution. For instance, in the CVRP, we could count how many times each customer has been moved from its current route. When an upper limit is reached, the idea could be to allow more complex moves, or to force a few rarely used components to be included in the current solution (or the best-known solution) and restarting the search from this point. For example, customers which have not yet been relocated frequently could be forced to move into new routes.

For a long time, TS methods have been the most employed and most effective metaheuristics for vehicle routing problems. In 2002, Cordeau and Laporte referred to the 10 most effective TSs at that time [COR 02]. Vehicle capacity and time windows are most often relaxed in these implementations of TS to treat an objective function with penalties, as in section 2.2.6.

Among the 10 referred TSs, the Taillard algorithm [TAI 93] defines a neighborhood based on the λ-interchange mechanism from Osman [OSM 93]. It applies no reoptimization, except occasionally by calling the exact algorithm for the traveling salesman problem (TSP) from Volgenant and Jonker [VOL 83] as intensification, and it passes only through feasible solutions. For Euclidean problems, the procedure uses a decomposition into sectors centered on the depot with concentric circles, and works in every sector. The latter are updated regularly to provide diversification. For non-Euclidean problems, the decomposition is defined by the smallest spanning tree rooted on the depot. Taillard also introduces a long-term memory by keeping track of past solutions and penalizing frequently performed moves.

Rochat and Taillard [ROC 95] apply another intensification concept based on adaptive memory. Using a population of good solutions gathered during TS, the authors combine non-overlapping routes. The search is then initiated from the partial solution resulting from these selected routes and the unrouted vertices.

Taburoute [GEN 94] employs a neighborhood defined by all solutions which can be reached from the current solution by removing a node from a tour and by inserting it into another containing at least one of its p closest neighbors with the GENI (Generalized Insertion) procedure developed for the TSP and this tour is reoptimized by the US (Unstringing and Stringing) TSP post-optimization local search [GEN 92]. Obtained solutions may violate capacity constraints, but this is penalized in the objective function.

Successful versions are available for many problems including the CVRP [REG 96, BAR 99, TOT 03], VRP with time windows (VRPTW) [COR 01a], CVRP and heterogeneous fleet VRP (HFVRP) with two-dimensional loading [LEU 11, LEU 13]. These algorithms typically involve classical moves, but Rego and Roucairol [REG 96] evaluate ejection chains which consist of moving vertices in a cyclic manner: a first vertex n_1 takes the place of vertex n_2 which is ejected at the position of a third vertex n_3, and so on (see Chapter 2).

Brandão et al. have developed TS for several variants of vehicle routing problems: the multi-trip vehicle routing and scheduling problem [BRA 97], the open VRP [BRA 04], the VRP with backhauls [BRA 06] and the heterogeneous fleet vehicle routing problem [BRA 09, BRA 11]. The TS algorithm starts with an initial solution, feasible or infeasible, generated by a dedicated heuristic. The neighborhood of the current solution is defined through a set of candidates to change their present position. For the Open VRP (OVRP) for instance, Brandão uses only relocate and exchange moves operated in interroutes (applied to distinct routes). A strategic oscillation between feasible and infeasible solution spaces is implemented, with a penalty term in the objective function that is dynamically adjusted according to the number of consecutive iterations within a space. An iteration consists of choosing the non-tabu move that generates the minimum cost solution (including the penalty). However, the tabu status of a move can be overruled in two cases:

– if it generates a feasible solution that is better than any feasible solution known so far;

– or if it is infeasible with a cost lower than the cost of any infeasible solution already known.

A tabu move is defined by the prohibition during a specified number of iterations to insert back a customer in a route it left in the past. Since a move modifies two routes of the current solution, each of those is improved by dedicated TSP local search methods.

A more detailed implementation of TS for the CVRP is offered in section 3.9.2, elaborated on the granular version.

3.4. Variable neighborhood search

The *variable neighborhood search* (VNS) and its simpler variant the *variable neighborhood descent* (VND) are fast and compact metaheuristics. They are often designed to replace the local search within another metaheuristic. The approach was introduced by Mladenovi and Hansen [MLA 97].

3.4.1. *Principle*

The main idea of variable neighborhood search is inspired by a simple principle: a systematic change of neighborhood each time no improvement is found by a local search algorithm in the current one. In fact, a local optimum in a particular neighborhood is not bound to be so in another one. Most of the time, VNS explores increasingly distant vicinities of the incumbent solution, which implies being able to evaluate the distance between any two solutions when performing a move, or at least to define neighborhoods with growing cardinalities. However, the way to jump into another neighborhood can be done through different options: (1) deterministic, (2) stochastic, (3) both deterministic and stochastic.

With a deterministic change, the method is reduced to a VND. If a finite set of k preselected neighborhood structures is $N = \bigcup_i N_i$, for $i = 1..k$, the set of solutions in the ith neighborhood of S can be denoted as $N_i(S)$. Then, the VND can be sketched by algorithm 3.3.

When the local search does not find a better solution in the current neighborhood (the solution is at a local optimum within this neighborhood), the next one is explored and the method proceeds in that way with the successive neighborhoods until finding an improving move or achieving a stopping criterion (here, $i = k$). However, when a better solution is achieved, the algorithm restarts its search around the new solution within the closest neighborhood ($i = 1$) before exploring more distant solutions.

Algorithm 3.3: VND principle on a solution S

---

1 build an initial solution S
2 $i := 1$
3 **while** $i \leq k$ **do**
4 $\quad$ $S' := \text{LocalSearch}(N_i(S))$
5 $\quad$ **if** S' improves S **then**
6 $\quad\quad$ $S := S'$
7 $\quad\quad$ $i := 1$
8 $\quad$ **else**
9 $\quad\quad$ $i := i + 1$

In a stochastic manner, random points are selected from $N_i(S)$ by a procedure called *shaking* applied on the current solution, resulting in the reduced VNS (RVNS) method (see algorithm 3.4). This version is useful for very large instances for which local search is costly.

Algorithm 3.4: RVNS principle on a solution S

---

1 build an initial solution S
2 $i := 1$
3 **while** *the stopping criterion is not met* **do**
4 $\quad$ **while** $i \leq k$ **do**
5 $\quad\quad$ $S' := \text{Shaking}(N_i(S))$
6 $\quad\quad$ **if** S' improves S **then**
7 $\quad\quad\quad$ $S := S'$
8 $\quad\quad\quad$ $i := 1$
9 $\quad\quad$ **else**
10 $\quad\quad\quad$ $i := i + 1$

The VNS method further enhances the RVNS by a local search called after the shaking procedure. The neighborhood visited during the local search must be different from the ones defined for the shaking to not cancel the move. This leads to the VNS described in algorithm 3.5. Most of the time, VNS combines deterministic and stochastic changes of neighborhood by replacing the local search by a VND involving its own moves.

The stopping criterion can be a maximum computational time, a maximum number of iterations or a maximum number of iterations between two improvements. In practice, the local search called in line 7 of algorithm 3.5 is often a VND.

Algorithm 3.5: VNS principle on a solution S

---

1 build an initial solution S
2 $S := \text{LocalSearch}(S)$
3 $i := 1$
4 **while** *the stopping criterion is not met* **do**
5   **while** $i \leq k$ **do**
6          $S' := \text{Shaking}(N_i(S))$
7          $S' := \text{LocalSearch}(S')$
8   **if** S' improves S **then**
9              $S := S'$
10             $i := 1$
11   **else**
12             $i := i + 1$

Details on the methodology can be found in [HAN 99, HAN 10].

3.4.2. *Variable neighborhood search in vehicle routing problems*

Although previous metaheuristics may apply different types of moves (relocate, swap, etc.) to search the solution space, they are not particularly presented to identify several neighborhoods. However, VND/VNS clearly require us to distinguish them. Mostly, it is even necessary to make a ranking. In practice, this can be made by measuring their cardinality and ordering them in increasing size. Another option can be to evaluate the complexity to explore each neighborhood. For instance, the best relocation move of a customer in a solution can be determined in $o(n^2)$, while a 3-opt is in $o(n^3)$. Thus, solutions in the second case are considered as belonging to a wider neighborhood than in the first case. In addition, moves performed in intraroutes and interroutes are also often differentiated. In the VNS from Kytöjoki *et al.* [KUO 12], seven frequently used operators are chosen:

– three are intraroute moves (2-opt, Or-opt and 3-opt);

– four others are interroute moves (exchange, relocate, 2-opt* and cross-exchange).

However, in their VNS for the open VRP, Fleszar *et al.* prefer two operators [FLE 09]: (1) an intraroute local optimization that consists of reversing a segment and (2) an interroute that considers exchanging pairs of segments between routes.

Kuo *et al.* in the multi-depot VRP [KUO 12] select four operators (relocate, exchange, arc exchange – similar to a 2-opt and sequence exchange). The proposed VNS applies a criterion like in SA as neighborhood solution acceptance.

Other effective VNSs are available, for example, for problems such as the VRP with loading constraints [WEI 15], in which a ruin-reconstruct mechanism is utilized to diversify the search process (see section 3.7), the inventory routing problem [POP 12], where the shaking procedure is based on the deliveries transfer between days of planning horizon, the periodic routing problems [HEM 12], with relocate and cross-exchange shaking procedures as well as a neighborhood that changes the visit combinations for customers, and the capacitated arc routing problems [HER 01, POL 08].

These methods are often surpassed by more complex metaheuristics, but their simplicity is particularly attractive. Furthermore, their speed often makes them the only candidates for large problems [KYT 07].

3.5. Iterated local search

The *iterated local search* (ILS) [LOU 10] is a very effective method for vehicle routing problems. Its generates a sequence of local optima by alternating local search and perturbation.

3.5.1. *Principle*

Historically, ILS appeared in the literature a few years before VNS: it was put forward under the name of iterated descent by Baum in 1986 [BAU 86]. In fact, a VNS in which a single neighborhood is used in the shaking phase is a particular case of ILS. However, the shaking procedure is now called perturbation, which may involve more complex moves. The idea is to search the solution space using a walk that explores the attraction basin around a solution (local search) before leaving it (perturbation), as illustrated in Figure 3.2.

Algorithm 3.6 provides an overview of the process. More precisely, given the current solution S, first it operates a change or perturbation (line 5) that leads to an intermediate state S'. Then, the local search (line 6) is applied to S' to reach the local optimum of its attraction basin. If the resulting solution passes an acceptance test, it becomes the next element of the search otherwise, the algorithm stays S.

The perturbation needs to be well tuned to be neither too weak nor too strong. In fact, if changes are too weak, the local search might bring us back to the previous solution. However, information on the search history can be used to guide the perturbation and/or the acceptance of a solution. Too strong, it could lose good attributes of the solution and perform random fruitless jumps in the solution space.

A basic version could generate a random initial solution. However, it is often more promising to use a heuristic to provide a better starting point. An easy and effective perturbation can be made through a random move in a neighborhood different from the one used by the local search algorithm. This leads to *Markovian* walk on the set of local optima. Concerning the acceptance criterion, we can choose to check the improvement of the current solution, as well as to adopt a criterion adjusted empirically as in SA.

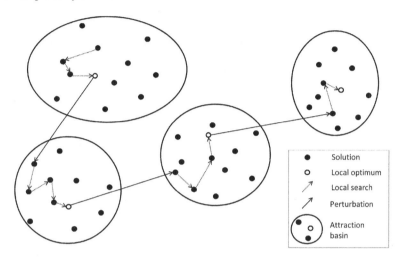

Figure 3.2. *Example of ILS trajectory in solution space*

Algorithm 3.6: ILS principle

---

1 build an initial solution S
2 $S := \text{LocalSearch}(S)$
3 $S^* := S$
4 **while** *the stopping criterion is not met* **do**
5 $\quad$ $S' := \text{Perturbation}(S, \text{history})$
6 $\quad$ $S' := \text{LocalSearch}(S')$
7 $\quad$ **if** $\text{AcceptationCriteria}(S,S',\text{history}) = true$ **then**
8 $\quad\quad$ $S := S'$
9 $\quad$ **if** S' improves S^* **then**
10 $\quad\quad$ $S^* := S'$
11 return(S^*)

Further enhancement on the perturbation phase is the possibility of modifying its strength by adapting it along the iterations. One idea is to exploit the search history to change it deterministically. This option brings both VNS and ILS ever closer: the strength modification is similar to a change of neighborhood, and the deterministic trigger could be the absence of improvement after the last perturbation. Finally, an even stronger perturbation may bring us near to another analogous method, presented in section 3.7: large neighborhood search.

Nevertheless, according to Lourenço *et al.* [LOU 10], a major difference between ILS and VNS is the philosophy underlying the two metaheuristics: ILS explicitly has the goal of building a walk in the set of locally optimal solutions, while VNS relies on the idea of systematically changing the neighborhood during the search. We can add another distinction. The perturbation called shaking in VNS is reduced to a single move, in a single neighborhood at a time, even if this neighborhood changes during the search. In most ILS algorithms, the perturbation consists of a given number of successive random moves, in one or several neighborhoods, e.g. two relocations, or two relocations plus two exchanges. Moreover, the strength of perturbation is increased by using wider neighborhoods in VNS, but augmenting the number of successive moves in ILS.

3.5.2. *Iterated local search in vehicle routing problems*

The four components of an ILS are: (1) generation of an initial solution, (2) local search, (3) perturbation and (4) acceptance criterion. As in the previous metaheuristics, the first two elements can be chosen from the standard algorithms for vehicle routing problems presented in Chapter 2. Thus, the key-points stand on the latter two components.

If the perturbation can be defined by a random move in a neighborhood different from the one used by the local search algorithm, it remains that the strength of a perturbation is crucial. In vehicle routing problems, common measures are the number of edges that are changed in the solution, or the number of relocated customers. Thus, we can perform several simple moves, such as relocate, in a raw. Another example is the use of the double-bridge move, which removes four edges and introduces four new ones in a route. Without disturbing the solution much, this kind of perturbation is strong enough to change the topology of the tour since it cannot be undone easily, neither by simple local search algorithms such as relocate and exchange moves, nor by 2-opt and 3-opt moves.

Concerning the acceptation criteria, as before, a particular strategy can be implemented in order to intensify or diversify the search by taking into account the history of the search.

Vansteenwegen *et al.* [VAN 09b] come up with an ILS for a team orienteering problem with time windows, a special vehicle routing problem in which a score is associated with each customer, as well as a service time and a time window. The goal is to maximize the sum of the collected scores by a fixed number of routes. In this problem, the score collected at a customer location and the distance to reach it are independent and often in opposition to each other. This makes it very difficult to solve since simple construction and improvement heuristics may end to undesirable directions. To escape from local optima, the perturbation removes one or more visits in each tour. Two parameters are needed: the first one defines the number of consecutive visits to remove in a tour, while the second one indicates the place in the tour from which to start the removing process. To control the strength, the maximum number of locations to remove depends on the number of customers and the number of routes.

For the two-echelon location-routing problem, Nguyen *et al.* [NGU 12a] implement a multi-start ILS. The principle is to restart the search from a new initial solution instead of losing time in unproductive iterations. In fact, recently visited solutions are stored and labeled as undesirable. Even if in ILS, encountering the same solution again does not imply cycling by means of the random perturbation, the authors interpret it as a lack of diversification penalized by reducing the number of ILS iterations before a restart. In addition, the acceptance criterion measures the gap to the best-known solution, which does not have to exceed a specified percentage. Then, in each ILS iteration, the algorithm alternates between the space of permutations of customers and the space of feasible LRP-2E solutions, using the split algorithm (see section 2.1.2). The perturbation operates on the giant tour by selecting at random one of the following moves: (1) randomly select p pairs of distinct customers and swap them, (2) determine the four longest edges (weak edges) and delete two at random. The substring between the two selected edges is removed and the cheapest insertion in the remaining sequence is performed; (3) add the edge linking the first and last customers of the giant tour, and then break the resulting cycle by randomly deleting one of the four weakest edges.

Silva *et al.* [SIL 15] design a novel perturbation mechanism for the split delivery vehicle routing problems, called *Multiple-k-Split*. Local optimal solutions are perturbed by removing a list composed of 5, 6 or 7 customers selected at random. Then, they are reinserted. To do so, a list of routes with non-zero residual capacity is initialized. If the sum of the residual capacities is enough to serve the demand of the customer to insert, a knapsack problem is solved. The aim is to decide how to split the demand to minimize the sum of the insertion costs. This is done by a greedy heuristic.

Allowing infeasible solutions can bring interesting results. Palhazi Cuervo *et al.* [PAL 14] take this option during the local search. The principle is to accept the solutions that violate the capacity constraint of the problem. The mechanism is guided by a dynamic adjustment of the penalty added to the cost of infeasible solutions. This *oscillating local search* (OLS) is applied on the VRP with backhauls. The perturbation mechanism iteratively removes a randomly selected customer, and inserts it back in a different randomly selected position, without considering capacity constraints. The strength of the perturbation relies on the number of relocated customers. Feasibility is brought back by the OLS.

Other excellent examples of ILS embedded in hybrid methods can be found for a vehicle routing problem. Some are described in Chapter 5.

3.6. Guided local search

As ILS, *guided local search* (GLS) [VOU 96] is adapted from a perturbation principle but with a penalized feature (qualifying one or several attributes of a solution). So, the solution does not directly undergo a change, but the landscape of the search space is modified and a local optimum is no longer optimal. It can also be seen as a penalty-based metaheuristic.

3.6.1. *Principle*

Instead of defining a neighborhood for a perturbation, a set of features of a solution is defined in a guided local search. So, when LS is trapped in local optima, some features are selected and penalized in the objective function. By doing so, a new call to LS will bring the search to a new area of the solution space.

In detail, GLS associates a cost and a penalty with each selected feature. The penalties are initialized to 0 and only increased after a call to a local search procedure. In fact, GLS assignes a new cost $g'(S')$ to the real value $g(S')$ of the local optimal objective function of S':

$$g'(S') = g(S') + \lambda \sum_i (p_i.l_i(S'))$$

where λ is a parameter, i ranges over the features, p_i is the penalty for feature i and l_i is a Boolean indicating whether i is in solution S'.

The aim is to penalize undesired features or features that would need to be changed to help in diversification. A highly penalized feature strongly affects the objective function. Thus, the utility of penalizing feature i at a local optimum needs to be defined, for example as follows:

$$utility_i(S') = l_i(S').\frac{c_i}{1 + p_i}$$

with c_i the cost and p_i the current penalty value of feature i, i.e. the higher the cost c_i of feature i, the greater the utility of penalizing it, and the more the penalized value p_i, the lower the utility of penalizing it again. Algorithm 3.7 provides an overview of the method. P is a vector of the penalty values p_i.

Algorithm 3.7: GLS principle

---

1 build an initial solution S
2 $S^* := S$
3 initialize P with penalty values p_i equal to 0
4 $S' := S$
5 **while** *the stopping criterion is not met* **do**
6 $\quad$ $S' :=$ LocalSearch(S',P)
7 $\quad$ **foreach** feature i **do**
8 $\quad\quad$ **if** $l_i = 1$ **then**
9 $\quad\quad\quad$ $utility_i(S') := l_i(S') \cdot \frac{c_i}{1+p_i}$
10 $\quad\quad$ **if** $utility_i(S')$ is maximum **then**
11 $\quad\quad\quad$ $p_i := p_i + 1$
12 $\quad$ **if** S' improves S^* **then**
13 $\quad\quad$ $S^* := S'$
14 return(S^*)

3.6.2. *Guided local search in vehicle routing problems*

The key-point of GLS is to define features for the problem, their costs and λ, since they will affect the efficiency of a search. Experience shows that the features and their costs normally come directly from the objective function, and that in many problems, the performance is not too sensitive to the λ value.

In vehicle routing problems, features could be the use of edges (so the fact that customer B is visited just after customer A in a route) with its associated cost. This is what was made in the first applications proposed in 1999 for the TSP [VOU 99] and the VRPTW [KIL 99].

A very efficient GLS has also been designed for the CARP [BEU 03]. In this version, two penalties are used: one for the GLS, and the other one for the infeasibility of the solution (the excess demand with respect to the vehicle capacity). The same is done for the VRP with backhauls and time windows [ZHO 05].

Tarantilis *et al.* [TAR 08] implement a GLS as post-optimization after a variable neighborhood search hybridized with a TS for the vehicle routing problem with intermediate replenishment facilities.

Another interesting application is for the team orienteering problem [VAN 09a], in which the objective is to maximize the total collected score at customers' locations. The authors suggest that heuristic procedures are made of a construction phase with local search. Two procedures first try to increase the total score of the solution by inserting and replacing (replace procedure) locations to be visited. Then, three other procedures tend to reduce the travel time between the selected locations by exchange and relocate moves between tours and 2-opt within each tour (the latter being denoted as TSP procedure). GLS is applied to replace and TSP procedures. In the replace heuristic, the actual score associated with a given customer is changed to an augmented score defined as GLS penalties updated as follows:

1) Increase the augmented score of the non-included location with the highest score;

2) Decrease the augmented score of an included location with a low score and remove it from the tour.

In TSP procedure, every time a local optimum is reached, the GLS framework penalizes the arcs (used in the current solution to connect two locations) with the highest utility as made in previous publications.

3.7. Large neighborhood search

The large neighborhood search (LNS) framework was described by Shaw in 1998 [SHA 98]. This is a search strategy that explores a (very) large neighborhood, which usually enhances the chance of finding a better quality of the locally optimal solutions, and in which the neighborhood is searched in an efficient manner (faster than a complete enumeration).

3.7.1. *Principle*

LNS decomposes the original problem by unfixing some decision variables, leading to a partial solution. The unfixed decision variables define a neighborhood of solutions that can be explored rather quickly by a specific procedure (e.g. a heuristic or a mixed-integer programming (MIP) solver). If the procedure finds an improved solution, it becomes the new current solution, and a new large neighborhood is defined around it. The scheme is repeated until reaching a stopping criterion. An iteration can also be seen as:

– partially destroying the incumbent solution by removing a certain number of elements;

– then repairing it by reinserting these elements.

A first key-point is the selection of variables to fix to obtain the partial solution. In fact, their number impacts the size of the neighborhood (the more fixed variables, the smaller the neighborhood). A common strategy is to vary dynamically the number of removed variables. A second key-point rests on the selection of fixed/removed variables: a random choice or a more sophisticated strategy to guide the search. Finally, the procedure that explores the neighborhood should provide good quality results in a short time.

Adaptive LNS (ALNS) is an extension of LNS, close to a VNS in the sense that ALNS operates on a predefined set N of (large) neighborhoods, with a number of different destroy (set $N^- \in N$) and repair (set $N^+ \in N$) operators. In comparison with LNS, an additional layer adaptively chooses among a set of removal and insertion heuristics. This approach has multiplied since that of Pisinger and Ropke [PIS 07], which can solve several vehicle routing problems such as CVRP and Pickup and Delivery Problems.

A pseudo-code of ALNS is detailed in algorithm 3.8. At each iteration, a randomly selected pair of operators (with procedures SelectDestruction and SelectRepair, lines 5 and 6) is applied to the current solution (line 7), with probabilities (respectively, sets π^d and π^r) updated by a learning process (line 12). The more a neighborhood $N_i^- \in N^-$ (respectively, $N_i^+ \in N^+$) has contributed to the solution process, the larger probability π_i^d (respectively, π_i^r) of being chosen it obtains. This approach is conceptually simple but requires quite tedious implementation because it typically uses around 10 heuristics.

Algorithm 3.8: ALNS principle

---

1 build an initial solution S
2 initialize π^d and π^r
3 $S^* := S$
4 **while** *the stopping criterion is not met* **do**
5 $\quad$ $d := \text{SelectDestruction}(N^-, \pi^d)$
6 $\quad$ $r := \text{SelectRepair}(N^+, \pi^r)$
7 $\quad$ $S' := \text{GenerateNewSolution}(S, d, r)$
8 $\quad$ **if** $\text{AcceptationCriteria}(S,S') = true$ **then**
9 $\quad\quad$ $\lfloor$ $S := S'$
10 $\quad$ **if** S' improves S^* **then**
11 $\quad\quad$ $\lfloor$ $S^* := S'$
12 $\quad$ update scores of π^d and π^r
13 return(S^*)

ALNS is particularly well suited when small neighborhoods show difficulties in escaping a local minima or certain areas of the solution space, such as for tightly constrained problems. However, it requires us to design each destruction and repair operator with, most often, sophisticated heuristics. In addition, it may have difficulties in handling very large problems since, to be efficient, destruction operators need to unfix some decision variables (commonly around 10%), which may represent a large subproblem to solve by the repair procedures. Details on large neighborhood search can be found in [PIS 10].

Another metaheuristic close to LNS is the very large scale neighborhood (VLSN) search [AHU 01, ERG 06]. The neighborhoods considered are often defined by a sequence of classical moves, such as swaps and relocations, and they have an exponential size. However, by building an auxiliary graph which models the possible sequences of moves, the best improving move can be determined in polynomial time, using a shortest path algorithm.

3.7.2. *Large neighborhood search in vehicle routing problems*

Successful ALNSs have been published very recently as for the VRP-2E and the LRP [HEM 12], the VRPTW in real time [HON 12], the cumulative VRP [RIB 12] and the inventory routing [COE 12, AKS 14]. These algorithms basically rely on several strategies to remove some customers before reinserting them with diverse procedures.

Coelho *et al.* [COE 12] pitch for a framework made up of five main components for inventory routing problems, reused by Aksen *et al.* [AKS 14]:

1) *Large neighborhood*: at each iteration, a number of customers are removed from their current route and are eventually reinserted.

2) *Adaptive search engine*: the choice of which operator to apply at a particular iteration is governed by a roulette-wheel mechanism in which each operator is assigned a weight depending on its past performance.

3) *Adaptive weight adjustment*: the search is divided into segments of φ iterations each, and weights are computed by taking into account the performance of the operators during the last segment.

4) *Periodic post-optimization*: at the end of each segment, apply a local search. The authors propose a 2-opt procedure to each vehicle route.

5) *Acceptance and stopping criterion*: the authors use an acceptance criterion inspired from SA.

The 2E-VRP is a two-level transportation problem where freight arrives at a major terminal and is shipped through intermediate satellite facilities to the final customers. Hemmelmayr *et al.* [HEM 12] consider this problem and the LRP, which is presented as a special case in which vehicle routing is performed only at the second level. They develop new neighborhood search operators that exploit the multi-level nature of the problems. Due to the decisions to handle in such problems, two types of destroy operators are used: three that change the number of satellites to open and five that only affect a few customers and routes. This results in eight procedures, and five repair algorithms. The operators are selected by a roulette-wheel mechanism based on their past success. A score is associated with each operator with respect to its success rate for finding new improving solutions. The first type of destroy operator explicitly changes the configuration of the open satellites (i.e. satellite removal, satellite opening and satellite swap). The second type affects a smaller part of the solution and removes a specified number of customers or some routes from the solutions. The repair operators may only insert customers into routes assigned to open satellites.

A more detailed implementation of the ALNS for the pickup and delivery problem with time windows from [ROP 06] is given in section 3.9.3.

Concerning the VLSN search, Ergun *et al.* [ERG 02] applied it to the TSP and the CVRP. The very large neighborhood is defined by the set of independent moves which can be simultaneously applied to the incumbent solution. For instance, it is possible to apply two relocations to a route if they do not interfere, i.e. if the two relocated nodes (and the nodes after which they are reinserted) are not consecutive. This independence of the moves is necessary to compute their cost variations individually. The problem of finding an improving move (not the best one) is polynomial and equivalent to finding a negative cost path in an *ad-hoc* auxiliary graph. For instance, Ergun *et al.* [ERG 02] show that the neighborhood defined by simultaneous relocations and swaps has a cardinality in $O(1.75^n)$ for the TSP but an improving move (if any) can be found in $O(n^2)$ only.

3.8. Transitional forms

There are transitional forms of the above methods to population-based metaheuristics detailed in the next chapter. For example, a tabu method can be reinforced by an *adaptive memory* that stores fragments of solutions to make periodic intensifications [ROC 95, TAR 02, TAR 05, LI 12]. We can also maintain a pool of good solutions in a GRASP and conduct periodic stages of path relinking, as made by Villegas *et al.* for the TTRP [VIL 11]. Another form of transition is the *evolutionary local search* (ELS).

3.8.1. *Evolutionary local search principle*

ELS was exposed by Wolf and Merz [WOL 07]. This can be seen as an ILS, where each iteration generates p children solutions by applying a perturbation and a local search to the current solution: the current solution S is replaced by the best child in case of improvement. The ILS particular case stands when $p = 1$. In our opinion, even if ELS corresponds to a $(1+p)$ evolution strategy, this is not really a population-based method since the set of children is not retained. Algorithm 3.9 provides the main ELS steps.

Algorithm 3.9: ELS principle

---

1 build an initial solution S
2 $S := \text{LocalSearch}(S)$
3 $S^* := S$
4 **while** *the stopping criterion is not met* **do**
5      $S' := S$
6   **for** $Child := 1 \ to \ p$ **do**
7          $S'' := \text{Perturbation } (S', \text{history})$
8          $S'' := \text{LocalSearch}(S'')$
9   **if** *AcceptationCriteria(S,S'')* = *true* **then**
10             $S := S''$
11   **if** S improves S^* **then**
12         $S^* := S$
13 return(S^*)

The method better explores the attraction basin around a solution than an ILS. Hence, for a certain number of iterations, it usually better improves the solution, but it may also discard too fast some search direction. This is why, generally, the perturbation strength needs to be adjusted dynamically through the iterations.

3.8.2. *Application to vehicle routing problems*

A family of recent and very effective ELS for vehicle routing problems relaxes the vehicle capacity to explore the solution space of TSP, and then applies a splitting procedure (see section 2.1.2) to derive feasible solutions for the original problem [PRI 09c, DUH 11, DUH 12].

For instance, the GRASPxELS from Prins [PRI 09c] can be seen as a multi-start ELS, in which a main iteration builds a solution with a greedy randomized heuristic, then improved by an ELS. The key-point of the effectiveness of the method rests on the alternation between the giant tour space and the complete solution space. Children are obtained through perturbations exchanging the position of two clients in the current giant tour T. The new generated giant tours are transformed into complete solutions by Split, and these solutions are improved by local search involving classical moves, including 2-opt, Or-opt and λ-interchange. Finally, the best child-solution S' replaces the parent solution S if it improves it and routes from S are concatenated to get a new giant tour T, which provides the pair (S, T) for the next iteration of the ELS.

3.9. Selected examples

Three examples of metaheuristics founded on generating a sequence of solutions and developed for vehicle routing problems are now detailed. The first one is elaborated on perhaps the simplest metaheuristic: a GRASP. However, to achieve state-of-the-art results, this method is often enriched with other components. Most of the time, the local search phase is replaced by another metaheuristic, giving birth to a hybrid method. Here, a learning process allows an alternation between diversification and intensification of the search. The second approach is based on the TS framework that has stood as the best one to tackle vehicle routing problems during more than 10 years from the middle of the 1990s. Now surpassed by others such as memetic algorithms, the first generation turns into more sophisticated versions, like the variant presented here, the granular tabu search. It is particularly fast and well suited to be part of a hybrid method. Finally, the third method is an adaptive large neighborhood search, very popular for vehicle routing problems since the publication of the version presented in the following.

3.9.1. *GRASP for the location-routing problem*

GRASP has been applied to several vehicle routing problems, including variants involving location decisions as the LRP, LRP-2E or the TTRP. More details on a GRASP developed by Prins *et al.* [PRI 06] and dedicated to the LRP are presented here. Given customers with known demands and possible depot locations, the LRP consists of determining the depots to be opened and the vehicle routes connected to these depots, in order to cover the demands at minimum total cost (fixed costs of depots, plus fixed and variable costs of the routes).

As explained before, a GRASP is an iterative method in two steps: (1) generation of a solution by a greedy heuristic, (2) improvement of the solution by a local search. Chapter 2 presents several constructive heuristics for vehicle routing problems. Among them, the Clarke and Wright saving algorithm [CLA 64], or CWA, is selected for its good usual results, and adapted for the first step of the algorithm. The improvement phase calls a local search procedure (LS) whose each iteration explores the following three neighborhoods, in the given order, and applied both in intra-routes and interroutes (belonging or not to the same depot), provided that capacities are respected: *relocate*; *exchange*; *md-opt* (a 2-opt procedure extended to the multi-depot case).

Originally designed for the CVRP, an extended version of CWA (called ECWA) has been designed for considering the location decisions. More precisely, at the beginning, several depots are available. They are all considered *a priori* open, and customers are treated in a random order. Each customer is assigned to its nearest depot with enough residual capacity to serve it. Then, unused depots are discarded. As in the original CWA, a dedicated route is created to link the customer to its selected depot, giving an initial solution looking like a bunch of flowers (see Figure 3.3).

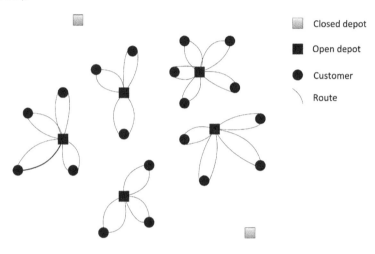

Figure 3.3. *Initial bunch of flowers*

For each pair of routes, $4m$ mergers (concatenations) are possible (with m, the number of available depots): four possible mergers per pair of routes (R, S) as in classical CWA, since each route may be inverted or not, multiplied by the number of possible assignments since the route resulting from a merger can now be assigned to any open depot with compatible capacity (see Figure 3.4).

When concatenating S after R for instance, the saving σ can be computed as follows:

$$\sigma = F + C_{ri} + C_{jr} + C_{sk} + C_{ls} - C_{jk} - C_{ti} - C_{lt} + O_r \lambda_r + O_s \lambda_s - O_t(1 - y_t) \quad [3.1]$$

where F is the fixed cost of a route, C_{ij} is the cost of arc (i, j), O_k is the opening cost of depot k, λ_r (respectively, λ_s) is a Boolean equal to 1 iff depot r (respectively, s) has no more routes after the merger and can be closed. The Boolean variable y_t is equal to 1 iff depot t is already opened before the merger.

The randomized version of ECWA adds a restricted candidate list (RCL) of a size randomly chosen in $[1, \alpha_{max}]$ at each merger. It is filled in by the α_{max} best savings calculated during the merger evaluations, and one is randomly chosen in this list.

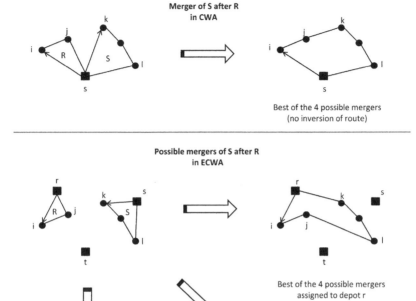

Figure 3.4. *Mergers in CWA and ECWA*

The items in the list of possible mergers are defined by:

– the two routes to merge;

– the direction of travel of each of them;

– the assignment of the obtained route to depot;

– the associated saving.

ECWA can have difficulties in selecting a good subset of depots to open. Thus, a learning process is added in the GRASP, allowing alternating phases of diversification and intensification. In a diversification phase, the algorithm works as described previously but at each iteration two depots are proscribed to be opened (procedure ChooseDepot in algorithm 3.10) and a list SD stores the depots used in the best solution of the phase. In the next intensification phase, the algorithm is allowed to introduce only depots from SD in the solution. An exception occurs if the constructive heuristic fails to affect all customers when creating the bunch of flowers, due to bin-packing issues. In such cases, an unrouted client will be assigned to its closest non-open depot, adding the latter into SD.

Algorithm 3.10: GRASP with learning process for the LRP

---

1   $divmode := true$; $itdiv := 0$
2   $bcostdiv := +\infty$; $bcostsoln := +\infty$
3   set all depots in SD
4   **for** $k := 1$ *to* $maxit$ **do**
5      $S := \text{ECWA}(SD)$
6      $S := \text{LocalSearch}(S)$
7   **if** *cost(S)* < *bsoln* **then**
8         $S^* := S$
9         $bcostsoln := \text{cost}(S)$
10   **if** *divmode = true* **then**
11   **if** *cost(S)* < *bcostdiv* **then**
12         $S' := S$
13         $bcostdiv := \text{cost}(S)$
14       $itdiv := itdiv + 1$
15       $\text{ChooseDepots}(SD)$
16   **if** *itdiv = maxitdiv* **then**
17         $divmode := false$
18         $itint := 0$
19         $SD := $ depots of S'
20   **else**
21       $itint := itint + 1$
22   **if** *itint = maxitint* **then**
23         $divmode := true$
24         $bcostdiv := +\infty$
25         $itdiv := 0$
26   return (S^*)

Algorithm 3.10 presents the GRASP with learning process, where S is a feasible solution of cost $cost(S)$, $maxit = 60$ is the number of GRASP iterations, $maxitdiv = 7$ is the number of iterations in a diversification phase, and

$maxitint = 5$ is the number of iterations in an intensification phase. The other parameter of the method is the maximum size of the RCL $\alpha_{max} = 7$. Note that in [PRI 06], a path relinking is also implemented as post-optimization. This method was among the best ones for the LRP in 2006, but has been rapidly surpassed by decomposition methods that cooperatively alternate between location and routing phases. The main lack is the computing time required to perform one iteration. By designing a heuristic able to handle both levels of decisions at the same time, the authors prevent hierarchical behavior resulting in the major default of previous methods. However, this option restrains the total number of iterations at a rather small value: 60, while hundreds or even thousands of iterations are generally recommended in a GRASP. Despite this limitation, results prove that the approach is valid, especially because of its learning process, which allows us to guide the search in promising directions.

3.9.2. *Granular tabu search for the CVRP*

On the one hand, reducing the size of the exploration space usually accelerates the search. On the other hand, the use of restricted neighborhoods may discard optimal solutions. The idea here is to inhibit the moves that involve elements which are unlikely to belong to good feasible solutions. So the reduction allows us to examine the neighborhoods in much less time, generally without significantly deteriorating the quality of the solution found.

Toth and Vigo [TOT 03] suggested applying this concept within TS, which is a metaheuristic that has been proven efficient for various vehicle routing problems. The resulting method is called the granular tabu search (GTS).

In vehicle routing problems, most of the moves in the local search are defined on the nodes (relocate, exchange, λ-interchange, ejection-chain, etc.), and some involve more specifically the edges (2-opt). However, to evaluate a move, the cost is based on the use of edges. It is also worth noting that, even if the problem is defined on a complete graph, arcs with the higher costs have a small probability of taking part of a high-quality solution.

Thus, the authors propose removing the larger arcs connecting the nodes from the initial graph to reduce the size of the neighborhoods. The new sparse graph $G' = (V, A')$ still has a node-set V made up of a depot and the n customers, but with $|A'| \ll n^2$. A' includes all arcs which should be considered for inclusion in the current solution during the local search. It should contain all the short arcs, plus a subset I of relevant arcs. The latter can be arcs incident to the depot, or belonging to a known good quality solution, for instance.

Then, the neighborhood consists of solutions generated by arcs belonging to G', i.e. only the moves involving at least one arc from G' can be performed. This does not mean that the current solution may not have any arcs with high cost. In fact, such an arc may already be in the current solution, but it may also be inserted: the prohibition is that moves introducing only arcs with high cost are not considered. Moves to visit the neighborhood should now be adapted. In fact, for an efficient management of allowed moves, relocate, for instance, should not be considered as such. Instead, the exploration of the neighborhood might be better done by browsing the list of non-tabu arcs and not used in the current solution.

In their implementation, Toth and Vigo selected the arcs to be included in A' in the following way. A' contains only the arcs (i, j) connecting customers and the depot, and those connecting two customers and having a cost lower than $\beta \tilde{d}$, where β is a constant and $\tilde{d}$ is the average cost of arcs connecting two customers in a good feasible solution S^*. $\tilde{d}$ can be evaluated as:

$$\tilde{d} = \frac{cost(S^*)}{(n + K)}$$

with K the size of the vehicle fleet. It thus excludes the arcs connecting two distant clients, which have little chance of appearing in an optimal solution. However, reducing the neighborhood must be temporary to avoid dismissing a good solution. If no improvement is achieved after a specified number of successive iterations of GTS with the initial value of β, granularity is amended to expand the neighborhood: arcs having a cost lower than $\beta' \tilde{d}$, where $\beta' > \beta$, are added to the reduced graph. The return to the initial granularity occurs when a new best solution is found or when a number of iterations have been executed. Such dynamic adjustment of granularity helps diversifying research.

To initialize A' at the beginning of the algorithm, a good feasible solution is obtained by the use of the Clarke and Wright heuristic [CLA 64]. If the result is a solution with more than K routes, the smallest ones are removed and their customers are inserted in the best position within the remaining K routes, without taking into account the capacity and length constraints. Then, every $2n$ iterations, A' is rebuilt from the current best solution.

In the local search, arcs are directly used as move generators by exchanging two, three or four arcs. When an arc is removed, it is set as tabu for the next t iterations (t being the tabu tenure, randomly chosen following a uniform distribution ranging from t_{min} to t_{max}). During the search, infeasibility is allowed, subject to a penalty dynamically udpdated in the objective function. Examples of possible moves are depicted in Figure 3.5.

A pseudo-code presents the main steps of the method in algorithm 3.11. Procedure *GranularGraph* reduces the initial graph, $Tabu$ is the set of tabu arcs of size t, $RemovedArcs_k$ are the arcs removed from the solution during the local search at iteration k, $MaxItNI$ is the maximum number of successive non-improving iterations before expanding the neighborhood, div states that the expanded neighborhood is used and $MaxItDiv$ is the maximum number of iterations in this mode.

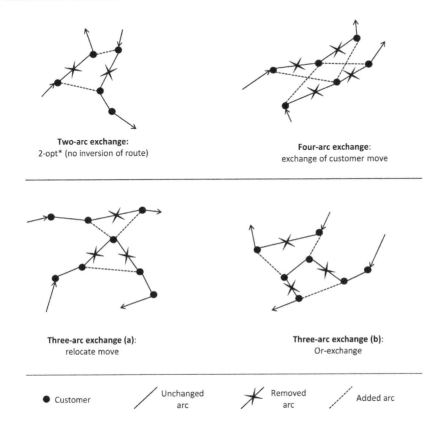

Figure 3.5. *Possible moves on two routes in the GTS for VRP [TOT 03]*

In their method, Toth and Vigo tuned the parameters as follows: $\beta = 1.25$, $\beta' = 1.75$, $t_{min} = 5$, $t_{max} = 10$, $MaxItNI = 15n$, $MaxItDiv = n$. In addition, since the visit of infeasible solutions is allowed during the search, two penalties are applied: α_C multiplied by the excess on capacity constraints and α_D multiplied by the excess on the route length. These values are dynamically updated: they are initialized at 100. Then, four exclusive cases are considered every $n_i = 10$ successive iterations:

– if all visited solutions are feasible with respect to capacity constraints, then set $\alpha_C = \max\{\alpha_{min}, \alpha_C/2\}$;

– if all visited solutions are infeasible with respect to capacity constraints, so set $\alpha_C = \min\{\alpha_{max}, 2\alpha_C\}$;

– if all visited solutions are feasible with respect to length constraints, so set $\alpha_D = \max\{\alpha_{min}, \alpha_D/2\}$;

– if all visited solutions are infeasible with respect to length constraints, so set $\alpha_D = \min\{\alpha_{max}, 2\alpha_D\}$;

with $\alpha_{min} = 1$ and $\alpha_{max} = 6400$.

Algorithm 3.11: Granular tabu search for the VRP

---

1 ClarkeWright(S)

2 initialize $\tilde{d}$

3 $G' :=$ GranularGraph($\beta, \tilde{d}$)

4 $S^* := S$; $S' := S$

5 $Tabu := \emptyset$

6 $itdiv := 0$; $div := false$

7 **for** $k := 1$ *to* $maxit$ **do**

8 $\quad$ LocalSearch($S, G', Tabu$)

9 $\quad$ **if** S improves S^* **then**

10 $\quad\quad$ $S^* := S$

11 $\quad$ $Tabu := Tabu \cup RemovedArcs_k$

12 $\quad$ **if** $(k \mod 2n) = 0$ **then**

13 $\quad\quad$ Update $\tilde{d}$ with S^*

14 $\quad$ $itdiv := itdiv + 1$

15 $\quad$ **if** S improves S' **then**

16 $\quad\quad$ $S' := S$

17 $\quad\quad$ $it := 0$

18 $\quad$ **else**

19 $\quad\quad$ $it := it + 1$

20 $\quad\quad$ **if** $it > MaxItNI$ and $div = false$ **then**

21 $\quad\quad\quad$ $G' :=$ GranularGraph($\beta', \tilde{d}$)

22 $\quad\quad\quad$ $itdiv := 0$

23 $\quad\quad\quad$ $div := true$

24 $\quad\quad$ **if** $itdiv > MaxItDiv$ and $div = true$ **then**

25 $\quad\quad\quad$ $G' :=$ GranularGraph($\beta, \tilde{d}$)

26 $\quad\quad\quad$ $it := 0$

27 $\quad\quad\quad$ $div := false$

28 return (S^*)

This method is somewhat less efficient than classic tabu methods (in terms of solution quality), but it is much faster. Thus, it is convenient for large-scale instances or when applied within a global framework as when tackling the LRP [PRI 07, ESC 14].

3.9.3. *Adaptive large neighborhood search for the pickup and delivery problem with time windows*

Adaptive large neighborhood search (ALNS) is a relatively efficient framework to solve variants of the vehicle routing problems, especially the so-called *Rich VRP* in which various, possibly tight, constraints need to hold. Rather than using one large neighborhood as in LNS, it applies several removal and insertion operators, selected dynamically according to their past performance, to a given solution. The new solution is accepted if it satisfies some criteria defined by the local search framework (e.g. SA) applied at the outer level. The main features of the ALNS algorithm offered by Röpke and Pisinger [ROP 06] for the pickup and delivery problem with time windows (PDPTW) are presented here.

The PDPTW is the problem of optimally moving a number of collection requests to delivery locations using a limited number of vehicles. Thus, paired pickups and deliveries must take place on the same route, and such that a pickup is performed before the corresponding delivery. Service times are associated with each pickup and delivery. Furthermore, in the present case, each request is assigned a set of possible vehicles, representing situations where some vehicles cannot enter a certain location because of their dimensions. However, the number of vehicles is limited. Thus, in situations where some requests cannot be assigned to a vehicle, they are placed in a virtual *request bank*. In addition, authors consider a multi-depot case and the start and end locations of a route do not need to be the same. As usual, time window and capacity constraints must be satisfied and the objective function is to minimize a weighted sum of three components: (1) the total distances traveled by the vehicles, (2) the total times spent by each vehicle, (3) the number of requests in the request bank.

In such problems with tight constraints, the search method can have difficulties in jumping from one promising area of the solution space to another. The authors propose the use of larger moves that can potentially rearrange up to 30–40% of all requests in a single iteration. The computation time needed becomes much larger but seems to produce very good solution cost on this problem. However, this performance and the robustness of the method are very dependent on the choice of removal and insertion procedures. Contrarily to previous works on LNS for vehicle routing problems using an exact approach in the insertion phase, here, heuristics are performed. Even if they may not provide such good solutions, the overall method achieves good results because of the diversification brought in the search process.

Three removal heuristics (N^-) are used, each taking a solution and removing q requests. Their principles are given in the following:

1) *Shaw Removal Heuristic*: this heuristic presented by Shaw [SHA 98] is slightly modified to tackle the PDPTW. The idea is to remove requests that are somewhat similar, according to a *relatedness measure*. For two requests i and j, it consists of the weighted sum of four terms: distance, time, capacity, plus one term that considers the vehicles that can be used to serve the two requests. It is equal to:

$$R(i,j) = \varphi(d_{A_i,A_j} + d_{B_i,B_j}) + \chi(|T_{A_i} - T_{A_j}| + |T_{B_i} - T_{B_j}|)$$

$$+\psi|l_i - l_j| + \omega(1 - \frac{|K_i \cap K_j|}{\min(|K_i|, |K_j|)})$$

where A_i and B_i are the pickup and delivery locations of request i. $d_{i,j}$ is the distance between locations i and j, T_i indicates the time when location i is visited, l_i is the amount of goods that must be loaded at node i and K_i defines the set of vehicles that are able to serve request i. φ, χ, ψ and ω are the weights related to each term in the measure. The procedure initially chooses a random request to remove, and the following are those similar to the already removed requests. Some randomness is introduced in the selection of the requests, with a parameter p.

2) *Random Removal*: this algorithm randomly selects q requests to remove.

3) *Worst Removal*: the worst removal is defined by the highest request cost. Given a request i served by some vehicle in a solution S, its cost is estimated as:

$$Cost(i, S) = f(S) - f_i(S)$$

where $f(S)$ and $f_i(S)$ are, respectively, the cost of solution S and its cost without request i. This procedure is also randomized to avoid always removing the same requests, with the degree of randomization controlled by the parameter p_{worst}.

The insert heuristics (N^+) are only of two types:

1) *Basic Greedy Heuristic*: this heuristic is a construction heuristic that inserts one request per iteration. The greedy criterion involves the best insertion principle within the current partial solution.

2) *Regret Heuristics*: the algorithm incorporates a type of look-ahead information when selecting the request to insert. For each request i, variable x_{ik} indicates the route in which it has its kth lowest insertion cost. Then, the regret value is the difference between the cost of inserting the request in its best route and its kth-best route. The request chosen to be inserted at a particular iteration is the one that maximizes this regret value, and it takes the positions involving the minimum cost. Ties are broken by selecting the insertion with the lowest cost. In their experiments, the authors use in fact five regret heuristics, with k equal to 1, 2, 3, 4 or m (the number of vehicles).

In addition, for the insertion of a request into a route, two costs are calculated: the real cost C and a modified cost $C' = \max\{0, C + noise\}$, where $noise$ is a random number from the interval $] - maxN, maxN]$. $maxN = \eta \max_{i,j \in V}\{d_{ij}\}$, where η is a parameter that controls the amount of noise. The decision of applying C or C' to evaluate the insertion is taken by the same adaptive mechanism as for the call to heuristics explain below.

The adaptive mechanism for the use of the removal and insertion procedures is influenced by a weight based on the score π_i associated with each heuristic i according to its past performance. High weight value corresponds to a successful heuristic. Every g iterations (g being the size of what authors called a *segment*), the weights w are updated and the scores are reset to zero. At the end of an iteration, scores π are modified by means of an evaluation of the solution. If heuristic i was able to find a new solution (never accepted before) that passed the acceptance criteria, and that was:

– a new overall best solution, thus π_i becomes $\pi_i = \pi_i + \sigma_1$;

– a better solution than the current one, $\pi_i = \pi_i + \sigma_2$;

– a worse solution than the current one, $\pi_i = \pi_i + \sigma_3$.

The weight of heuristic i used in segment j is defined as w_{ij}. In the first segment, all heuristics are weighted equally. Then, they are updated as follows:

$$w_{i,j+1} = w_{ij}(1 - r) + r\frac{\pi_i}{\theta_i}$$

θ_i is the number of times heuristic i has been called during the last segment. The factor r controls the adjustment of the algorithm according to the effectiveness of the heuristics. If $r = 0$, scores do not impact the choice of heuristics, while if $r = 1$, scores obtained in the last segment have a strong influence.

Thus, during the next segment t, heuristic i will be called with probability $\frac{w_{it}}{\sum_i w_{it}}$ by a roulette-wheel selection.

Another important feature is the acceptance criteria, inspired from SA. That is a solution S is accepted with probability $e^{-(\Delta f/T)}$ where T >0, and Δf is the cost difference between S and the current solution. T is initialized at the value T_{init} and is decreased at each iteration according to the cooling rate c.

The remaining components are both the construction of the initial solution and the management of the number of vehicles used. In fact, this last part does not take place in the objective function of the problem in hand, but is considered in most of the vehicle routing literature. Thus, the authors propose to manage it by a two-stage scheme: first minimizing the number of vehicles, second minimizing the other objectives.

An initial feasible solution is built using a sequential insertion method that constructs one route at a time until all requests have been planned. This provides an initial estimate on the number of vehicles required. Then, the algorithm removes one route and places the related requests in the request bank. The resulting problem is solved by the ALNS but with a higher weight than normal on the third term of the objective function concerning the unserviced requests. This favors assigning the latter requests into routes. If the heuristic is able to find a solution that serves all requests, a new candidate for the minimum number of vehicles has been found, and the process is repeated so on, removing a new route. However, if the ALNS heuristic does not find such a solution, the algorithm steps back to the last solution encountered with all requests served. This solution is used as a starting solution in the second stage of the algorithm, which consists of applying the ALNS for further iterations, with the original objective function. To limit the computational time, the total number of ALNS iterations in the first stage is restricted to a specified value Θ. Another reducing condition is to stop the ALNS when it seems unlikely that a solution exists in which all requests are planned. The authors judge it "unlikely" when five or more requests are unplanned and no improvement in the number of unplanned requests has been found in the last τ ALNS iterations.

Algorithm 3.12 details one ALNS iteration, and algorithm 3.13 shows how it takes place in the general ALNS structure. $Bank$ is the set of unrouted requests. *SelectDestruction* and *SelectRepair* are the procedures choosing the heuristics to be used in the current iteration among N^- and N^+ sets, respectively, and according to the vector w of weights. *GenerateNewSolution* applies both selected heuristics to build a new incumbent solution S'. In the computational experiments, the parameters are fixed at the following values: $maxit = 25000$, $\Theta = 25000$, $\tau = 2000$, $g = 100$, $\sigma_1 = 33$, $\sigma_2 = 9$, $\sigma_3 = 13$, $r = 0.1$, $T_{init} = 0.05$, $c = 0.99975$, $\varphi = 9$, $\chi = 3$, $\psi = 2$, $\omega = 5$, $p = 6$, $p_{worst} = 3$, $\eta = 0.025$. In each iteration, q requests are removed, with q randomly chosen in such a way: $4 \leq q \leq \min\{100, \eta\xi\}$, and $\xi = 0.4$.

As in most ALNS algorithms, the presented version is not easy to implement. Besides the removal and insert heuristics, several other components are added to the method and the number of parameters is rather large. Nevertheless, it must be recognized that the method was able to find very good solutions and to improve the results of previous heuristics. Its performance is demonstrated mainly on large instances as well as at the price of a dramatic increase in the computational time.

Algorithm 3.12: An iteration of ALNS for the PDPTW - IterALNS_PDPTW

---

1 $it := it + 1$
2 $d := \text{SelectDestruction}(N^-, w)$
3 $r := \text{SelectRepair}(N^+, w)$
4 $S' := \text{GenerateNewSolution}(S, d, r)$
5 $\Delta = f(S') - f(S)$
6 **if** $\Delta < 0$ **then**
7 $\quad \mid \quad S := S'$
8 $\quad \mid \quad NoImprov := 0$
9 **else**
10 $\quad \mid \quad$ **if** $e^{-\Delta f/T} < U \sim (0, 1)$ **then**
11 $\quad \mid \quad \mid \quad S := S'$
12 $\quad \mid \quad \mid \quad NoImprov := NoImprov + 1$
13 update scores of π
14 **if** $(it \mod g) = 0$ **then**
15 $\quad \mid \quad$ update weights of w
16 **if** S improves S^* **then**
17 $\quad \mid \quad S^* := S$

Algorithm 3.13: Whole heuristic for the PDPTW

---

1 build a solution S
2 $it := 0$
3 set a higher value to γ
4 $NoImprov := 0$
5 **repeat**
6 $\quad \mid \quad$ remove a route
7 $\quad \mid \quad T := T_{init}$
8 $\quad \mid \quad NoImprov := 0$
9 $\quad \mid \quad$ **repeat**
10 $\quad \mid \quad \mid \quad$ IterALNS_PDPTW($it,S,S^*,\gamma,NoImprov,T,\pi,w$)
11 $\quad \mid \quad$ **until** $it = \Theta$ **or** $Bank = \emptyset$ **or** ($|Bank| > 5$ **and** $NoImprov = \tau$)
12 **until** $it = \Theta$ **or** ($|Bank| > 5$ **and** $NoImprov = \tau$)
13 reset γ to its initial value
14 $T := T_{init}$
15 initialize π and w
16 **repeat**
17 $\quad \mid \quad$ IterALNS_PDPTW($it,S,S^*,\gamma,NoImprov,T,\pi,w$)
18 **until** $it = maxit$
19 return (S^*)

3.10. Conclusion

This chapter has presented the main metaheuristics working on a sequence of solutions, and their applications on vehicle routing problems. The main idea under these methods is to make evolve a solution through a particular iterative process. The walk in the solution space requires to define at least a neighborhood and a specific rule to jump from an incumbent (potentially locally optimal) solution to another one, by attempting to reach a new, hopefully better, attraction basin. The quality of the results mainly stands on the problem-specific elements included in the method, such as the heuristic building the initial solution, the moves used in the local search and the potential other extra components. Thus, the procedures presented in Chapter 2 have a great influence.

The simplest way to proceed is surely to rebuilt a complete solution at each iteration, as in GRASP. Nevertheless, GRASP hardly stands among the best efficient method on vehicle routing problems because of its independent iterations. To be more efficient, extra features need to complement the method, such as the learning process presented in section 3.9.1 for the LRP. To avoid a sampling without learning from the history of solutions found in previous iterations, another idea is to keep a part of the solution and rebuild the remainder as in ALNS. However, this method is not so easy to implement because it requires several heuristics and many tuning to work well, as shown in section 3.9.3 for the PDPTW. Furthermore, it often consumes a larger computational time than other metaheuristics. Then, even if it can provide good results, ALNS should be reserved for very constrained cases and/or when small neighborhoods show difficulties to escape certain areas of the solution space.

A good compromise is surely brought by methods that slightly modify the solution, but in a controlled manner to escape from local optima. This goes from the deterministic to the randomized versions. In a deterministic case, the TS looks for the best, possibly non-improving, move in a specified neighborhood, with a record of the last visited solutions to avoid cycling. The method has been for a long time the best metaheuristic for vehicle routing problems and a very fast and efficient version was presented in section 3.9.2. Another option, for instance, is to modify the objective function with a penalized feature as in GLS, or to change the type of neighborhood each time a local optimum is achieved in the current one, as in VND. In randomized versions, random moves are performed. Founded on the same idea as VND, RVNS (and its close version with a local search, VNS) iteratively changes of neighborhood but selects a random move (not necessarily improving). A similar method, but possibly applying several moves for the perturbation, each one involving the same neighborhoods over the iterations, is ILS. All these randomized cases have proven to be good methods for vehicle routing problems. However, they often need to be hybridized with other components to increase their efficiency even more. In fact, they are mainly used to replace a simple local search within any other metaheuristic. The

SA also performs random moves in a predefined neighborhood, under a dynamic accepting criterion, but does not use any local search (except in hybrid versions).

Finally, the method making the link with evolutionary metaheuristics is the ELS. Its principle is the same as ILS, but the perturbation tool generates several new solutions to keep only the best one among the incumbent solution and the new ones. As ILS, this method is often called to replace a simple local search in another metaheuristic, giving birth to a hybrid algorithm. This will be presented in a dedicated chapter on hybrid metaheurisics (see Chapter 5), but for now, Chapter 4 will present metaheuristics based on a set of solutions.

Metaheuristics Based on a Set of Solutions

This chapter is dedicated to metaheuristics evolving a set of solutions and generating new solutions by either combining existing ones or by making them cooperate through a learning process. Here are distinguished population-based approaches, which combine solutions selected from a population stored in memory (such as genetic algorithms (GAs), memetic algorithms (MAs), scatter search (SS) and path relinking (PR)) from swarm methods based on a cooperation of homogenous agents in their environment (such as particle swarm optimization (PSO) or ant colony optimization (ACO)).

4.1. Genetic algorithm and its variants

Genetic algorithms (GAs) are subsumed on population-based approaches. Three variants are identified: the basic version (GA), its advanced variant using local search procedures, called memetic algorithm (MA), and a further enhanced method which includes a population management mechanism (MA|PM).

4.1.1. *Genetic algorithm*

GAs are population-based metaheuristics that mimic the processes of biological evolution in order to solve problems and to model evolutionary systems. Introduced for the first time by Holland in 1975 [HOL 75], they can be considered among the pioneer metaheuristics since they were proposed just after simulated annealing and tabu search methodologies (see Chapter 3). Figure 4.1 illustrates the principle of this approach.

The evolution process of GA consists of three major operators: selection, crossover and mutation. Based on a population of solutions represented as chromosomes, the selection step consists of choosing two parents among the population with a bias in favor of the best parents (with the best fitness). The parents are then combined using a crossover operator to provide offspring solutions. Finally, the mutation modifies some characteristics of the child solution with a certain probability to ensure the diversity of the population. The general structure of a GA is presented in algorithm 4.1.

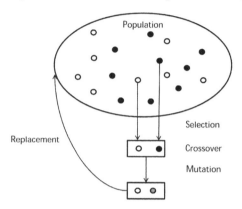

Figure 4.1. *Main steps in genetic algorithm*

Algorithm 4.1: Genetic algorithm principle: incremental version
1 build an initial population *Pop*
2 **while** *the stopping criterion is not met* **do**
3   selection: draw randomly two parents P_1 end P_2
4   reproduction: apply a crossover to get children
5   mutation: randomly perturb children solutions (with small probability)
6   replacement: select some solutions in the population and replace them by the children
7 return the best solution

There exist two GA types depending on the way old individuals are replaced when creating new ones: the generational GA and the incremental GA. Generational GA is the standard form and consists of using non-overlapping generations and optionally an elitism mechanism. For each generation, the algorithm creates a new population of individuals. If an elitism mechanism is applied, the best individuals are kept in the next generation. Incremental GA does not create an entirely new population. It simply adds children to the population each time they are generated, as in algorithm 4.1. To keep a population size constant, the individuals to be replaced by the children are selected according to a chosen replacement strategy. For more details and extensive information on GAs, interested readers can refer to the textbooks from Goldberg [GOL 89] and Michalewicz [MIC 96].

4.1.2. *Memetic algorithm*

GAs, as proposed by Holland [HOL 75], are not aggressive enough for combinatorial optimization problems compared to other metaheuristics such as tabu search. *Memetic algorithms* (MAs) proposed by Moscato [MOS 89] are more powerful versions which apply a local search procedure to each new child-solution improving hence the performance on many optimization problems. Local search in memetic algorithms brings intensification [MOS 99]. Indeed, the solutions resulting from crossover are improved by local search before undergoing mutation.

Algorithm 4.2 shows the general structure of an MA in its incremental version.

Algorithm 4.2: Memetic algorithm principle

---

1   build an initial population Pop
2   **while** *the stopping criteria is not met* **do**
3   selection: draw randomly two parents P_1 end P_2
4   reproduction: apply a crossover to get children
5   improvement: apply local search to the children with a given probability
6   mutation: randomly perturb children solutions (with small probability)
7   replacement: select some solutions in the population and replace them by the children
8   return the best solution

4.1.3. *Memetic algorithm with population management*

Memetic algorithm with population management (MA|PM) is a more powerful version of MA which uses a strategy to ensure the diversity of the population. This version, proposed by Sörensen and Sevaux in 2006 [SOR 06], consists of accepting new solutions in the population only when they are sufficiently different from those already present in the population.

The first implementations of population management strategies were based on costs as differentiating criterion, which means that a solution is accepted in a population if and only if the gap between its cost and that of solutions already included in the population is at least equal to a value Δ. Later, distance measures in solution space were used instead. Let δ be a distance measure (a metric) in solution space. The distance D between a child-solution C to a current population Pop is given by $D(C, Pop) = \min\{\delta(C, S) \mid S \in Pop\}$. After local search, a child-solution C is accepted in the population if $D(Pop, C) \geq \Delta$, where Δ is a parameter that can be fixed at the beginning of the algorithm or dynamically readjusted during the search process to control diversity.

Examples of distance measures used in vehicle routing problems include Hamming distance. This distance consists of computing for two permutations of n customers the number of positions for which the corresponding customers are different. For instance, Hamming distance $\delta(p_1, p_2)$ equals 4 for $p_1 = (2, 1, 6, 5, 4, 3, 7)$ and $p_2 = (2, 4, 7, 5, 1, 3, 6)$. Another measure often used in vehicle routing problems is the broken pairs distance proposed by Martì [MAR 05]. For two permutations of n customers, it consists of computing the number of pairs of consecutive customers from the first permutation which are broken in the second one. For the previous example, $\delta(p_1, p_2)$ takes the maximal value 6 since all pairs are broken.

4.1.4. *Genetic algorithm and its variants in vehicle routing problems*

Pure genetic algorithm (GA) implementations have shown mitigated results except in the works of [THA 95] and [POT 96], both dedicated to the vehicle routing problem with time windows. In the early 1990s, all published papers on capacitated vehicle routing problems (CVRP) used complete representation of solutions by considering, for example, the list of customers with route delimiters. These delimiters can be, for instance, the symbol 0 (the depot index), which means that the route must be ended by going back to the depot node. Crossovers such as route based crossover (RBX), sometimes generating children with routes that violate capacity constraints, were used in some studies [POT 96]. Reparation procedures were applied to restore feasibility, however, since they are based on relocating customers, the genetic transmission of good properties from parents to children was deteriorated. This fact can explain the inconclusive results obtained by the first GAs applied to several vehicle routing problems. The absence of improvement methods (local searches) in GAs is another reason that contributed to this limited performance.

In the MA of Berger and Barkaoui [BER 03] also dedicated to capacitated vehicle routing problem (CVRP), complete solution representations were also used but fair results were obtained. The capacity constraints violations were avoided by Baker and Ayechew [BAK 03] by using a *cluster-first route-second* approach (see section 2.1.2 for the details). These authors proposed a pure GA and a MA which were compared to establish the impact of adding the local search component. In this work, each chromosome defines a partition of customers into clusters by assigning a sector (vehicle) index to each customer. It is then decoded by solving a traveling salesman problem (TSP) for each cluster, using a constructive heuristic. In the proposed MA, 2-opt and λ-interchange moves were used in the local search part.

However, the real trigger of genetic-based algorithms for vehicle routing problems appeared in 2001 with the first good results obtained on CVRP and capacitated arc routing problem (CARP) due to memetic algorithms developed by Prins [PRI 01] and Lacomme *et al.* [LAC 01]. This has been particularly the case after the publication from Prins [PRI 04a] who proposed an MA for the CVRP where the *route first, cluster second* approach was used. To decode the chromosomes coded as *giant tours*, i.e. permutations containing all customers without route delimiters, a procedure called *Split* is proposed (for more details, see section 2.1.2 of Chapter 2). This procedure is able to establish optimally the limits between routes with respect to the imposed sequence. The MA of Prins [PRI 04a] was the first to improve upon the results of tabu search methods.

Later, other MAs using *giant tours* encoding were proposed to solve several vehicle routing problems. We can cite the works of Lacomme *et al.* [LAC 04] for the CARP, Labadi *et al.* [LAB 08b] for the VRP with time windows, El Fallahi *et al.* [ELF 08] for the multi-compartment VRP, the MA of Boudia *et al.* [BOU 09] for a production-distribution problem and the study from Ngueveu *et al.* [NGU 10b] developed to solve the cumulative VRP.

The OX crossover is used in most of these works, therefore we will detail its principle in a small example below. Figure 4.2 shows two parents P_1 and P_2 constituted of nine customers. OX consists of randomly selecting two positions i and j with $(i < j)$. The customers from positions i to j are copied in the same positions in the child C_1. Then, P_2 is circularly scanned from position $j + 1$ to j in order to complete C_1. Indeed, each time a customer is not already at this child, it is added in a circular way from $j + 1$ to i. A second child can be generated by changing the roles of parents P_1 and P_2.

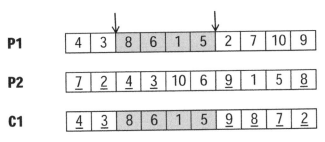

Figure 4.2. *Example of OX crossover*

Nagata and Bräysy proposed the first efficient MA for the CVRP not using *giant tours* encoding. It is based on a sophisticated crossover operator called *edge crossover assembly* [NAG 09]. Some more recent MAs are designed to solve a large class of vehicle routing problems [VID 13b, VID 14]; the last reference provides the current best metaheuristic for more than 20 vehicle routing problems.

Within population management strategies, MA|PMs often perform best, as indicated by [PRI 09a] and [PRI 04b], developed to solve, the heterogenous fleet

VRP (HVRP) and the CARP, respectively. As the best method for 26 variants of routing problems, Vidal *et al* approach [VID 13b] which also uses a population management mechanism that is based on both solution costs and diversity measures. Details on this work are given in section 4.7.3.

4.2. Scatter search

Scatter search (SS) also follows a reproduction scheme that combines solutions in a systematic way. This method is detailed in the following sections.

4.2.1. *Scatter search principle*

SS is a population-based metaheuristic that uses diversification strategies as in tabu search. Unlike GA, it usually operates on a smaller set containing good and diversified solutions. This method, introduced by Glover in 1977 [GLO 77], maintains in a pool some high-quality solutions encountered during the search process and also ensures diversity by adding well-scattered solutions, to drive the exploration to other regions when the optimization process is trapped in a local minimum.

The general principle of SS, given in algorithm 4.3, consists of repeating the following steps until a stopping criterion is met. First, an initial population with well-scattered solutions is built to ensure the diversity of the solutions. This step requires to define a distance measure to evaluate how solutions are different from each other. A local search is then executed to improve the population and a reference set $RefSet$ is constituted with the $RefSize$ best solutions in the population.

The second While loop consists of combining all pairs of different solutions in the reference set and improving the resulting solutions by a local search procedure. The reference set is then updated by keeping $RefSize$ best solutions among the union of $RefSet$ and the set of improved solutions. This second While loop ends when no new solutions enter to the reference set. If the stopping criterion is not met, a new population is generated and the reference set is refreshed by keeping the best half part from the current $Refset$ and to complete the missing part from the new population by adding the more dispersed ones.

SS shares many similarities with memetic algorithms insofar as it also uses crossover operators and local search. The difference between these two methods lies in the management of the population. Indeed, the SS uses a distance measure to control diversity of a smaller population, the crossover operator can be deterministic, systematic and tailored to combine more than two parent and mutation is never used.

Algorithm 4.3: Scatter search principle

---

1 **while** *the stopping criterion is not met* **do**

2   apply a diversification Generation method to build an initial population Pop

3   improve solutions in Pop by a local search method

4   build the reference set $RefSet$ with a $RefSize$

5      $BS:=$ best solution in $RefSet$

6   **while** *new solutions in* $RefSet$ **do**

7   combine all pairs of solutions in $RefSet$ where at least one solution in the pair is new

8   apply local search to improve resulting solutions

9   choose the best $RefSize$ solutions from the union of the current $RefSet$ and the set of improved solutions

10   remove from $RefSet$ the $\frac{RefSize}{2}$ worst solutions

11   generate a new population Pop

12   add from Pop the $\frac{RefSize}{2}$ more diverse solutions to $RefSet$

13 return the best solution

4.2.2. *Scatter search in vehicle routing problems*

SS has been applied to many combinatorial optimization problems, such as graph coloring, the linear ordering problem, scheduling problems, etc. Applications to vehicle routing problems are rather scarce. This is likely due to the fact that the method is reputed to be time-consuming, especially with its initial design where crossover and local search operators are systematic.

Some successful applications of SS are proposed by Russel and Chiang [RUS 06] for the vehicle routing problem with time windows, Chu *et al.* [CHU 06] for the periodic capacitated arc routing problem and by Zhang [ZHA 12] for the stochastic travel-time vehicle routing problem with simultaneous pickups and deliveries. In the work from Belfiore and Yoshida Yoshizaki [BEL 09], a SS was developed to deal with a real-life heterogeneous fleet vehicle routing problem with time windows and split deliveries. The paper from Chu *et al.* [CHU 06] is detailed in section 4.7.1.

4.3. Path relinking

Another metaheuristic approach uses two solutions from a population to generate new ones, but without crossover operators. It is path relinking (PR), discussed herafter.

4.3.1. *Principle*

PR is an evolutionary search strategy which explores the trajectory connecting two solutions, generally of high quality. It was proposed for the first time by Glover to intensify a tabu search or a SS [GLO 97b, GLO 00]. PR can be considered as an evolutionary method since it creates new solutions by combining elements from existing ones. However, unlike the GAs family, randomness is not a key factor to generate offsprings: PR generates new solutions by exploring paths that connect elite solutions.

The search starts from an initiating solution U and it is further guided toward a guiding solution V, while several intermediate solutions are generated progressively. Each intermediate solution is generated by incorporating more attributes from the guiding solution. These attributes are generally elementary modifications, as in local search moves. Several alternatives are possible for a couple (U, V), for example:

– unidirectional PR: made only from solution U to solution V;

– bidirectional PR: made from U to V and from V to U;

– randomized PR: the choice of the attribute introduced in U is randomly chosen among those leading to V;

– PR truncated: the transformation of U into V is only partial and the path is not, therefore, completely explored.

Any PR implementation must contain the following three components that are crucial in the design of the algorithm:

– rules to build the reference set;

– rules to choose the starting and guiding solutions;

– distance measure and a neighborhood structure for moving along paths.

The general structure of a PR procedure for a minimization problem is given in algorithm 4.4. It starts with the creation of an initial set of elite solutions ($RefSet$). As in the SS method, the solutions in $RefSet$ are ordered according to their quality and all possible pairs of different solutions are considered. For each pair of solutions, the relinking method is applied to move from the initiating solution to the guiding one and new solutions in the path are generated. An improvement method can be applied during the relinking process in each step of the path. All solutions generated (including those obtained after the application of the improvement method) are checked to see whether they improve upon the best solution currently recorded in $RefSet$. If so, the best solution is updated.

A PR is rarely used alone: it is either used as an external component or as an internal procedure within another metaheuristic [RES 05]. The first case (*external*

PR) uses PR for post-optimization, on a small pool of elite solutions called a reference set, collected during the main metaheuristic [PI 04]. The second case (*internal PR*) consists of applying PR as an intensification to each local optimum during the embedded search method, by exploring the path which links it to an elite solution randomly chosen in the reference set built during iterations [LAG 95]. These last authors showed that the best strategy for building the pool consists of both keeping good and diversified solutions in it, i.e the solutions must be sufficiently different with respect to each other. A distance measure is hence required to measure the similarities between solutions. Typically, the distance can be defined as the minimum number of some basic operations required to convert the starting solution into the guiding solution.

Algorithm 4.4: Path relinking principle

---

1 build an initial reference set *RefSet*
2 $BS :=$ best solution in $RefSet$
3 **foreach** *pair* $(S_1, S_2) \in RefSet \times RefSet$ **do**
4 $\quad$ $S := S_1$
5 $\quad$ **while** $S \neq S_2$ *do* **do**
6 $\quad\quad$ build a solution S^* with $dist(S^*, S_2) < dist(S, S_2)$
7 $\quad\quad$ **if** S^* improves BS **then**
8 $\quad\quad\quad$ $BS := S^*$
9 $\quad\quad$ $S := S^*$
10 return (BS)

Figure 4.3 shows an example of trajectories (see solid lines) linking two solutions in the search space. It is possible, after applying a metaheuristic, to create a trajectory according to the objective function value as depicted in the same figure by the dotted lines. In this event, the new trajectory created by PR is likely to be somewhat different from the one initially established, giving the opportunity to find better solutions not already encountered (left part of Figure 4.3).

4.3.2. *Path relinking in vehicle routing problems*

As already mentioned, path relinking (PR) is often used in post-optimization phases within other metaheuristic frameworks. Its use provides good results in vehicle routing problems, as will be detailed in Chapter 5 (dedicated to hybrid metaheuristics). Ho and Gendreau have applied PR in a tabu method for the CVRP [HO 06]. In Labadi *et al.* PR was used within a greedy randomized adaptive search procedure (GRASP) to solve the capacitated arc routing problem with time windows (CARPTWs) [LAB 08a].

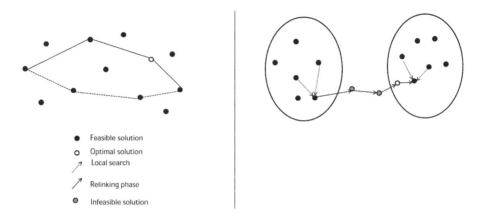

● Feasible solution

○ Optimal solution

↗ Local search

↗ Relinking phase

◉ Infeasible solution

Figure 4.3. *Example of path relinking trajectories*

Souffriau *et al.* [SOU 10] proposed a PR to solve a team orienteering problem, which was also hybridized with a GRASP. To the best of our knowledge, the first and unique stand-alone version of PR has been proposed for a multi-depot periodic vehicle routing problem by Rahimi *et al.* [RAH 13]. This work will be detailed in section 4.7.2.

4.4. Ant colony optimization

In addition to GAs, other bioinspired methods involving a population are those which resemble swarm animal behaviors. One example is ant colony optimization.

4.4.1. *Principle*

The *ant colony optimization* (ACO) approach [DOR 04] is inspired by the social behavior of ants using pheromone-based strategies when foraging for food. Figure 4.4 shows the principle of the methods: ants first randomly depose pheromone to alert each other about food sources. After some time, the quantity of deposed pheromone on some trajectories either increases if more and more ants follow them or disappears if less ants go through them.

ACO is the swarm-based algorithm most used in combinatorial optimization. ACOs are especially well suited to problems where the construction of a solution can be assimilated to building paths in a given graph as is the case in vehicle routing problems. As a matter of fact, the first application of the method was on the TSP.

The general ACO framework consists of three main steps. The first step is to use artificial ants to construct solutions by probabilistic rules that add components from heuristic information of the problem and pheromone trails. The second step consists of building centralized actions that cannot be performed by ants individually. For example, to activate local improvement procedures or to decide additional pheromone deposal according to global information that cannot be collected by single ants. The final step updates the pheromone trails and the trace values are reinforced for the features contained in good solutions and reduced for the attributes which are rarely used. The general structure of an ACO is given in algorithm 4.5.

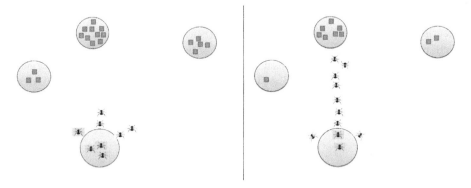

Figure 4.4. *Ant colony principle*

Algorithm 4.5: Ant colony optimization principle

---

1 initialize pheromone trails
2 **while** *the stopping criterion is not met* **do**
3 | construct solutions
4 | call Daemon Actions (optional)
5 | update pheromone trails
6 |_   global update pheromones
7 return best solution

At the beginning of the algorithm, parameters and pheromone trails are initialized to an initial value of τ_0. A set of m artificial ants builds solutions to the considered problem starting from an initially empty partial solution $s_p = \emptyset$. At each construction step, the current partial solution is extended by adding a feasible solution component $C_i^j \in \mathcal{N}(s_p)$ where $\mathcal{N}(s_p)$ is the set of solution components that can be added while maintaining feasibility. The choice of the solution component to add is done probabilistically at each construction step. Various ways for defining the probability distributions have been considered. The most widely used rule is that of an ant system (AS) [DOR 04] given by equation [4.1]:

$$P(C_i{}^j|s_p) = \frac{\tau_{ij}{}^\alpha [\eta(C_i{}^j)]^\beta}{\sum\limits_{C_i{}^j \in \mathcal{N}(s_p)} \tau_{il}{}^\alpha [\eta(C_i{}^l)]^\beta}, \forall C_i{}^j \in \mathcal{N}(s_p).$$ [4.1]

The function $\eta(.)$ assigns to each feasible solution component $C_i{}^j \in \mathcal{N}(s_p)$ a heuristic value, which is usually called the heuristic information. Parameters α and β determine the relative influence of the pheromone trails and the heuristic information. Deamon action, which is often used as a local improvement procedure, is optional, however, most of the successful ACO applications to NP-hard problems use local search to enhance their performance. Without this component, the method tends to be less competitive as is the case for pure GAs. The pheromone global update aims to make solution components belonging to good solutions more attractive for subsequent iterations.

There are essentially two mechanisms that are used to achieve this goal. The first is pheromone deposit, which increases the level of the pheromone of solution components that are associated with a chosen set $\mathcal{S}_{upd}$ of good solutions. The second is pheromone trail evaporation, which is the mechanism that decreases over time the pheromone deposited by previous ants. Pheromone evaporation is needed to avoid a rapid convergence of the algorithm to local optimum and allows exploration of other regions. The pheromone update is commonly implemented through the following equation:

$$\tau_{ij} = (1 - \rho)\tau_{ij} + \sum\limits_{s \in \mathcal{S}_{upd}|C_i{}^j \in S} g(s)$$ [4.2]

where $\mathcal{S}_{upd}$ is the set of solutions that are used to deposit pheromones, the parameter $\rho \in [0, 1]$ is the evaporation rate, g is a positive function defined on the search space such that $f(s) < f(s') \Rightarrow g(s) \geq g(s')$. It determines the quality of a solution and it is called the evaluation function. Several variants exist in the literature depending on the update rules used, the most popular ones being:

– ant system (AS): uses a random proportional state transition rule, while the pheromone is deposited by all ants proportionally to their solution quality and is evaporated in all the components;

– ant colony system (ACS): is based on pseudo-random state transition rule, and the pheromone is only deposited and evaporated on the components of the best solution. It generally uses local pheromone update during the solution construction, allowing the exploration of unused components;

– MAX–MIN ant system (MMAS): includes lower and upper bounds on the pheromone, which is only deposited on the components of the best solution.

4.4.2. ACO in vehicle routing problems

For vehicle routing problems, an ant can, for example, build successive routes on the graph, using for instance a nearest-neighbor heuristic completed by pheromone deposits.

ACO was applied to the CVRP by Bullnheimer *et al.* [BUL 99], Bell and McMullen [BEL 04], Doerner *et al.* [DOE 04], Reimann *et al.* [REI 04] and Yu *et al.* [YU 09, YU 11a, YU 11b]. For the CARP, Santos *et al.* proposed an ACO enhanced with a local search, currently one of the best metaheuristics for the CARP [SAN 10]. Ting and Chen [TIN 13] also proposed a multiple ACO to solve the location routing problem (LRP). The method was effective and able to improve several best-known solutions.

4.5. Particle swarm optimization

Another well-spread swarm-based algorithm is particle swarm optimization. Its principle is presented in the following section.

4.5.1. Principle

Particle swarm optimization (PSO) is based on a population of individuals called particles. It was proposed for the first time by Kennedy and Eberhart in 1995 [KEN 95] for continuous optimization problems and then adapted to discrete optimization ones [KEN 97]. A particle represents a potential solution which moves in the search space with the goal to reach the global optimum. The overall learning process of the swarm results in local interactions between the different particles that constitute it. Each particle has a memory of its best visited solution and its ability to communicate with the particles around it. From this information, a speed is computed for each particle which will condition the changes that would be done on it for the next iteration.

In each PSO iteration, each particle moves from its original position to a better position in an N-dimensional space with a specific velocity. Particles' velocity is influenced by the cognitive and social information of the particles. The cognitive information of a particle is the best position *pbest* that it has already visited. The social information of the particles is controlled by the swarm best position *sbest*: the best position encountered by considering all the particles in the swarm. In the first iteration, for each particle i the position x_i is generated randomly and the velocity v_i

is initialized to zero. For the next iteration, these values are updated according to equations [4.3] and [4.4]:

$$v_i^{k+1} = \omega v_i^k + c_1 \times \alpha_1(pbest_i - x_i^k) + c_2 \times \alpha_2(sbest_i - x_i^k) \qquad [4.3]$$

$$x_i^{k+1} = x_i^k + v_i^{k+1} \qquad [4.4]$$

The weighting factors c_1 and c_2 are used to balance the move toward positions *pbest* and *sbest*. α_1 and α_2 are random variables generated from uniform distribution in [0,1], ω is the inertia weight and it is used to control intensification and diversification phases during the PSO. This parameter is usually adjusted linearly through the algorithm; decreasing from ω_{max} to ω_{min} according to equation [4.5]. max_{iter} and $iter$ are, respectively, the maximum number of iterations and the current iteration in the PSO. The general structure of the method is given in algorithm 4.6.

$$\omega = \omega_{max} - \frac{(\omega_{max} - \omega_{min})}{max_{iter}} \times iter \qquad [4.5]$$

Algorithm 4.6: Particle swarm optimization principle

---

1 initialize the speed v_i and position x_i of each particle
2 **while** *the stopping criterion is not met* **do**
3 | update positions and speeds
4 | update best positions
5 return the best solution

Since PSO was originally proposed for continuous problems, the general design scheme presented in this section requires some adaptations to deal with combinatorial problems. Kennedy and Eberhart [KEN 97] proposed a discrete binary PSO (DPSO), so that it could solve some binary problems in discrete research spaces. As a result, binary PSO is commonly used to solve CVRP.

4.5.2. *PSO in vehicle routing problems*

PSO started to be used on vehicle routing problems only 10 years ago, its early applications being on continuous optimization problems. The first published work using PSO on vehicle routing problems was by Chen *et al.* [CHE 06], who proposed this approach to solve CVRP. The developed method is in fact a hybrid that uses simulated annealing to solve a TSP for each vehicle, the assignment of customers to vehicles being conducted in the PSO part. Just after that, Ai and Kachitvichyanukul

[AI 07] used the classical version of PSO without any hybridization to solve the same problem (CVRP). In terms of computational results, Chen's PSO provides high-quality solutions for some benchmark problems with less than 134 customers. However, it is time-consuming (half an hour for the more difficult instances). On the other hand, Ai and Kachitvichyanukul's PSO is relatively fast on some benchmark problems with less than 199 customers; however, their method is not stable.

Ai and Kachitvichyanukul [AI 09] presented a second pure PSO algorithm to solve the vehicle routing problem with simultaneous pickup and delivery (VRPSPD), considered to be a rare non-hybrid PSO that competes with other metaheuristics dedicated to the same problem. Marinakis et al. obtained good results for CVRP but their method is also a hybrid combining PSO, GRASP and PR [MAR 10b, MAR 10a]. On CVRP with stochastic demands, we can cite works from Marinakis et al. [MAR 13] and Moghaddam et al. [MOG 12]. Very recently, Norouzi et al. [NOR 15] designed a PSO to solve a periodic VRP with time windows where the objective is to minimize the travel cost and maximize the sales while serving customers before the arrival of rival vehicles.

When examining the literature dealing with PSO methodology, except in rare cases, only hybrid PSO methods are competitive compared to other metaheuristics approaches and this observation is still valid for vehicle routing problems.

4.6. Other approaches and their use in vehicle routing problems

This section describes some population or swarm-based methods that were used for solving vehicle routing problems but which are still not widespread. Among these methods, we can cite approaches similar to ACO and PSO which are also inspired from the social behaviors of insects and animals, for example the artificial bee colony (ABC) method.

ABC is a swarm-based heuristic which mimics the foraging behavior of a honey bee swarm. This method was introduced by Karaboga in 2005 [KAR 05] for solving continuous optimization problems. The main idea of this evolutionary algorithm is that complete or partial solutions are considered as food sources and the bees try to exploit the food sources in the hope of finding good quality nectar, i.e. high-quality solutions. In addition, bees communicate between themselves about the search space and the food sources. The first application of this methodology was by Marinakis and Marinaki [MAR 11] and Szeto et al. [SZE 11], who used it to solve the CVRP.

The *imperialist competitive algorithm* (ICA) is also a recent swarm-based method, introduced in 2007 by Atashpaz-Gargari and Lucas [ATA 07]. This method is derived from the field of sociopolitical behaviors where solutions are assimilated to countries, where the best ones are the imperialists and the others are considered as colonies.

Yousefikhoshbakht and Sedighpour [YOU 14] proposed the first ICA to solve the TSP. Results indicated that the ICA competes with other evolutionary algorithms.

Harmony search is another relatively new population-based metaheuristic which achieved good results in some combinatorial optimization problems. Proposed by Geem in 2000, it mimics the behavior of a music orchestra when aiming to compose a harmonious melody. Some applications of this methodology on vehicle routing problems can be found in the literature, such as the papers by Geem [GEE 05a, GEE 05b]. To overcome the slow convergence of the initial version of harmony search, Taha Yassen *et al.* [YAS 15] proposed a version enhanced by a local search procedure that was applied to solve the VRP with time windows.

4.7. Selected examples

This section is devoted to the presentation of three examples of population-based metaheuristics. The first one is an SS designed to solve the periodic capacitated arc routing problem [CHU 06]. The second is a PR proposed for multi-depot periodic VRP (MDPVRP). The last one is a memetic algorithm with population management which is currently the best method, competing with existing metaheuristics over 26 different variants of vehicle routing problems [VID 13b].

4.7.1. *Scatter search for the periodic capacitated arc routing problem*

Chu *et al.* [CHU 06] investigated the periodic capacitated arc routing problem (PCARP) raised, for instance, by municipal waste collection. In this problem, the objective is to assign a set of service periods to each required edge in a given network and to solve the resulting CARP for each period, in order to minimize the fleet size and the total cost of the routes over the whole horizon. The authors proposed an SS which was evaluated on two sets of PCARP instances derived from the well-known *GDB* and *VAL* benchmarks; initially designed for the CARP. In this section, the main principles of the method are recalled.

In the periodic CARP, a multi-period horizon H of np periods and a connected undirected network $G = (X, E)$, with a set X of n nodes and a set E of m edges, are considered. A fleet of identical vehicles with limited capacity is based at a depot node. Each edge $e = [i, j]$ has a traversal cost $C(e)$. A subset E_R of t edges, the tasks, must be serviced. Each task e has a frequency $f(e)$, and a set of allowed day combinations $comb(e)$. A combination is a set of $f(e)$ distinct service periods. For instance, $np = 7$ days and $comb(e) = \{(1, 4), (2, 5)\}$ means that e must serviced twice along the 7-periods horizon either on Monday and Thursday or on Tuesday and Friday. The demand $Q(e, k, p)$ for each edge e, each day combination k in $comb(e)$ and each day p in k, is assumed to be known.

As mentioned before, the objective function consists of minimizing the fleet size in priority and then the total distance traveled. The fleet size is defined as the maximum number of vehicles used in each period. For a given solution S, the objective function value is hence defined as $Z(S) = M \times nvu(S) + Cost(S)$ where $nvu(S)$ is the fleet size, $Cost(S)$ is the total traveled distance over the time horizon (it can also correspond to the total traveled time or any other cost) and M is a positive large constant. If the fleet is already fixed, by setting M to 0, it falls back to the classical objective function usually used in periodic VRP (the node-routing counterpart of the PCARP).

In the proposed SS, a solution is coded as a set of *giant tours*, one for each time period, as done for the single-period CARP by Lacomme *et al.* [LAC 04]. The solutions are decoded due to a generalization of the Split algorithm (see section 2.1.2 for more details).

Each required edge $[i, j]$ is coded by two opposite arcs (i, j) and (j, i) representing the two possible service directions. These two arcs are linked by a pointer inv. Hence, when u and v represent a same edge, we set $inv(u) = v$ and $inv(v) = u$. A PCARP solution is encoded as an ordered list S of arc-tasks. S contains np daily sublists $S(1)$, $S(2)$, $S(np)$. Each sublist $S(p)$ contains the k_p tasks performed in period p, without trip delimiters. Each task u occurs in S a number of times equal to its frequency, either as u or $inv(u)$, but at most once in each sublist. The optimal evaluations of S for $M = 0$ and M set to a large value are possible through a splitting procedure inspired from that of Prins *et al.* [PRI 04b, LAC 04].

When M equals 0, the method consists of applying the procedure explained in Chapter 2 for each sublist $S(k), k = 1, 2, ..., np$ (see section 2.1.2). If the fleet size is limited to K vehicles per period, the splitting procedure can be adapted very quickly since Bellman's algorithm for general graphs can be used for this purpose. Indeed, this algorithm computes in its iteration i the shortest paths with at most i arcs. Therefore, the algorithm may be stopped at the end of iteration K. The cost of the optimal solution with respect to the sequence imposed by the list S is derived as the sum of the costs of the np daily solutions.

When $M \neq 0$, the splitting procedure can be done in two steps: a first step consists of computing the minimum number of vehicles needed to serve the customers. For this purpose, the splitting procedure is performed in each period to obtain the minimum number of necessary vehicles. The fleet size is set as the maximal value obtained over the np periods. A second step applies Bellman's algorithm to obtain the detailed routes for each period with respect to the sequence order and the fleet minimum size obtained in the first step. Figure 4.5 shows the principle on a small example with two periods. Tasks a, b, f must be serviced in each period in contrast to tasks c, d, e, g which require only one visit. To simplify the computations, we assume in this example that the vehicles have a common capacity equal to 10 and that all the required arcs (represented by continuous lines in the top and bottom figures) require three units of demand. The travel costs are given between brackets near the arcs. The figures in the middle show the auxiliary graphs and are built as explained in Chapter 2.

The first step of the splitting procedure ignores the costs of the trips and associates instead a unitary cost with them, which means a vehicle is used for each arc in the auxiliary graph. The first phase finds 2 as minimum number of vehicles and the second phase computes optimally the routes of each period under sequence and fleet size constraints. The obtained routes for the considered example are illustrated in the lower part of Figure 4.5.

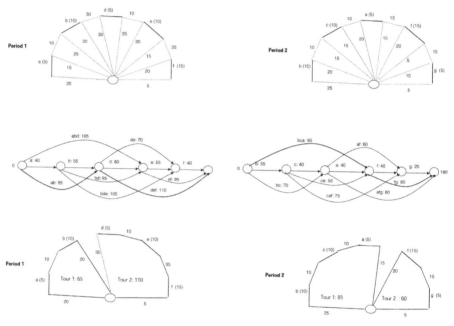

Figure 4.5. *Two-phase split for PCARP*

A distance measure that generalizes the R-permutations distance proposed by Campos [CAM 05] was considered in this work. Let $D(S_1, S_2)$ be the distance between two PCARP solutions S_1 and S_2. Define this distance by:

$$D(S_1, S_2) = \sum_{p=1}^{np} \left[\sum_{u \in S_1(p)} B(S_1, S_2, p, u) + |p - F(S_1, S_2, p, u)| \right] \qquad [4.6]$$

$B(S_1, S_2, p, u)$ is a binary function defined for each time period p and each required arc (task) u scheduled in both sublists $S_1(p)$ and $S_2(p)$ which takes the value 1 if and only if: u immediately occurs before a task v in $S_1(p)$, and S_2 contains either the subsequence (u, v) or $(inv(v), inv(u))$, where $inv(x)$ is the opposite arc of x.

The function $F(S_1, S_2, p, u)$ is defined for each arc u serviced in $S_1(p)$ but not in $S_2(p)$. It is computed as follows: for $p = 1, ..., np$, the first tasks present in both $S_1(p)$ and $S_2(p)$ are virtually deleted. Let $S_1{}^*$ and $S_2{}^*$ be the resulting subsequences and k be the occurrence number of $u \in S_1(p)$ in $S_1{}^*$. $k = 2$ means that the second service on arc u is accomplished in period p. Hence, $F(S_1, S_2, p, u)$ indicates the kth service period of u in $S_2{}^*$. Figure 4.6 shows the computation of this distance on a small example with six tasks and five periods. For the sake of simplicity, the opposite arcs are not represented in this solution. The distance takes the value 10: the first term in equation [4.7.1] equals 2 and the second equals 8.

Day	1	2	3	4	5
S_1	4, 5, 2	1, 5, 3	6, 1, 4	2, 4	1, 5, 4
S_2	5, 1, 2	1, 4, 5	4, 5	2, 1, 3, 4	4, 6
$S_1{}^*$	4	3	6, 1		1, 5
$S_2{}^*$	1	4	5	1, 3	6

Figure 4.6. *Distance measure used in the scatter search for PCARP*

The initial population contains $PopSize$ solutions, encoded as explained previously. All initial solutions were randomly generated except the first one that was obtained by a best insertion heuristic. This last is directly added to the population after concatenating its trips day by day to obtain the same encoding as the other solutions. To ensure diversity, nt random solutions are generated and the one maximizing the distance to the solutions already present in the population is kept.

The local search is executed with a probability π on detailed solutions (those obtained after the splitting procedure) during the SS. It involves the following actions:

– M_1: permute u and v over the entire horizon if they have the same frequency but are not assigned to the same periods on the horizon;

– M_2: flip u in its trip, i.e. replace u by $inv(u)$;

– M_3: move task u after v (v may be the depot for this move);

– M_4: move u and its successor on the trip after v (v may be the depot for this move);

– $M5$: permute u and v.

The two possible directions are evaluated each time a task is inserted into a new position. Neighborhood exploration stops at the first instance of improvement. The whole search stops when no more improvement can be detected. The trips are then concatenated day by day to obtain an encoded solution, which is reevaluated by the splitting procedures. To speed up the local search, a list is precomputed for each arc sorted in the increasing order of distance to its final extremity. Then, the search can be restricted by limiting the choice of v in the moves to a fixed percentage of the list.

The recombination operator was inspired from the LOX crossover usually used in genetic algorithms. Given two solutions P_1 and P_2 with k tasks, $PLOX$ starts by randomly selecting two cutting positions p and q, with $1 \le p \le q \le k$. To obtain the first child solution C_1, the tasks between p and q are first copied from the first parent, while keeping their respective service days. Then, C_1 is completed by scanning P2, starting from the first day. There are three possible cases for the current task u of P_2:

– if u is already serviced the required number of times in C_1, the task is not copied;

– otherwise, u is appended to the tasks which are in the same day in C_1, provided that there exists at least one period combination over the horizon compatible with this day assignment;

– if there is no such combination, u is appended to the earliest period compatible with a period combination. Such a period always exists.

The second child is obtained by exchanging the roles of the two parents. The general structure of the SS developed for PCARP is similar to algorithm 4.3. It was intended to solve both CARP and PCARP. The parameters set to the same values in both problems (CARP and PCARP) are: population size $PopSize = 60$, reference set size $RefSize = 20$, number of trials to obtain a diversified solution $nt = 10$. The local search rate was set to 75% in CARP and 10% in PCARP. The percentage of neighborhoods examined during the local search is 100% for CARP and 25% for PCARP.

Numerical tests in the single-period case (CARP) on two sets of standard instances indicate that the SS is competitive with state-of-the-art algorithms published for CARP at this period, however, it requires larger running times. When applied to PCARP instances derived from these two sets, the SS strongly improves the solutions obtained by greedy heuristics. The results were improved only 5 years later by Mei *et al.* [MEI 11] who developed a memetic algorithm to solve the problem.

4.7.2. *PR for the muti-depot periodic VRP*

Rahimi *et al.* [RAH 13] were the first to propose a pure PR for a vehicle routing problem, namely the multi-depot periodic VRP. Their approach incorporates exploitation and exploration strategies in order to solve the considered problem in two different manners: as a stand-alone algorithm and as a part of a cooperative search method, called integrative cooperative search (ICS). In the following, the main features of this work are given.

The key idea of this approach is to use several independent reference sets: the first one, called *complete set*, corresponds to elite solutions of the main problem (MDPVRP); while the others, named *partial sets*, consist of elite solutions dedicated either to the periodic VRP or to multi-depot VRP: two subproblems of the MDPVRP. Each of these subproblems is then solved by a dedicated solution algorithm called *partial solver*.

The main advantage of the decomposition procedure is that working on each attribute at a time (either multi-depot or multi-period) quickly provides high-quality solutions. Elite solutions obtained by each partial solver are added to partial sets that can be either kept unchanged during the path relinking process (static scenario) or iteratively updated by adding better solutions in terms of diversity and quality (dynamic scenario). Another trick used in this work is to allow traversing infeasible regions during the search process. For this purpose, a penalty function, associated with a new solution x generated during the search mechanism, is defined as:

$$z(x) = c(x) + \alpha q(x) + \beta t(x) \qquad [4.7]$$

where $q(x)$ and $t(x)$ are, respectively, the total violation of the load and duration constraints, and α and β are positive parameters that are adjusted dynamically. Parameter α is set as follows: if there is no violation of the capacity constraints, its value is divided by $1 + \gamma$, otherwise it is multiplied by $1 + \gamma$, where γ is a positive parameter. The same adjustment rule is also applied to β.

After building the initial reference list, the proposed PR starts constructing high-quality solutions for the main problem, by exploring trajectories that link solutions chosen from different subsets, partial and/or complete. Two variants of PR are obtained by discarding either complete or partial sets. In the first case, PR generates complete solutions using partial solutions only, while in the second case the method reduces to the general PR described in algorithm 4.7.

As mentioned before, the PR uses three reference sets: two partial corresponding either to the multi-depot or to the multi-period attribute; the third one corresponds to complete solutions of the MDPVRP. The three subsets have the same maximum size $Size_{max}$. Four strategies are used to define the starting and guiding solutions.

Algorithm 4.7: General PR to solve MDPVRP

---

1 **while** *stopping criterion is not met* **do**
2 | generate an initial set of solutions
3 | **while** *reference set contains at least a solution* **do**
4 | | select two solutions from the reference list
5 | | identify the initial and guiding solutions
6 | | remove the initial solution from the reference list
7 | | generate intermediate solutions by moving from initial toward guiding
   | | one
8 | └   update the reference set

9 return the best solution

The first strategy, called *partial relinking strategy*, selects two partial solutions, each from a different partial set of the reference list, and sends them to the neighborhood search phase. The main idea involved in implementing such a selection strategy is to produce complete solutions by integrating the best characteristics of the chosen partial solutions. To attain this goal, four possible ways of choosing pairs that will undergo the relinking phase are tested:

– the ith pair is constituted by taking the ith best solution of the jth $j = 1, 2$ and kth $k = 1, 2, k \neq j$ partial sets, as guiding and starting solutions, respectively. The main idea behind is that high-quality solutions have some common characteristics with optimum solutions;

– the ith pair is generated by determining the guiding solution as the ith best solution of the jth $j = 1, 2$ partial set, while the initial solution is defined as the ith worst solution of the kth $k = 1, 2, k \neq j$ partial set;

– the ith pair is constructed by randomly choosing the guiding and initial solutions from the jth $j = 1, 2$ and kth $k = 1, 2, k \neq j$ partial sets, respectively;

– the ith pair is constructed by defining the guiding solution as the ith best solution of the jth $j = 1, 2$ partial set, whereas the initial solution is chosen as the solution of the kth $k = 1, 2, k \neq j$ partial set with maximum Hamming distance from the guiding solution. Here, the aim is to select the initial and guiding solutions not only according to the objective function value but also by considering diversity.

The second strategy, called *complete relinking strategy*, consists of using two different complete solutions taken from the complete reference set. The following three manners of selecting pairs of complete solutions are tested:

– the ith pair is constructed by defining the guiding and initial solutions as the best and ith complete solutions of the complete set, respectively;

– the ith pair is built by determining the guiding and initial solutions as the ith and $i+1$th best solutions of the complete set, respectively;

– the ith pair consists of taking as guiding solution the ith best solution of the complete set, whereas the initial solution is chosen as the solution of the same set with maximum Hamming distance from the selected guiding solution.

Another strategy, called *mixed strategy*, selects a partial and a complete solution as the inputs of the neighborhood search phase. This selection strategy aims to improve selected partial solution by introducing good characteristics from the chosen complete solution. Two ways of realizing this are tested:

– the ith pair is constructed by defining the guiding and initial solutions as the ith best solution of the jth $j = 1, 2$ partial set and complete set, respectively;

– the ith pair contains as guiding solution the ith best solution of the complete set, whereas the initial solution is chosen as the solution of the jth $j = 1, 2$ partial set with maximum Hamming distance from the selected guiding solution.

The last strategy, called *ideal point strategy*, considers the two-dimensional ideal point whose ith coordinate is the objective function value of the best partial solution of the ith partial set $i = 1, 2$. This strategy first selects two different guiding solutions so that the ith guiding solution is the best solution of the ith coordinate. Then, each of the solutions in the global reference list (partial or complete) serves, respectively, as the initial solution. This strategy aims to simultaneously introduce on new solutions appropriate characteristics of multiple high-quality guiding solutions.

The general PR sketched in algorithm 4.7 updates the reference list each time a new solution is generated. Two methods are used to make the update: the first method, called *internal update* method, adds each new generated complete solution S_{new} to the complete reference set if this latter does not achieved yet its maximal size $Size_{max}$. Otherwise, the diversity contribution of S_{new} is calculated as the minimum Hamming distance to the complete reference set (i.e. $D_H(S_{new}, P) = \min_{X \in P} D(S_{new}, X)$ where P denotes the complete reference set.

First, a solution S_{max} is computed such that:

$$S_{max} = \arg\max_{\{S \in P: Z(S) < Z(S_{new})\}} \frac{Z(S)}{D_H(S_{new}, P \setminus \{S\})}, \text{ where } Z \text{ denotes the objective}$$

function.

If $\dfrac{Z(S_{new})}{D_H(S_{new}, P \setminus \{S_{max}\})} < \dfrac{Z(S_{max})}{D_H(S_{max}, P \setminus \{S_{max}\})}$ then S_{new} replaces S_{max}; otherwise, it replaces the worst solution in the set $\{S \in P : Z(S) < Z(S_{new})\}$.

The second method, called *external update*, is dedicated to the partial reference sets. Whenever a new partial solution x_{new} is generated by the ith partial solver, the method updates the corresponding reference set as follows: first, if x_{new} is better than the worst solution in the corresponding reference set, it replaces this latter. Otherwise, x_{new} is added to the corresponding set if it increases the Hamming distance between the two partial subsets.

Another important issue in PR implementation is the path generation method, in other words, the neighborhood structure used in order to move from starting solutions to guiding ones. As in the PR components detailed previously, two strategies working either on partial solutions or on complete ones are developed. The first strategy consists of selecting partial solutions from the first and second partial reference sets. These two solutions deal with either muti-depot attribute or periodic VRP attribute: they exhibit (1) good characteristics of depots assignments to customers, and (2) good characteristics of periods assignments to customers. The authors define *good complete solution* as a solution generated by the neighborhood search phase in which all customers are eligible. A customer is said to be eligible if assigned to the same depot as in the first partial solution and to the service period as in the second partial solution.

The first θ iterations are executed in order to make customers, randomly selected from the starting partial solutions, eligible. At the end of this process, if the customer is eligible, two moves are iteratively applied:

– *intraroute relocate move*: an eligible customer is first removed, for each period, from the route by which it is visited. He/she is then inserted into the best position, based on the penalty function 4.7 in the same route;

– *interroute relocate move*: the chosen customer is first removed, for each period, from its current route and, then, is inserted into the best position of the other routes assigned to the depot from which the customer is served.

If the selected customer is ineligible, an attempt is made in order to prevent ineligibility by applying the relocate moves in this following way:

– the depot to which the selected customer is currently assigned is replaced by the depot for which that customer is served in the solution selected from the first partial set;

– the current visit pattern of the selected customer is replaced by the visit pattern of the customer in the solution chosen from the second partial set;

– the customer is removed from the routes by which he/she is visited;

– finally, at each period of the new visit pattern, the removed customer is inserted into one of the routes assigned to the new depot. The position is chosen so that the penalty function [4.7] is minimal.

The second strategy shares the same ideas as the first one and is also a memory-based strategy which explores trajectories between starting and guiding solutions. However, these solutions are selected according to the *complete* or the *mixed* or the *ideal point* strategies. As for the case detailed just before, the notion of eligibility is used and the interrelocate and intrarelocate moves are executed in order to establish it when it is missing for some customers.

The algorithm is stopped when a maximum number of successive iterations are executed without finding improving solutions or when a maximum allowable running time is attained.

The authors used in this paper as local solver the hybrid GA proposed by Vidal *et al.* [VID 12a] to rapidly generate fairly good (not necessarily high quality) partial solutions (either for MDVRP or PVRP). Finally, the obtained partial solutions are sent to the PR in order to generate solutions for the main problem. A design of experiments was used to tune the algorithm parameters based and different exploration and exploitation strategies were tested. The PRA performs considerably well, for all the problem instances.

4.7.3. *Unified genetic algorithm for a wide class of vehicle routing problems*

Vidal *et al.* [VID 13b] proposed a unified genetic algorithm with population management to deal with a large class of vehicle routing with time windows (VRPTWs), route-duration constraints and additional attributes involving requirements for customer assignments to particular vehicle types, depots or planning periods. The method, called by the authors HGSADC for hybrid genetic search with adaptive diversity control, owes its success to several new tricks such as the use of a double population: one for feasible individuals and the second for infeasible ones. HGSADC allows accepting infeasible solutions not respecting route-related constraints such as load and maximum duration. Fleet size constraints are always kept verified and the method uses an adaptive penalty function control.

The method is not described in Chapter 5 dedicated to hybrid metaheuristics because, in our opinion, it can be considered as a memetic algorithm. The general framework of the proposed approach is given in algorithm 4.8.

The method generates feasible and infeasible solutions that are put into two different subpopulations. First, two parents are selected and then combined to get a child solution. This last is improved by a local search and then inserted into the corresponding subpopulation if the size of this latter has not reached its maximum value. Infeasible solutions are repaired with a given probability π_{rep}.

Algorithm 4.8: General structure of the HGSADC

---

1 build Population
2 **while** *max. number of iteration without improvement (It_{Ni}) is not attained and running time less then a threshold* **do**
3   generate two parents P_1 and P_2
4   select two solutions from the reference list
5   create offspring solution C from P_1 and P_2
6   improve C with a local search procedure
7   **if** *C is infeasible* **then**
8   add C to the infeasible sub-population
9   repair C with a probability π_{rep}
10   **if** *C is feasible* **then**
11   add C to the feasible sub-population
12   **if** *maximum sub-population size reached* **then**
13   select survivors
14   **if** *best solution not improved since It_{Div}* **then**
15   diversify population
16   adjust penalty parameters for infeasibility
17   **if** *number of iteration is a multiple of It_{dec}* **then**
18   decompose the master problem
19   use HGSADC on each subproblem
20   reconstitute three solutions and insert them in the population
21 return best feasible solution

A survivor selection is applied when the subpopulation achieves its maximum size. This phase is followed by a diversification step if no improving solutions is met during It_{div} successive iterations. Then, penalty parameters are updated. After each It_{dec} iteration, the main problem under consideration is decomposed to subproblems and a recursive call is made to HGSADC to solve each subproblem. The method stops after It_{Ni} successive iterations without improving the best solution.

As mentioned before, the method allows infeasible solutions, however the violated constraints are penalized. The constraints that can be violated are related to route duration, route load and time windows if any in the main problem. The fleet size is always respected to avoid sophisticated repair procedures that can consume large amount of time to reduce the number of vehicles. For clarity's sake, the components of the approach are explained on a restricted set of vehicle routing problems, the VRPTW and its periodic extension PVRPTW, in what follows as done by the authors.

The penalty function for a route r with a schedule t_r is defined as the sum of its total distance plus the weighted sum of its excess on duration, load and time warp. Time warp is computed as in Nagata *et al.* [NAG 10]. The principle is explained on a small example given in Figure 4.7. In this example, the route visits five customers in the order V_1, V_2, V_3, V_4, V_5. The arrival time at those customers is shown according to the horizontal axis of the figure. At customer V_2, a waiting time holds since the vehicle arrives at its location before the beginning of the time window. However, at customer V_4, a time wrap occurs since the customer is reached after the closure of its time window.

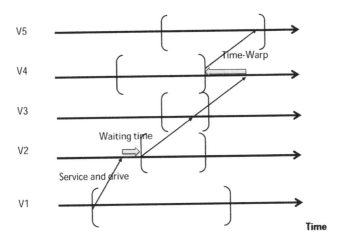

Figure 4.7. *Illustration of time warp computation*

Note that time windows violations are not necessary propagated to subsequent customers with this method, since each time a late arrival to a customer is observed, the departure time to the following client is set equal to the upper limit of the current time window.

Equation [4.8] provides the expression of the penalty function, where D and Q are, respectively, the maximum duration of routes and the vehicles' capacity. $\tau(r)$ and $q(r)$ indicate, respectively, the total length and the total load of route r.

$$\phi(r) = c(r) + \alpha \max\{0, \tau(r) - D\} + \beta \max\{0, q(r) - Q\} + \gamma tw(r) \quad [4.8]$$

The single-period single-depot solution is represented by a list of customers without trip delimiters as proposed in Prins [PRI 04a]. Depending on the nature of the problem, this representation is slightly modified to capture the other attributes of the main problem. For example, for the periodic VRP, two chromosomes are used: one to indicate for each customer the visit-period choices and the second provides the sequence of services to be done in each period. This representation allows us to use simple combination operators. Furthermore, detailed routes can be derived from this encoding by a polynomial time splitting algorithm as done by Chu *et al.* for the periodic CARP [CHU 06] (see section 4.7.1 for details). For the PVRTW, some tricks are used in the splitting procedure: penalized routes are included in the auxiliary graph, and the value $2Q$ is considered as the maximal load that cannot be exceeded for the vehicle capacity.

The developed HGSADC includes a population management mechanism that is based on the use of a distance measure δ. Depending on the nature of the main problem, the distance used can be different. For example, the Hamming distance is considered for the PVRPTW and SDVRPTW and the distance of broken pairs proposed by Martì [MAR 05] is selected for both VRPTW and MDVRPTW.

A diversity contribution $\delta(P)$ measured by equation [4.9] is computed for each individual P by considering only the set of closest neighbors N_{close} in its subpopulation.

$$\delta(P) = \frac{A}{|N_{close}|} \sum_{P_1 \in N_{close}} \delta(P, P_1) \qquad [4.9]$$

The authors considered a biased fitness BF measure that involves both cost and diversity contribution. For an individual P, with a fitness $fit(P)$ and a rank $dc(P)$ in the population, $BF(P)$ is given by equation [4.10].

$$BF(P) = fit(P) + (1 - \frac{N_{elite}}{N_{indiv}}) \times dc(P) \qquad [4.10]$$

The rank $dc(P)$ is computed according to the diversity contribution measure $\delta(P)$, N_{indiv} is the current number of individuals in the subpopulation and N_{elite} is a parameter that controls elitism during the survivor selection.

To generate a child, two parents are first selected by binary tournament in the union of both feasible and infeasible populations and then they are combined with a crossover operator. For the VRPTW for instance, the crossover OX is used whereas it is replaced by the combination operator PIX in the periodic version of the VRPTW.

Once a child individual is generated, it undergoes the splitting procedure to obtain the detailed routes and then the repair phase is executed with a probability π_{rep} if the obtained solution is infeasible.

The local search procedure is based on *route improvement RI* or *pattern improvement PI* that is called in the order RI, PI, RI. The objective of these moves is to efficiently address both service sequencing and assignment characteristics. The *PI* procedure evaluates for each customer in a random order the best combination of reinsertions within periods. Any improving move is directly performed until no more improvement can be found. The *RI* procedure explores for each period a series of moves based on relocations and/or exchanges of customer visit sequences:

– M_1 (swap and relocate): swap, with or without sequence inversion, two disjoint visit sequences containing between 0 and 2 customers;

– M_2 (2-opt*): swap two visit sequences from two different routes;

– M_3 (2-opt): reverse a sequence of customers in the same route.

To improve computational efficiency of the local search phase, neighborhoods are also pruned by means of customer correlation measures. This strategy is usually used in the TSP and CVRP and takes into account spatial proximity measures, for time contained VRP (such as VRPTW), the authors propose in addition to include time proximity. For a customer v_i, the set of $\Gamma(v_i)$ correlated customers is defined as the $|\Gamma(v_i)|$ closest customers computed by equation [4.11]:

$$\gamma(v_i, v_j) = c_{i,j} + \gamma^{WT} \max\{0, e_j - \tau_j - \delta_{ij}\} + \gamma^{TW} \max\{0, e_i + \tau_i + \delta_{ij} - l_j\}[4.11]$$

This measure includes the distance, the minimum waiting time and the minimum penalty if v_j is directly serviced after customer v_i. The role of the parameters γ^{WT} and γ^{TW} is to balance the temporal and spatial proximity characteristics. For the VRPTW, neighborhoods M_1 and M_2 are restricted to sequences $(\sigma_i{}^r, \sigma_{i+1}^r, ..., \sigma_j{}^r)$ and $(\sigma_k{}^{\hat{r}}, \sigma_{k+1}^{\hat{r}}, ..., \sigma_l{}^{\hat{r}})$ such that $\sigma_i{}^r \in \gamma(\sigma_{k-1}{}^{\hat{r}})$ or $\sigma_k{}^{\hat{r}} \in \gamma(\sigma_{i-1}{}^r)$. For move M_3 and a sequence $(\sigma_i{}^r, \sigma_{i+1}^r, ..., \sigma_j{}^r)$, only moves with $\sigma_j{}^r \in \gamma(\sigma_{i-1}{}^r)$ or $\sigma_{j+1}{}^r \in \gamma(\sigma_i{}^r)$ are tested.

The feasibility tests are efficiently implemented according to the techniques explained in 2 (see sections 2.2.3 and 2.2.4). To efficiently tackle large instances and complex time constrained variants of the VRPTW, a decomposition phase is performed. The procedure follows four main steps: features from one elite solution are exploited to define subproblems, in the second step initial individuals for the subproblems are created from the genetic material of the complete problem population. After that, the HGSADC algorithm is called to solve the subproblems, and finally the complete solution is reconstituted.

The developed HGSADC is compared to state-of-the-art methods and was able to improve the results on a large class of instances dedicated for several VRP variants. Decomposition phases contribute significantly to the search performance on large PVRPTW instances, for which subproblems can involve up to 560 customers. The impact is less important on problems such as MDVRPTW and SDVRPTW, especially when the number of customers per depot or vehicle type is not large.

The performance of this method lies in the combination of several ideas and tricks that originate from several methodologies: a biased fitness that includes measures from genetic algorithms and from scatter search (fitness and distance measure), local searches using speed-up techniques which not only consider the geographic proximity of customers in neighborhoods, but also their temporal proximity (see equation [4.11]), an efficient decomposition phase and the use of partial (thus infeasible solutions) and complete ones, and last but not least, the method is generic and uses the same code (same Split procedure and local search) for all the 26 VRP variants. This is made possible due to an object-programming design.

4.8. Conclusion

This chapter gathers the main population-based metaheuristics; their principles are first exposed and some of their applications on vehicle routing problems are given. Three successful implementations are further detailed with an emphasis on the key points that contributed to their performance.

We should notice that population-based metaheuristics are widely used in combinatorial optimization in general and in vehicle routing problems in particular. The most effective ones are without a doubt those using local improvement procedures especially when they are completed by diversification techniques. These strategies can be based on population management as it is the case in MA|PMs, or on the use of a distance measure in solution space, as done in scatter search and path relinking.

Throughout this chapter, we can see that a number of aspects in methods such as scatter search and path relinking deserve more investigation. The design of an appropriate distance measure to quantify the diversity is one of these issues. In fact, all distance measures used in those methods until now are based on solution encoding which depends finally on the choices made by authors. One important research direction is really to derive a distance which better reflects the distribution of the solutions in the search space.

The two key components of the search process in metaheuristics are intensification and diversification. Approaches performing well are those balancing these two components. Nevertheless, a number of these metaheuristics are implemented in an increasingly similar way. Indeed, methods exploiting some form of collective learning such as PSO and ACO, basically different from evolutionary algorithms, are often combined with local improvement procedures to boost their performance and, in some recent implementations, a chromosome-like encoding is also used in such methods.

In real word applications, researchers and practitioners are facing many more complex problems with high dimensionality. Metaheuristic approaches are expected to be increasingly used in the future and especially in their hybrid form combining some of them. Chapter 5 aims in its first part to give an overview of these hybridization schemes.

5

Metaheuristics Hybridizing
Various Components

Research in metaheuristics for combinatorial optimization problems, and thus for vehicle routing problems, significantly shifts toward a trend of hybridization. The main motivation of this trend is to take advantage of the complementarity of different optimization strategies and to make them cooperate in synergy. Different definitions of hybrid metaheuristics can be found as explained, for example, by Blum *et al.* [BLU 11]. In this chapter, only two main classes are examined: either by combining components from several standalone metaheuristics, or by crossbreeding exact algorithms and metaheuristics, leading to matheuristics.

Nevertheless, designing an efficient hybrid metaheuristic can be a difficult task. Indeed, to have a real interest, the resulting method has to be efficient both in terms of solution quality and computational time, without being too specific to the problem at hand and/or complicated to implement. Thus, the choice of an appropriate combination of cleverly chosen components is surely the key to success.

The motivation for development of hybrid metaheuristics has been noticed in the early 2000s with the first dedicated workshops (Hybrid Metaheuristics in 2004 and Matheuristics in 2006). The first book especially dedicated to hybrid metaheuristics was published in 2008.

5.1. Hybridizing metaheuristics

Very widespread hybridization techniques consist of using local search methods within classical metaheuristics not originally including them. This is particularly the case for methods working on a set of solutions such as genetic algorithms, resulting in memetic algorithms (see section 4.1 in Chapter 4). Such a simple scheme is not detailed here.

5.1.1. *Principle*

Over the last decades, a large number of metaheuristics have been developed to solve several optimization problems raised in different application areas. This category of approaches has proven its effectiveness in terms of quality of results and running times.

Recent trends encourage researchers to focus more and more attention on solving complex problems on large-scale and real-size benchmarks. This has inevitably led to develop more powerful approaches taking advantage from components originating from different metaheuristics in order to solve the problem considered in the most efficient way. Naturally, a first form of hybridization appeared by putting together different metaheuristics in a main framework with the objective to complement each other and to produce better results than when they are run separately. This kind of hybridization, although it seems simple, is not so easy to implement efficiently.

Hybridization design can be based on enrichment of a given metaheuristic by adding restart procedures (as in greedy randomized adaptive search procedure (GRASP)), with a population generation (as in genetic algorithms (GAs)), probabilistic acceptance of deteriorating moves (a main component of simulated annealing, tabu search), variable neighborhood structures (as in variable neighborhood search (VNS)) or long-term memories and penalty functions (as in guided local search (GLS)). The main hybridization usually employed to combine metaheuristics can be classified in four forms:

1) The first form of hybrids consists of embedding elements specific to a given metaheuristic into another one. For instance, employ a population of solutions for which a single-solution metaheuristic is run on each individual. As an example, we can cite the population-based iterated local search (ILS) that consists of generating an initial population as in genetic algorithms, and then, and then for each solution in the population an ILS iteration is applied. The new population generated with this process is then merged with the initial one to keep for the next generation only the best individuals in the union. In this example, components are taken from the GA (population generation and replacement) and the single solution metaheuristic is kept unchanged. This approach is suited for problems with local minima scattered in the search space.

2) The second form of hybrids consists of replacing a component of the original metaheuristic by another complete metaheuristic. For instance, Lozano and García-Martínez [LOZ 10] applied an evolutionary algorithm as a perturbation technique in an iterated local search (ILS). Hybrid GRASP-ELS or GRASP-ILS, in which an evolutionary local search (ELS) or an ILS (respectively) replaces the local search in a greedy randomized adaptive search procedure (GRASP) iterations, follows the same idea. In the same vein, Resende *et al.* [RES 05] designed several versions of

hybrid algorithms based on greedy randomized adaptive search procedures and path relinking.

3) The third scheme consists of calling two or more metaheuristics in a sequential way, which means that the output solutions of the first metaheuristic are given as inputs to the second to get better results. An example of such a hybridization is to call an external path relinking (PR), as a post-optimization procedure, to explore trajectories between solutions in a pool that is built by another metaheuristic such as a GRASP.

4) The last form is based on a decomposition of a main complex problem into subproblems. These problems are solved afterward by different metaheuristics that cooperate and exchange information within an upper-level method to get high-quality complete solutions for the entire problem. The upper-level method must be designed so that complete solutions inherit good features from solutions of the subproblems.

5.1.2. Application to vehicle routing problems

A large variety of hybrid methods have been proposed for a large class of vehicle routing problems (VRPs). The aim of this section is not to address an exhaustive survey of existing hybrid metaheuristics; only some references are given.

For the capacitated vehicle routing problem (CVRP), we can cite the hybrid simulated annealing (SA) – tabu search (TS) developed by Osman [OSM 93], the hybrid GRASP-ELS due to Prins [PRI 09c], a combined ILS-variable neighborhood descent (VND) [CHE 10] and a tabu-ILS proposed by Cordeau and Maischberger [COR 12] among others. Other advanced hybrids involve, for instance, both GA and tabu search as in the paper by Perboli et al. [PER 08], hybrid GA with particle swarm optimization (PSO) [MAR 10b] and combined PR-PSO [MAR 10a].

Many hybrids were also designed by combining GRASP with ELS or ILS to solve extensions of the CVRP. Nguyen et al. [NGU 12a] elaborated a GRASP-ILS for solving the two-echelon location-routing problem. The same form of hybrids was also used by Michallet et al. [MIC 14] to deal with a periodic vehicle routing problem with time windows. For the team orienteering problem with time windows detailed in section 5.2.3.3, Labadie et al. [LAB 11] presented an effective GRASP-ELS. The method was able to improve the results on a large number of instances from the literature in terms of solution quality and computational time. As an illustrative example of GRASP-ELS application, the work of Duhamel et al. [DUH 11] is further discussed in section 5.1.3.2.

Some studies in the VRP literature used GRASP combined to PR. For instance, Nguyen et al. [NGU 12b] employed this kind of hybrids to solve the two-echelon location routing problem. In [VIL 11], the same approach is proposed to tackle the truck and trailer routing problem. Labadie et al. [LAB 08a] also employed a GRASP-PR to deal with the CARP with time windows.

5.1.3. *Selected examples*

This section details some successful applications of hybrid metaheuristics to vehicle routing problems. The first example is a hybrid tabu search-guided local search proposed by Zachariadis *et al.* [ZAC 09] to solve the VRP with simultaneous pickups and deliveries. The second paper detailed is a GRASP-ELS designed by Duhamel *et al.* [DUH 11] for the two-dimensional loading CVRP. The last example is a reactive tabu search enhanced by an evolutionary strategy for solving the open VRP [REP 10].

5.1.3.1. *Hybrid tabu search-guided local search for the VRP with simultaneous pickups and deliveries*

Zachariadis *et al.* [ZAC 09] studied the VRP in which customers require simultaneous pickup and delivery services. This variant of vehicle routing problems is denoted as VRPSPD in the sequel. To solve the VRPSPD, the authors combined two metaheuristics, a tabu search and a guided local search, to design a hybrid form that they called guided tabu search (GTS). The GTS method was able to well balance the intensification and diversification phases. The performance of the method was tested on benchmark instances with customer numbers ranging from 50 to 400, on which new best-known solutions were achieved. This section details the main components of the method and how the hybridization was designed.

In addition to the classical VRP data, in the VRPSPD each customer is associated with both a pickup and a delivery quantity. The first one must be picked up at the customer and transported to the central depot, while the second one must be provided to the customer from the depot. At any node of a given route, the total transported amount must be less than the vehicle capacity.

The proposed approach starts by building an initial feasible solution thanks to a cost-saving heuristic, and then the hybrid GTS is called. The constructive heuristic consists of evaluating the insertion of customer v_k between customers v_i and v_j by the following formula:

$$Cost_{ijk} = c_{ik} + c_{kj} - g \times c_{ij} + f \times |c_{ik} - c_{kj}| \qquad [5.1]$$

where g and f are the two stochastic parameters distributed in intervals $[0, 3]$ and $[0, 1]$, respectively. The initial solution built with the constructive heuristic then undergoes the GTS phase.

As in the case of the local search method, the GTS phase explores the solution space by performing a series of moves. Four types of intraroute and interroute moves defining four neighborhood structures $N_i(S)$, $i = 1, ..., 4$ are considered:

– N_1: customer relocation that moves a customer from its current position to another in the same or into another route.

– N_2: customer exchange that exchanges the positions of a pair of customers pertaining to the same or to different routes.

– N_3: route interchange that consists of deleting two arcs and replacing them with two new ones. This move reduces to 2-opt when only one route is involved and costs are symmetric. When two routes are considered, the starting part of the first route is connected to the terminating part of the second one, while the starting part of the second route is linked to the terminating part of the first one, which returns to a first 2-opt* case.

– N_4: route interchange used only for the symmetric case and evolving two routes. The routes are divided into their initial and final parts. The initial part of the first route is connected to the initial part of the second route, the final part of the first route is connected to final part of the second route (second case of 2-opt*).

To limit the computational time, reduced size neighborhoods are considered. For customer i, a quantity avg_i and a set of neighboring vertices NV_i are defined. The value avg_i is computed as the average cost of arcs adjacent to i, while the set NV_i contains all vertices $j \neq i$, such that $c_{ij} < avg_i$. The exploration of the neighborhood of a solution S is hence reduced by generating arcs connecting vertices m and n, such that $m \in NV_n$ and $n \in NV_m$.

The GTS approach starts from the solution obtained by the constructive heuristic. At each GTS iteration, one of the four neighborhoods listed before is selected. The cost for implementing every possible move toward a solution in the reduced neighborhood is evaluated. The considered moves must lead to feasible solutions; they are not declared tabu unless they lead to higher quality solutions than the best solution encountered so far. When a move is executed, the reversal move is declared tabu for *tabuTenure* number of GTS iterations. This tabu search process is continuously coordinated by an algorithmic component incorporating some GLS ideas. At each GTS iteration, the arc of the candidate solution maximizing utility function [5.2] is penalized. In this formula, P_{ij} denotes the number of times the arc (i, j) has been selected for penalization.

$$U(i,j) = \frac{c_{ij}/avg_{ij}}{1 + P_{ij}} \qquad [5.2]$$

Let pa be the arc selected for penalization. The cost of this arc is updated to a new value Cp_{pa}^* as follows: $Cp_{pa}^* = Cp_{pa} + P_{pa} \times \lambda \times avg_{ij}$.

The value of λ plays a key role in the effectiveness of the proposed metaheuristic methodology, as it controls the balance between the intensification and the diversification phases in the conducted search. The GTS algorithm is ended after mni iterations without any improvement of the best solution encountered during the search.

After several numerical tests, the *tabuTenure* parameter was fixed at 20. The value $\lambda = 0.05$ proved to be rather robust yielding to the best average solution cost for test problems of various scales. The parameter mni was set equal to 6000.

The added value of hybridization was evaluated by testing three algorithmic configurations (pure TS, pure GLS and hybrid GTS) on seven benchmark problems proposed by Salhi and Nagy [SAL 99]. For the pure GLS, the *tabuTenure* parameter was fixed to zero, while in the TS configuration the penalization component was removed.

The results indicate that the hybrid GTS provides better solutions with a lower average cost than those obtained by the pure TS and GLS methods, especially on large-scale instances. Furthermore, regarding the efficiency of the hybridization, the additional computational time demanded by the GTS algorithm was negligible. The hybrid GTS was also compared with tabu search methods, which were the best state-of-the-art methods for solving VRPSD, on other sets of instances proposed by Dethloff in 2001 and Tang Montané and Galvão in 2006 for the VRPSPD. In both sets, GTS was able to improve the results regarding the route costs. As a conclusion, the GTS constitutes an example of successful hybridization: it is simple, uses few parameters and produces good results on a large set of instances.

5.1.3.2. *Hybrid GRASP-ELS for the VRP with two-dimensional loading constraints*

The two-dimensional loading CVRP (2L-CVRP) is an extension of the classical VRP in which each customer asks for two-dimensional weighted items. In this problem, in addition to the classical data provided in a CVRP instance, with each customer i is associated a set of m_i items to be delivered (or collected) with a total weight d_i. Each item $k = 1, ..., m_i$ has a width w_k and a length l_k. The vehicles have a common capacity D and a platform size $L \times W$, where W, L are, respectively, the vehicle width and length. As in the CVRP, each customer must be visited by exactly one vehicle, which means that it is not allowed to split the demands.

Duhamel *et al.* [DUH 11] proposed a hybrid GRASP-ELS to solve the problem. More precisely, they studied the two-dimensional *unrestricted oriented* loading VRP (noted 2|UO|LCVRP), a variant in which there is no restriction on the order in which the items are packed in a vehicle, conversely to the *sequential* case. This latter case imposes to pack the items into the vehicle in such a way that unloading the items for each customer scheduled in a route can be achieved through a sequence of straight movements (one per item). In oriented loading variants, no rotation of items is possible while this is permitted in rotated loading cases.

A vehicle trip T is a sequence $T = (t_0, t_1, ..., t_{n(T)}, t_{n(T)+1})$ of customers where t_0 and $t_{n(T)+1}$ correspond to the depot and $n(T)$ is the number of customers scheduled in route T. A route must be *weight-feasible* and *packing-feasible*. The first constraint means that the total weight of items carried by a vehicle cannot exceed its capacity and the second one ensures that customer items can be loaded into the vehicle without overlapping and exceeding its area $L \times W$. The objective consists of determining a set of routes that minimizes the total transportation cost such that each vehicle route is weight feasible and packing feasible.

A solution of the 2L-CVRP must indicate for each customer i scheduled in a given route, the coordinates (x_k, y_k) in the corresponding vehicle of its kth item bottom left corner ($k = 1, ..., m_i$). Note that the loading surface of the vehicle is mapped onto a positive quadrant of a Cartesian coordinate system, whose origin (0,0) corresponds to the bottom-left corner of the loading surface in the vehicle, and that the x-axis and y-axis correspond, respectively, to its bottom and left sides.

The proposed framework works in two steps: in the first step, the bin-packing problem is relaxed into a resource-constrained project scheduling problem (RCPSP). The resulting problem denoted as RCPSP-CVRP is easier to solve and this is achieved by a GRASP-ELS metaheuristic. The second step consists of converting a RCPSP-CVRP solution into a 2L-CVRP solution.

Some key features are considered in the resolution approach proposed by Duhamel *et al.*: to limit unsuccessful conversion of RCPSP solutions to 2L-CVRP solutions, the load of each vehicle is limited by a coefficient p in the first step. Since the best solution generated in this phase can be infeasible with regard to the loading constraints, nb best solutions (instead of only one) are kept in memory. At the end of the GRASP-ELS, these solutions are iteratively investigated and the best that can be transformed into a 2L-CVRP solution is kept as the best solution found during the process.

During the optimization, solutions violating the fleet size can be encountered, such solutions are considered but penalized as shown in equation [5.3]. In this formula, $N(S)$ is the number of vehicles used in solution S, N is the imposed fleet size, α is the penalty cost, $R(S)$ is the set of routes in solution S and $f(T)$ is the total cost of route T.

$$f(S) = (N(S) - N)\alpha + \sum_{T \in R(S)} f(T) \qquad [5.3]$$

The initial solutions are generated by means of four heuristics: a randomized version of Clarke and Wright, path scanning, randomized path scanning and a basic random generation. The general skeleton of the GRASP-ELS is given in algorithm 5.1. The outer For loop corresponds to the iteration of the GRASP, S being the incumbent solution and S^* is the global best solution. The While loop implements the ELS. The second For loop (lines 21–27) applies mutation and local search to generate nd child-solutions and records the best child in S.

Algorithm 5.1: General structure of the GRASP-ELS for the 2L-CVRP

1 **Global parameters**;
2 np: maximum number of GRASP iterations;
3 ns: maximum number of ELS iterations;
4 nr: maximum number of iterations without improvement in ELS;
5 nd: number of mutations;
6 nb: number of best solutions saved during the search;
7 **begin**
8      $f^* := \infty$;
9      $Pool := \emptyset$;
10   **for** $p := 1$ *to* np **do**
11          $S :=$ Initial _solution ();
12          $T := \text{Concat}(S)$;
13   **if** $f(S) < f^*$ **then**
14              $f^* := f(S)$; $S^* := S$;
15   **else**
16   **if** *intensification = true* **then**
17                  $S := S^*$;
18          $i, r := 0$;
19   **while** $i < ns$ *and* $r < nr$ **do**
20              $i := i + 1$; $f'' := \infty$;
21   **for** $j := 1$ *to* nd **do**
22                  $T' := \text{Mutation}(T)$;
23                  $S' := \text{Split} (T')$;
24                  $S' := \text{Local \_Search}(S')$;
25                  $T' := \text{Concat}(S')$;
26   **if** $f(S') < f''$ **then**
27                      $f'' := f(S')$; $T'' := T'$, $S'' := S'$;
28   **if** $f'' \geq f(S)$ **then**
29                  $r := r + 1$;
30   **if** $f'' < f^*$ **then**
31                  $Pool := Pool \cup \{S\}$;
32                  $S^* := S''$;
33              $T := T''$
34   convert the solutions in $Pool$ into 2L-CVRP solutions;

The GRASP-ELS alternates between the exploration of two search spaces: the *giant tour* space where solutions are encoded as permutations of the customers and the RCPSP-CVRP solutions. A solution S to the latter problem is obtained by using a splitting procedure (see Chapter 2) that cuts the ordered sequence to feasible routes respecting the RCPSP constraints.

The local search is based on first improvement strategy and involves the classical CVRP neighborhoods: 2-opt, 2-opt* and Swap that can be applied to one or two different routes. The mutation operator is executed on giant tours. It consists of generating a new concatenation order and to exchange the position of some customers in the giant tour.

During the GRASP-ELS, an RCPSP with a single resource and without precedence constraints is addressed. In a general RCPSP instance, a set of na activities and m resources is considered. Each activity i is characterized by its duration d_i and its resource requirement $r_{ik}, k = 1, ..., m$. Activities are linked by precedence constraints: if i precedes j, the latter activity cannot be started before the end of activity i. A source activity s and a sink activity u are usually added to the project. They correspond, respectively, to the project start and the project end. The aim of the RCPSP is to determine a schedule of the activities minimizing the total duration of the project (the makespan) so that both precedence and resource constraints are satisfied.

The variant of RCPSP involved considers one resource (the vehicle length) and no precedence constraints. In RCPSP, the resource consumption over time depends on the starting time x_i of each activity i. For each trip, an RCPSP must be solved considering that an item corresponds to an activity, and activity duration and resource requirement are the item lengths and widths, respectively. A route is RCPSP-feasible if the makespan of the corresponding RCPSP does not exceed the vehicle length L. Each time a route is modified in the local search and each time the splitting procedure generates a new route, a procedure that checks the feasibility of the RCPSP constraint must be called. Due to the particular structure of the RCPSP raised in this study, the authors used a random activity selection rule that provided better results.

The splitting procedure is inspired from that of Prins [PRI 04b], it builds the auxiliary graph in a similar way as explained in Chapter 2. The difference lies in the labels considered at each node. For the CVRP, the splitting procedure can be performed by a simple shortest algorithm, however, in this work optimally splitting a sequence into feasible RCPSP routes returns to a resource constrained shortest path problem. Hence, for each node i in the auxiliary graph several labels are defined. Let $L_i^p = (N_i^p, z_i^p, k, j)$ the p-th label be associated with node i. N_i^p is the number of available vehicles remaining, z_i^p is the cost of the trips previously built and (k, j) is the reference to its father label. The initial label at the initial node (node 0) in the auxiliary graph is defined as $L_0^1 = (N, 0, -1, -1)$.

Given an arc (i, j) in the auxiliary graph, label L_j^q can be extended from label L_i^p by setting $N_j^q = N_i^p + 1$ and $z_j^q = z_i^p + z_{ij}$ where z_{ij} is the cost of the arc linking i to j in the auxiliary graph. This process is completed by dominance rules that allow pruning dominated labels at a given node in the auxiliary graph. A label L_i^p dominates a label L_i^q if and only if either $((L_i^p > L_i^q)$ and $(z_i^p \leq z_i^q))$ or $((z_i^p < z_i^q)$ and $(L_i^p \geq L_i^q))$.

The final step of the GRASP-ELS consists of transforming an RCPSP-CVRP solution to a 2L-CVRP one. The method investigates iteratively all the y-positions starting from 0 until all items are packed or until the vehicle width is reached. Note that computing a feasible packing solution depends on the starting time x_i assigned to the items and that several successive attempts can be performed to get a feasible packing from an RCPSP feasible one.

The GRASP-ELS was tested on the well-known benchmark proposed by Iori in his PhD thesis and was compared to state-of-the-art methods. GRASP-ELS was able to improve the average results on all problem sets (classes 2–5). Furthermore, it provided the largest number of new best solutions, improving therefore the results on many instances. In Class 1, which corresponds to a pure CVRP, the method obtained 34 best solutions on the 36 instances compounding the class and provided 10 new best solutions.

5.1.3.3. *Hybrid reactive tabu search enhanced by an evolutionary strategy for the open VRP*

This section presents an effective hybrid metaheuristic proposed by Repoussis *et al.* [REP 10] to solve the open VRP (OVRP). The proposed method is in fact a kind of memetic algorithm where the local search is replaced by a reactive-guided tabu search.

The OVRP consists of designing least cost routes from a depot to a set of customers. The difference with the CVRP is that each route ends at a customer.

As in the CVRP, consider a graph $G = (V, A)$ where $V = \{0, 1, ..., n\}$ is the node set and A is the arc set. Node 0 is the depot in which a homogeneous fleet of m vehicles is based. With each customer are associated a demand d_i and a service time e_i. Each vehicle has a capacity Q and a maximum travel time L. C_{ij} denotes the travel time from i to j.

The objective considered is first to find the minimum number of vehicles required and second to determine the route of each vehicle such that the total traveled distance is minimized. The routes must satisfy the maximum load and length constraints, and each customer must be serviced by one and only one vehicle.

This problem is solved with a population-based evolutionary algorithm combined with a guided local search approach. Starting from an initial population of μ adequately diversified individuals, at each generation a new intermediate population of λ individuals is produced by combining pairs of parents and then applying a mutation operator on the offspring. A guided reactive tabu search is then executed on each obtained solution and the resulting one is added to the new population. For the next iteration, the population is updated by applying a selection mechanism to the $\lambda + \mu$ individuals. This process is repeated until a stopping criterion is met. The general structure of the hybrid method is provided in algorithm 5.2.

Algorithm 5.2: Hybrid Evolutionary Strategy for the OVRP

---

1 $t := 0$;
2 $P(t) :=$ Initialization();
3 Evaluation($P(t)$);
4 **begin**
5   **while** *stopping conditions not met* **do**
6   **for** *all individuals* $(\overrightarrow{x}, \overrightarrow{\sigma}) \in P(t)$ **do**
7              $(\overrightarrow{x}, \overrightarrow{\sigma'}) :=$ Recombination $(P(t), \overrightarrow{x}, \overrightarrow{\sigma})$;
8   **for** *all individuals* $(\overrightarrow{x}, \overrightarrow{\sigma'})$ **do**
9              $(\overrightarrow{x'}, \overrightarrow{\sigma'}) :=$ Mutation$(\overrightarrow{x}, \overrightarrow{\sigma'})$;
10             $(\overrightarrow{x'}, \overrightarrow{\sigma'}) :=$ ReGTS$(\overrightarrow{x'}, \overrightarrow{\sigma'})$;
11             $P'(t) := (\overrightarrow{x'}, \overrightarrow{\sigma'})$;
12   Evaluation $P'(t)$;
13         $P(t+1) :=$ Selection $(P'(t) \cup P(t))$;
14         $t := t + 1$;
15   return best solution;

To get the initial population, a probabilistic insertion heuristic based on an adaptation of the well-known Clarke and Wright method (see Chapter 2 for more details) is used. Since in the OVRP the routes do not return to the depot, the merging phases of two routes $r = (0, v_1, ..., v_k, v_{k+1}, ..., v_i)$ and $r' = (0, v'_1, ..., v'_j)$ consist of testing the following concatenation orders $(0, v_1, ..., v_k, v_{k+1}, v_i, v'_1, ..., v'_j)$, $(0, v'_1, ..., v'_j, v_1, ..., v_k, v_{k+1}, ..., v_i)$ and $((0, v_1, ..., v_k, v'_1, ..., v'_j, v_{k+1}, ..., v_i)$ for all positions k such that $1 < k < i$. The cost variations corresponding to these cases are, respectively: $C_{v_i, v'_1} - C_{0, v'_1}$, $C_{v'_j, v_1} - C_{0, v_1}$ and $C_{v_k, v'_1} + C_{v'_j, v_{k+1}} - C_{v_k, v_{k+1}} - C_{0, v'_1}$. Negative costs correspond to merges that provide better solutions. As the priority is given to the minimization of the fleet used, positive cost variations can also be accepted.

The probabilistic mechanism first consists of considering n single customer vehicle routes. Subsequently, for all possibles pairs of routes, the associated cost variations are computed and sorted in a list called a *restricted savings list* (RSL), constituted by the most beneficial mergers. At each iteration, a merger is randomly selected from the list and applied just after. This process is repeated until no further feasible merger is possible. The cardinality of the RSL is a parameter which is set to a fixed value at the beginning of the algorithm.

A solution $\omega = \{r_1, r_2, ..., r_k\}$, constituted of k routes, can be represented as a vector $\overrightarrow{X}_{node} = (0, v_1, v_2, ..., 0, v'_1, v'_2..., 0, ...)$ or by its corresponding vector of arcs: $\overrightarrow{X}_{arc} = (a_{0,v_1}, a_{v_1,v_2}, ..., a_{0,v'_1}, a_{v'_1,v'_2}, ...)$ of $n + k$ elements. Each element of $\overrightarrow{X}_{arc}$ is associated with a binary vector $\overrightarrow{\sigma} \in \{0, 1\}^{n+k}$ that controls the mutation. If the value of the element σ_i is 1, the corresponding arc in $\overrightarrow{X}_{arc}$ will be maintained to the next generation offspring; otherwise, it will be subject to mutation.

A multi-parent recombination operator is applied to the strategy parameters of each solution vector. Initially, the frequency of appearance $\theta_{i,j}$ of each arc $a_{i,j}$ within the population is determined. A threshold frequency of acceptance $\kappa \in \mathcal{N}$ is also defined with respect to the size and the current diversity of the population. This threshold indicates the least number of individuals in the current population that must include a given arc. Hence, the element $a_{i,j}$ of a solution vector $\overrightarrow{x}$ is considered as promising, if this arc is present in more than κ individuals. Therefore, σ_i is set to 1, if and only if the value θ of the corresponding element $x_i \in \overrightarrow{x}$ is at least equal to κ. Otherwise, it is set to 0.

The measure of similarity $D(s, s')$ of two individuals s and s' is defined as the number of arcs that they share. The median position (or average similarity of an element s with respect to a population P) is defined as:

$$M(s, P) = \frac{\sum_{s' \in P \setminus \{s\}} D(s, s')}{|P| - 1} \qquad [5.4]$$

The threshold κ is set as given in equation [5.5], with $M(s^*, P)$ the average similarity of the fittest individual s^*, ψ the number of arcs contained in the vector $\overrightarrow{x_{s^*}}$ and μ the population size.

$$\kappa = \frac{M(s^*, P)}{\psi} \times \mu \qquad [5.5]$$

The mutation consists of removing some customers from a solution and reinserting them in a probabilistic way. Formally, the arc-based solution vector $\overrightarrow{X}_{arc}$ is converted into its equivalent node-based solution vector $\overrightarrow{X}_{node}$. Next, node customers are removed from this latter vector such that arcs with corresponding strategy σ equal to zero are removed from $\overrightarrow{X}_{arc}$. The resulting $\overrightarrow{X}_{arc}$ will thus correspond to a strategy vector σ with all σ_i equal to 1. Finally, single customer vehicle routes are generated to service the removed customers, while the partially ruined solution vector is reconstructed by employing the probabilistic constructive heuristic described previously (it is an adapted randomized version of the Clarke and Wright heuristic).

The reactive guided tabu search (ReGTS) uses the short-term memory TS framework to control a trajectory local search process, while the exploration of the neighboring space is performed on the basis of a guided local search algorithm (GLS). The idea in the GLS is to penalize long arcs that are unlikely to occur in an optimum solution.

GLS associates a cost and a penalty with each arc in the set A and augments the objective function by adding these penalties. Let s and $f(s)$ be a solution and its objective function value. GLS considers a new augmented function $h(s)$, which replaces $f(s)$, defined by equation [5.6] where δ is a scaling parameter, $p_{i,j}$ is the penalty on (i,j) and $l_{i,j}$ takes the value 1 if (i,j) is present in s, 0 otherwise.

$$h(s) = f(s) + \delta \sum_{(i,j) \in A} (p_{i,j} l_{i,j}(S)) \qquad [5.6]$$

The number of times an arc has already been penalized is also taken into account. The more often it appears and is penalized, the less likely it is to be penalized further. For this purpose, the utility $U_{i,j}(s^*)$ of penalizing an arc (i,j), under a local optimum solution s^*, is defined as follows: $U_{i,j}(s^*) = \frac{l_{i,j}^{(s^*)} C_{i,j}}{1 + p_{i,j}}$.

The parameter δ has a key role in the efficiency of the search process. This parameter was dynamically tuned through equation [5.7], where s^* designates the current local optimum and γ is a scaling factor which is instance-dependent.

$$\delta = \gamma \frac{f(s^*)}{\sum_{(i,j) \in A | p_{i,j} \geq 1} l_{i,j}(s^*)} \qquad [5.7]$$

Given a solution s, all penalties $p_{i,j}$ are set to 0 and the basic TS solution framework is called. First, a neighborhood structure is selected randomly and the set of allowed non-tabu neighboring solutions is examined. Let s' be the best solution in the current neighborhood of s according to the objective function f, and $f(s')$ is its cost. Let s'' be best solution in the neighborhood according to the function $h(s)$ for a given δ. If s' improves the best encountered solution s^* in terms of objective function, it replaces both s and s^* and δ is updated just after. Otherwise, s is replaced by s''.

Next, the short-term memory is updated and the new incumbent solution s is stored. If s corresponds to a new local optimum, solution penalties are reset to zero.

Finally, the values $U_{i,j}(s)$ are recomputed and the arc with the highest value is penalized.

The neighborhood structures used within ReGTS are based on the edge-exchange moves: 2-opt, 2-opt*, relocate and exchange. They are called randomly with equal selection probabilities.

The evaluation and selection strategies are purely deterministic: three criteria are considered in a hierarchical order for evaluating individuals: the fleet size, the total traveling cost and the number of different arcs when compared to the fittest individual.

To build the next population (iteration $t + 1$), all individuals s of $P(t)$ are added into $P(t + 1)$. Then, each offspring generated in iteration t is compared to its parent and added to $P(t + 1)$ if it is better. The best and worst individuals (s^* and w^*) in $P(t + 1)$ are then computed and the average similarity measure $M(s^*, P(t + 1))$ is determined. Each remaining offspring s' generated at step t is compared to each solution s_r present in $P(t + 1)$ and replaces it if it performs better and the similarity measure $D(s^*, s')$ is lower than the average value $M(s^*, P(t + 1))$.

The whole framework is iterated until a maximum number of iterations without improving the best solution is attained. The method was tested on data sets of Christofides et al. [CHR 79], Fisher [FIS 94] and Li et al. [LI 07]. In the first two data sets, the number of customers ranges from 50 to 199, in the last one it varies between 200 and 488. In the first two sets, the approach produced two new best solutions and achieved 10 out of 16 best known from the literature. For the fleet size, it provided the least values for all instances. On the large-scale instances, the hybrid algorithm was able to improve half of the best-known results and achieved the lower bound on the fleet size for all instances.

5.2. Matheuristics

The other widespread form of hybrid metaheuristics in a routing context consists of combining exact algorithms and metaheuristics, to give a matheuristic. According to Boschetti et al. [BOS 09], a definition of this approach is "heuristic algorithms made by the inter-operation of metaheuristics and mathematical programming techniques". However, this definition may be too restrictive and a few other hybrids employing other forms of exact resolution have also been designed in the literature: dynamic programming, graph algorithms and constraint programming, in particular. A representative sample of them is the class of route-first cluster-second algorithms involving the Split algorithm described in Chapter 2 and adopted in many efficient vehicle routing methods. This scheme, introduced before the definition of matheuristics, is rarely considered as such in the literature. Yet, it involves an exact approach to solve a shortest path in an auxiliary directed acyclic graph, and thus, in our opinion, it perfectly fits the characteristic of this family of hybrid methods. However, being already widely presented in previous chapters, first as a heuristic, and then as a component of metaheuristics, the scope of this section will not expand too much on them. More detailed surveys on matheuristics for vehicle routing problems are available [DOE 10, ARC 14].

5.2.1. *Principle*

Incorporating exact approaches within resolution schemes can be interesting. In fact, several particular problems can be extracted as subproblems of the VRP in hand, and then be optimally solved by a specific exact algorithm. In addition, mixed integer linear programming (mixed integer LP or MILP) models can be solved to (close) optimality within a reasonable amount of time due to the advances in exact solution methods and hardware technology. Thus, reducing the model sizes through decomposition approaches allows us to tackle smaller and simpler (sub-)problems, in an exact manner.

The first step is to choose a problem representation, which would be suitable from the model/mathematical point of view. The main decomposition approaches encountered in the VRP literature are:

1) *Structural decomposition*: this consists of choosing among the variables of the original problem, those to be fixed to certain values (according to some criteria) and those to be optimized over the resulting restricted search space. This can be seen as a large neighborhood search (LNS – see section 3.7), but here the idea is often not to change the set of fixed/optimized variables over the iterations, but rather to identify a subproblem that could be relatively easily solved to optimality, while the other decisions are tackled heuristically. The decomposition may be chosen on the basis of an implicit hierarchy among the decision levels involved, or of a natural separation into partial problems. It can also be considered as close to an approach called local branching [FIS 03], in which a generic MIP solver is called to effectively explore some areas of the solution space defined at an upper level by an external framework.

2) *Set covering and partitioning approaches*: the idea stands on modeling the problem as a set covering/partitioning problem whose columns correspond to possible routes. Due to the exponential number of feasible routes, which here are the variables, the Dantzig-Wolfe decomposition can be applied with the slave subproblem that searches the solution of the linear relaxation through a column generation. The scheme may be complemented by a branching to close the optimality gap (branch-and-price approach). In a heuristic version, the method is modified by heuristically tackling a part of the approach, such as the column generation.

3) *LP-based neighborhood reduction techniques*: not based on a problem decomposition, but on choosing which local dimension of the solution space will be explored, a matheuristic may guide the search by an exact approach.

The following section is devoted to the description of the three classes of approaches, with a sample of methods on the vehicle routing literature.

5.2.2. *Application to vehicle routing problems*

A certain amount of matheuristics have appeared since the 2000s to solve vehicle routing problems. We propose a classification in three main classes. They are motivated on the way of decomposing the search to be able to exploit an exact approach.

5.2.2.1. *Structural decomposition*

In this class of approach, the original problem is decomposed into smaller subproblems, which can be solved to optimality relatively easily. The main option is the hierarchical decomposition, followed by the natural separation into partial problems.

The *hierarchical decomposition* is not recent since a first method for routing problems can be found in [FIS 81]. Besides other optional decisions related to a particular version of the problem, the two basic settlements in VRP are the assignment of customers to each vehicle and the sequencing of customers in each route. In [FIS 81], the authors opt for what will be one of the most common decompositions in matheuristics for VRP: a solution scheme that leads to exactly solve a generalized assignment problem. They employ the cluster-first route-second paradigm: after selecting heuristically seed customers, the clustering is done by exactly solving an assignment problem. Then, a traveling salesman problem (TSP) is tackled in each cluster. In the same vein, but built on the ruin-and-recreate concept, an approach is to remove some customers from routes, and optimally reassign them using an integer linear program. This has been done, for instance, on the distance constraint VRP [DEF 06], and the open VRP [SAL 10]. As already mentioned, the other paradigm founded on route-first cluster-second algorithms and involving the Split algorithm also belongs to the hierarchical scheme.

For complex problems combining several kinds of decisions, the problem can be naturally decomposed into subproblems related to each family of decision. Hence, the hierarchical decomposition is particularly suitable for complex and integrated problems, such as inventory routing problems, production routing problems and the location routing problems. The first attempts were mainly *one-shot* approaches, i.e. once each decision level has been completed, the algorithm terminates. This was the case for the production routing problems [CHA 94] where the production schedule and the delivery quantities were first optimally determined before building the routes with a TSP heuristic. Sometimes, the whole problem is solved heuristically, but some decisions are reoptimized at the end of the algorithm by an exact resolution scheme used as post-optimization [SAV 08, ARC 13].

Other recent research is also based on a simple two-phase scheme to handle various routing problems (e.g. [YI 07] with an LRP arising in disaster logistics, or [YU 08] for the inventory routing problem (IRP) with split deliveries). However, the cooperation between each decision level needs to be well shaped to be efficient, and often requires an iterative process. Campbell and Savelsbergh [CAM 04] consider an inventory routing problem with a long time horizon and no inventory costs. The solution approach decomposes the problem into two hierarchical phases: an integer program that solves the assignment of customer deliveries to days, and heuristics for the daily vehicle routing problems. The solution obtained in the second phase is used to update the input of the first phase. A cooperative approach has been developed to solve the capacitated location routing problem [PRI 07]. This problem combines two NP-hard problems: the facility location problem and the multi-depot VRP. The two decision levels are closely related and cannot be solved independently without the risk of losing the global optimality. The authors suggest solving the facility location problem optimally using Lagrangian relaxation and the routing part by a tabu search. Besides the matheuristic feature, the key-point relies on the cooperation between the two subproblems in order to alternate iteratively and to exchange information in a simple and efficient manner that avoids prematurely converging.

This method stands among the best approach for the LRP, reaching very good quality solutions in a very short time. A deeper description is provided in section 5.2.3.1. In Guerrero et al. [GUE 13], a cluster first-route second approach is designed for an inventory location routing problem (ILRP) where two phases alternate. In the first phase, a MILP model is solved to determine the locations of the supplier plants and the distribution plan. Routes are constructed heuristically in the second phase. In the two-dimensional loading vehicle routing problem (2L-CVRP), Gendreau et al. [GEN 06] call a tabu search algorithm with an embedded branch-and-bound for the packing component, while Fuellerer et al. [FUE 09] design a hybridization of ant colony optimization and branch-and-bound.

In the same vein, but inspired by the adaptive large neighborhood search (ALNS) principle (see section 3.7), some authors solve an MILP, not to reassign customers to routes as in [DEF 06] or [SAL 10], but to reconsider a type of decision. This is more a partial optimization than a decomposition with a cooperation spirit, but a type of decision is still fully handled by an exact approach. For example, in [COE 12], every time a heuristic operator is applied to the current solution of the IRP with transshipment, an MILP model is solved to determine the optimal quantities to deliver at each customer. For the solution of the pollution routing problem, that is a VRPTW where the speed on each route has to be determined in order to minimize fuel consumption, emission and driver costs, Demir et al. [DEM 12] involve an MILP model to determine the best speed for each route segment during iterations of ALNS.

The other option is the *natural separation into partial problems* that relies more on spatial or temporal aspects. Instead of handling different kinds of decisions separately, the idea is to divide the same family of decisions into subfamilies with relatively little interaction between each other. A good illustration is the rolling horizon heuristics for multi-period problems. The idea is to solve the subproblem defined on a smaller number of periods than the entire horizon. The decision taken for the subproblem is used to update the information for the following subproblem. Rakke *et al.* [RAK 11] solve an IRP arising in maritime logistics through this approach, using one frozen period. An MILP model is solved for each interval where the values of the variables in the frozen period are inherited from the previous interval.

5.2.2.2. *Set covering and partitioning approaches*

A well-spread way to deal with vehicle routing problems is to resort to a set covering/partitioning model, in which binary variables are associated with feasible routes and are equal to one for the routes taking part of the solution, zero otherwise. However, the number of feasible routes to include in the model is exponential. Therefore, the Dantzig-Wolfe decomposition is a good option to overcome this drawback. In fact, the principle is to exploit the dual variables of the LP relaxation of a so-called master linear program that has an exponential number of variables (columns). To manage the master problem efficiently, the whole set of variables is not explicitly defined, but is handled using dynamic column generation (slave problem). It can also be seen as a reformulation technique that leads to a mixed integer master program, which facilitates the development of branching and cutting plane approaches in the master program [VAN 06].

Column generation technique (also called pricing problem) progressively extends sets of variables introduced in the mathematical model until an optimality criterion ensures that the value of the optimal solution of master problem is also the value of the optimal solution of original problem. Otherwise, new variables (columns) are introduced in the master problem, based on the optimal solutions of the dual programs. In routing problems, new columns of minimum marginal cost are produced by solving the shortest path problem with constraints defined using the dual variables of the LP relaxation of the master problem. The scheme may be complemented by a branching (branch-and-price approach) allowing the relaxation of the integer variables when solving the master program. Used in a matheuristic, the aim is no longer to prove the optimality, but to provide good quality solutions. Several options are thus possible, mainly founded on the way to generate columns, to solve the master program or to branch.

The first option, about a heuristic manner of generating routes for the set covering/partitioning model, is the most common of this class of matheuristic. For instance, instead of building a new column by solving the shortest path problem, a large number of good routes are heuristically produced. A lot of examples are available in the literature, for many variants of the VRP. One of the first attempts is due to Foster and Ryan [FOS 76], who generate a set of petal routes and then solve the set partitioning problem (SPP). In the same spirit, other authors pitch for storing all the routes generated during the search in a first phase, and then handle the set partitioning model [ROC 95, KEL 99]. The principle has been applied to the IRP [AGH 06], the split delivery VRP (SDVRP) [ARC 08], the dial-a-ride problem (DARP) [PAR 12], the VRP with stochastic demands [MEN 13] and the truck and trailer routing problem [VIL 13], for instance. A more elaborate scheme is suggested by Parragh and Schmid [PAR 13] for the DARP. In their method, VNS is iteratively run to find negative reduced cost columns that are then passed to a set covering formulation. Each time a given number of iterations is reached, an LNS is called to improve the best solution found so far. Subramanian *et al.* [SUB 12] expose a two-phase approach made up of an ILS and the resolution of an SPP, but the set partitioning model is solved by a mixed integer programming solver that interactively calls the ILS heuristic during its execution whenever a new best solution is found. This method is fully detailed in section 5.2.3.2. In Yildirim and Çatay [YIL 14], an iterative procedure for the VRP alternates between a set covering formulation, which chooses the best routes generated by an ant colony optimization algorithm, and the ACO guided by the solution obtained through the MILP model to update the pheromone trails. A matheuristic is developed in Archetti *et al.* [ARC 15] for the team orienteering arc routing problem. It is adapted from a VNS in which two MILP models are solved before changing the neighborhood size. The first is a set partitioning model which chooses the best routes among all routes generated so far by the VNS. The second MILP model modifies the current solution inserting and removing chains of customers.

In the second option, this is the master problem that is solved heuristically to produce a feasible solution. This approach is exploited by Sierksma and Tijssen [SIE 98] to solve the SDVRP. A relaxed solution is obtained through a pricing problem as column generation and the fractional solution is rounded to obtain a feasible solution. Another example can be found in [JIN 08], where a feasible solution for the SDVRP is obtained by successively fixing the value of subsets of variables in a set covering formulation.

The last option stands on heuristic branching approaches. The aim is to prune a large number of nodes of the branch-and-bound tree and consequently obtain a good solution quickly. This is what is done by Cordeau *et al.* [COR 01b] for the solution of an aircraft routing and crew scheduling problem. The objective is to determine a minimum-cost set of aircraft routes and crew pairings such that each flight leg is covered by one aircraft and one crew, and side constraints, on maximum flight time and maintenance requirements, are satisfied. The authors work with a Benders decomposition approach which iterates between a master problem that solves the aircraft routing problem and a subproblem that solves the crew pairing problem. Both subproblems are solved through column generation.

5.2.2.3. *LP-based neighborhood reduction techniques*

An LP-based neighborhood reduction technique denotes an exact approach used to guide the search in order to avoid unpromising moves. It can be seen as a branching which reduces the neighborhood.

In [NGU 10a], an exact method is elaborated to guide and accelerate a tabu search for solving an m-peripathetic VRP (problem of finding a minimum cost set of routes over m periods such that each customer is visited exactly once, no edge is traversed more than once and vehicle capacity holds). As in the granular tabu search (see section 3.9.2), the neighborhood used within the search is reduced to a set of promising edges. The latter is identified by solving a *b-matching* problem.

A similar approach is the one provided by Wolfler Calvo and Touati-Moungla [WOL 11] for a dial-a-ride problem where the granularity of the solution space is determined through the solution of an assignment problem which identifies most promising edges.

The team orienteering problem (TOP) is a known NP-hard problem that typically arises in vehicle routing and production scheduling contexts. In [LAB 12b], a variable neighborhood search (VNS) procedure is exposed to solve the TOP with hard time window constraints (TOPTW). Once again, the method is based on the idea of exploring, most of the time, granular instead of complete neighborhoods in order to improve the algorithm efficiency without loosing effectiveness. The method provides a general way to deal with granularity for those routing problems based on profits and complicated by time constraints.

Details on this kind of approach are presented in section 5.2.3.3 through an extended description of the method developed by Labadie *et al.* on the TOP [LAB 12b].

5.2.3. *Selected examples*

An example from each class of matheuristic (as defined above) is described in this section. The first is dedicated to a problem that involves several levels of decisions facilitating the hierarchical decomposition. The second deals with the heterogeneous fleet VRP which is tackled by a set partitioning approach. The third example exposes an LP-based neighborhood reduction technique for the TOP with time windows.

5.2.3.1. *A hierarchical decomposition-based matheuristic for the LRP*

A hierarchical decomposition is now presented for a complex problem combining several kinds of decisions: the capacitated location-routing problem. The LRPs are problems where we have to decide simultaneously the location of depots and the distribution of goods from these depots to a set of customers, making the problems remarkably harder to solve. Thus, two subproblems naturally emerge, a capacitated facility location problem (CFLP) and a multi-depot VRP (MDVRP), and these are the decompositions followed in the method called Lagrangian relaxation – granular tabu search (LRGTS) offered by Prins *et al.* [PRI 07]. However, to be efficient, the target of the authors is to provide synergy between each component, in addition to the reduction in the size of the problems to be solved.

Instead of solving the location part by an assignment of each customer individually, Prins *et al.* note that it would be more suitable to assign routes. Two advantages are drawn up: (1) the size of the resulting CFLP is rather small, making it possible to call an exact resolution as often as desired, and (2) the solution of the CFLP may change when varying the routes, allowing an iterative scheme. To do so, the original problem is simplified by aggregating customers from a same route k into a *supercustomer* k of demand D_k to be assigned to a depot. Its distance C_{ik} to depot i is computed as the minimum insertion cost of this depot between two consecutive customers j and l of the original route as follows:

$$C_{ik} = c_{ij} + c_{il} - c_{jl}$$

Let M be the set of m locations for potential depots, W_i be the capacity of depot i and K be the set of supercustomers, the aim is to minimize the opening cost of the depots (O_i, $\forall i \in M$) and the assignment cost of the supercustomers to them while respecting depot capacity constraints. The problem can be modeled as follows, where the binary decision variables $X_{ik}, \forall i \in M, k \in K$ equal one iff supercustomer k is assigned to depot i, and $y_i, \forall i \in M$ equal 1 iff depot i is open:

$$\min Z = \sum_{i \in I} O_i y_i + \sum_{i \in I} \sum_{k \in K} C_{ik} X_{ik} \qquad [5.8]$$

Subject to the constraints:

$$\sum_{i \in I} X_{ik} = 1 \qquad \forall k \in K \qquad [5.9]$$

$$\sum_{k \in K} D_k X_{ik} \leq W_i y_i \qquad \forall i \in I \qquad [5.10]$$

$$X_{ik} \in \{0, 1\} \qquad \forall i \in I, \forall k \in K \qquad [5.11]$$

$$y_i \in \{0, 1\} \qquad \forall i \in I \qquad [5.12]$$

[5.8] is the objective-function, [5.9] ensures that supercustomers are assigned to a single depot, [5.10] stands for the depot capacity constraints, while [5.11] and [5.12] state the Boolean nature of the decision variables.

The CFLP is then relaxed in a Lagrangian manner on the capacity constraints and solved by a subgradient optimization, complemented by a Lagrangian heuristic when the optimization fails to converge quickly.

In fact, given the Lagrangian multipliers $u_k \in I\!R$ ($\forall k \in K$) associated with each constraint [5.9], the model becomes:

$$\min g(u) = \sum_{i \in I} O_i y_i + \sum_{i \in I} \sum_{k \in K} C_{ik} X_{ik} + \sum_{k \in K} u_k \left(1 - \sum_{i \in I} X_{ik}\right) \qquad [5.13]$$

Subject to the constraints:

$$\sum_{k \in K} D_k X_{ik} \leq W_i y_i \qquad \forall i \in I \qquad\qquad [5.14]$$

$$X_{ik} \in \{0, 1\} \qquad \forall i \in I, \forall k \in K \qquad\qquad [5.15]$$

$$y_i \in \{0, 1\} \qquad \forall i \in I \qquad\qquad [5.16]$$

By fixing all y_i to 1, this linear program can be decomposed into m independent knapsack problems, one for each depot i, which can be solved by an ILP solver. However, the authors opt for a classical dynamic programming algorithm. For specified values of u_k, a lower bound to the CFLP can be deduced from the m optimal solutions by considering their values as the reduced cost for each associated depot i. If it is negative, then depot i is open ($y_i = 1$) and the values of the $X_{ik}, \forall k \in K$ are those found by solving the knapsack problem for depot i. Otherwise, the depot i is closed, and the associated y_i and X_{ik} are set to zero.

The relaxation allows a supercustomer to be assigned to several depots. To improve this lower bound, the subgradient optimization modifies the values given to the Lagrangian multipliers. First initialized in order to favor an assignment of supercustomers to their closest depots, multipliers are set to $u_k = \min_{i \in M}(C_{ik}), \forall k \in K$. Then, at each iteration, they are updated before solving the m models again. If each supercustomer is assigned to a single depot, the result is optimal for the CFLP. Otherwise, a new lower bound is obtained, from which an upper bound can be deduced by means of Lagrangian heuristic that gives a feasible solution by a repair procedure on supercustomers assigned to zero or several depots.

Once a subset of depots is selected to be opened, and the supercustomers are assigned, the routes are reshaped and an MDVRP solution is available. The latter is improved by a metaheuristic: *Granular Tabu Search – GTS* (see section 3.9.2). Even if it does not provide the best results on VRP benchmark instances, GTS has proven to be able to be both fast and efficient, and seems well suited in the case of a call within an iterative procedure.

Tabu search is a local search metaheuristic that performs the best move in a particular neighborhood even if it does not improve the current solution, enabling the search to escape from local optima. A list of recent moves, settled as tabu, is recorded to avoid loops resulting from returning to already visited solutions. The granularity reduces the list of possible moves in the neighborhood, removing elements that have no real chance of belonging to the optimal solution. Unlike the GTS proposed by Toth and Vigo [TOT 03], in LRGTS, the neighborhood consists of all the solutions that can be obtained by transferring one node from its current position to another one (instead of solutions visited by exchanging of two, three or four arcs). This transfer requires the insertion/removal of arcs. Thus, the search tests the insertion of a non-tabu and non-used arc (i, j) in the current solution. This induces two possible moves in the neighborhood, as shown in Figure 5.1. To restore feasibility, three edges must be deleted, and two others have to be added. Once a move is executed, the three deleted edges are considered tabu during a small constant tenure.

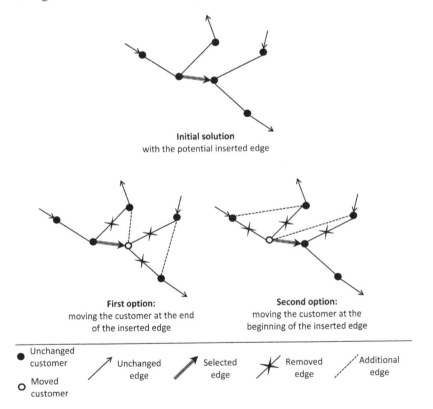

Figure 5.1. *Possibles moves in GTS for the LRP*

The granularity shortens the list of edges (i, j) allowed to be tested for insertion. In fact, it removes those having a cost greater than a given value $\tilde{d}\beta$, with β which varies dynamically, as suggested by Toth and Vigo, to intensify or diversify the search. $\tilde{d}$ is the average cost of the edges linking two customers in a good feasible solution, here obtained by several calls to a randomized version of a constructive algorithm based on the nearest neighbor (see Chapter 2). Still as in [TOT 03], the search allows visiting infeasible solutions but with a penalty mechanism. In this manner, if capacity constraints on both depots and vehicles are violated by an amount $OverCapa$, a penalty term $P.OverCapa$ is added to the objective function value, where P is a unit penalty factor dynamically adjusted. The GTS principle is executed during $GTSit$ iterations, and then, a post-optimization by a local search involving other types of moves (such as 2-opt) is performed.

At the end of the routing phase, the customers of a route are aggregated into supercustomers and the method iterates with a new location phase. Figure 5.2 illustrates the evolution of the solution over the iterations. This scheme rests on a natural cooperation between the components. Unfortunately, the method may converge too quickly to a local optimum: in fact, the routing strongly depends on the open depots, and the choice of depots is highly dependent on the route shape. A perturbation of the solution is required to escape from the current attraction basin. Hence, a cooperative restart simultaneously frees up and guides the search by exploiting information on the visited solutions. New routes are built by a heuristic that limits the number of edges introduced in the solution, with a choice bias in favor of their frequency in good solutions. This technique can be seen as a branching on the more promising edges.

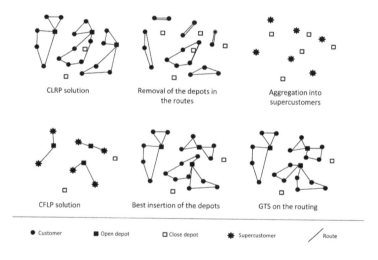

| CLRP solution | Removal of the depots in the routes | Aggregation into supercustomers |

| CFLP solution | Best insertion of the depots | GTS on the routing |

● Customer   ■ Open depot   □ Close depot   ✳ Supercustomer   ╱ Route

Figure 5.2. *LRGTS principle*

An overview of the global pseudo-code is exposed in algorithm 5.3. The main parameters are:

– the initial number of edges introduced in the solution during the cooperative restart equals $3 + (n - \hat{k}).025$ with $\hat{k}$ being the minimal number of routes in a solution, with respect to vehicle capacity. Then, at each new restart, this number increases by a factor $g = 1.15$. The introduced edges come from a list of edges sorted in decreasing frequency order. The probability of introducing a given edge is 80%;

– during the subgradient optimization, 200 iterations are allowed before using the best feasible solution from the Lagrangian heuristic;

– the GTS performs n iterations, $\beta = 1.20$, $\beta' = 1.85$, and the tabu tenure equals to $0.15n$;

– the overall algorithm runs $MaxIt$ iterations.

Algorithm 5.3: Matheuristic for the *LRP - LRGTS*

---

1   build an initial solution S and evaluate its average edge cost ;
2   Create the granular graphs by using β and β';
3   $It := 0$;
4   $S^* := S$;
5   build an initial solution S by the cooperative restart procedure (introducing a limited number of edges) ;
6   $S' := S$;
7   **repeat**
8   create the supercustomers from S ;
9   solve the resulting CFLP with Lagrangian relaxation ;
10   convert the supercustomers into routes to have a feasible LRP solution S ;
11   GTS(S) ;
12   LocalSearch(S) ;
13   update edge frequency for each edge used in S ;
14   **if** (S improves S^*) **then**
15         $S^* = S$;
16   **if** (S improves S') **then**
17         $S' := S$;
18   **else**
19   build a new solution S by the cooperative restart procedure ;
20         $S' := S$;
21         $It := It + 1$;
22 **until** ($It > MaxIt$);
23 return (S^*) ;

The method has been tested on three sets of small-scale, medium-scale and large-scale instances with up to 200 customers. The results obtained by the LRGTS improved over 80% of the best-known solutions at that time, even on instances with uncapacitated depots. In addition, LRGTS is particularly fast, and until now, the method remains among the best to deal with the capacitated location-routing problem.

5.2.3.2. *Set partitioning-based matheuristic for the heterogeneous fleet vehicle routing problem (HFVRP)*

In the HFVRP, m different vehicle types, with distinct capacities $Q_v, v \in \{1, \ldots, m\}$, fixed costs $f_v, v \in \{1, \ldots, m\}$ and variable costs $r_v, v \in \{1, \ldots, m\}$ are available. The variable cost induced by a vehicle of type v traversing an arc (i, j) is $c_{ij}^v = d_{ij} r_v$, where d_{ij} is the distance between the nodes i and j. The number of available vehicles of type v is m_v. The objective is to determine the best fleet composition as well as the set of routes to minimize the total cost.

Subramanian *et al.* [SUB 12] handle this problem by an algorithm, which hybrids an iterated local search (ILS) with the resolution of a set partitioning problem (SPP). Routes are generated by ILS that calls a procedure developed as a variable neighborhood descent with random neighborhood ordering (RVND) in the local search phase. A mixed integer programming (MIP) solver handles the SPP model and interactively calls the ILS heuristic during its execution. The resulting approach is called ILS-RVND-SP.

The vehicle routing problem is thus modeled by a set partitioning formulation, in which columns represent a set R of feasible routes. Due to the heterogeneous features of the fleet, $R_v \in R$ defines the subset of routes associated with vehicle type $v \in \{1, \ldots, m\}$. $R_i \in R$ is the subset of routes that visit customer i. A binary variable y_j is associated with each route $j \in R$, with cost c_j. The problem can be defined as follows:

$$\min \sum_{j \in R} c_j y_j \qquad\qquad [5.17]$$

Under the constraints:

$$\sum_{j \in R_i} y_j = 1 \qquad \forall i \in V \setminus \{0\} \qquad\qquad [5.18]$$

$$\sum_{j \in R_v} y_j \leq m_v \qquad \forall v \in \{1, \ldots, m\} \qquad\qquad [5.19]$$

$$y_j \in \{0, 1\} \qquad \forall j \in R \qquad\qquad [5.20]$$

Objective function [5.17] minimizes the costs by selecting the best combination of routes. In constraints [5.18], a single route from R_i must visit customer i. Constraints [5.19] limit the number of vehicles of each type to the maximum possible value according to the fleet composition. Constraints [5.20] state the binary nature of the decision variables.

Obviously, a complete formulation (with all possible routes) would require an exponential number of variables and would not be easily solved. The authors come up with an alternative to the common branch-and-price or related methods, which remains time-consuming for certain instance sizes. Their algorithm restricts the SPP to a few thousand routes generated by the ILS-RVND heuristic, inspired by Penna *et al.* [PEN 13].

ILS principle (see section 3.5) is to generate a sequence of local optima by alternating local search and perturbation. In this version, in addition to the limited number of total iterations, a maximum number of consecutive perturbations without improvements $MaxIterILS$ are allowed in the core procedure, before performing a restart from a new solution. The $MaxIterILS$ value depends on the quality of the initial solution.

A new solution is built by a constructive procedure that first initializes empty routes associated either with each available vehicle (when the fleet is limited), or with a vehicle of each type (when the fleet is unlimited). In the second case, a new route, associated with a random vehicle type, is opened whenever it is necessary to satisfy capacity constraints while inserting the customers. Then, a seed customer is assigned to each route. The insertion criterion and insertion strategy are chosen at random among the following ones:

– two insertion criteria: the modified cheapest feasible insertion criterion (including an insertion incentive for customers located far from the depot) or the nearest feasible insertion criterion;

– two insertion strategies: the sequential insertion strategy (routes are filled sequentially with customers) and the parallel insertion strategy (all routes are considered while evaluating the insertion criteria).

Three perturbation mechanisms are involved: multiple-swap, multiple-shift and split. One is randomly selected at each iteration. In multiple-swap, several exchange moves are executed randomly. Multiple-shift is similar but a customer k from a route r_1 is transferred to a route r_2, whereas a customer l from r_2 is transferred to r_1. Split divides a randomly chosen route r (not already assigned to vehicle with the smallest capacity) into smaller routes (assigned to vehicles with a smaller capacity than originally) by sequentially transferring its customers while respecting the capacities. The procedure is employed only on instances with unlimited fleet and is repeated a given number of times chosen at random from the interval $\{1, 2, \ldots, v\}$.

The local search is designed in the spirit of a VND (see section 3.4). The idea of VND is to change of neighborhood each time no improvement is found in the current one. The randomized version (RVND) utilizes a random neighborhood ordering. Two lists of neighborhoods are initialized: one with a predefined number of interroute moves (N_1), and one with a given number of intraroute moves ($N2$). The search begins by randomly selecting a neighborhood q_1 in N_1. The best admissible move is performed, and q_1 is removed from N_1. Then, the involved routes are improved by intraroute moves. Consequently, while N_2 is not empty, a neighborhood q_2 is randomly selected before being removed from N_2 and an exhaustive local search is performed (until no more improvements are found in q_2). When N_2 is empty, the search goes back to the N_1 list and iterates by selecting a new neighborhood $q_1 \in N_1$ until N_1 is empty.

Seven interroute neighborhood structures are included in N_1:

– two shift moves (Or-opt) where x adjacent customers (with x equal 1 or 2) are transferred from a route r_1 to a route r_2;

– three swap moves where x adjacent customers (with x equal 1 or 2) from a route r_1 are exchanged with y adjacent customers (with y equal 1 or 2, $y \leq x$) from a route r_2, relatively similar to a λ-interchange move;

– cross moves (2-opt*) where the arcs between two adjacent clients from route r_1, and the one between two adjacent clients from route r_2 are both removed. The feasibility of the routes is repaired by adding two new arcs as in Figure 5.3;

– K-shift where a subset of K consecutive customers is transferred from a route r_1 to the end of a route r_2 with variable and fixed costs smaller than those of r_1. Note that the move is also evaluated when r_2 is an empty route.

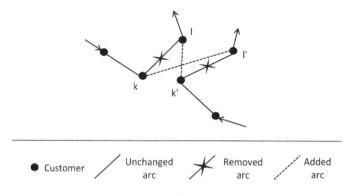

Figure 5.3. *Cross moves*

Five intraroute neighborhood structures are considered in N_2: relocate, exchange, 2-opt and Or-opt with either 2 or 3 adjacent customers removed and inserted in another position of the route.

For each neighborhood, all possible moves are examined, and the best feasible improving one is performed.

To provide a set of columns to the set partitioning formulation of the problem, the algorithm stores a pool P of routes during its execution. After each local search phase, the pool of routes is updated by adding routes that are not already in P. The SPP can be solved at the end. Each time the MILP solver finds a new best solution, it calls the ILS-RVND heuristic again (callback mechanism), but without updating P. When the resolution of the restricted SPP by an MIP solver exceeds the time limit imposed or the gap between the linear relaxation of the root node and the incumbent solution S is larger than a specified limit (this usually happens when fixed costs are considered), the algorithm forces the fleet composition to be equal to the one requested by S.

Algorithm 5.4: ILS-RVND *HFVRP*

---

1 **repeat**
2   **if** $S := NULL$ **then**
3   build an initial solution S ;
4      $MaxIterILS := n + v;$
5   **else**
6      $MaxIterILS := 1000;$
7    $ItILS := 0$;
8    $S' := \text{RVND}(S)$;
9   UpdateRoutePool(P, S')
10   **repeat**
11     $S' := \text{Perturb}(S)$;
12     $S' := \text{RVND}(S')$;
13   UpdateRoutePool(P, S') ;
14   **if** S' improves S **then**
15       $S := S'$;
16       $ItILS := 0$;
17   **else**
18       $ItILS := ItILS + 1;$
19   **until** $(ItILS \leq MaxIterILS);$
20   **if** S improves S^* **then**
21     $S^* = S$;
22 **until** $(It > MaxIt);$
23 return (S^*) ;

An overview of the ILS-RVND is provided by algorithm 5.4, while the global pseudo-code is given in algorithm 5.5. ILS-RVND has two arguments: (1) the pool of routes, which is not used and consequently set as NULL during the callback in the set partitioning phase (see line 4), (2) the initial solution transmitted to the procedure that is the incumbent solution found by during the set partitioning phase, NULL otherwise (see line 2 of algorithm 5.4). The main parameters are $MaxIt = 30$ and a maximal time in the solver equals 30 s.

Algorithm 5.5: Matheuristic for the *HFVRP - set partitioning approach*

---

1 $P := \emptyset$;
2 $S^* :=$ ILS-RVND(P,NULL) ;
3 SPP := CreateSetPartitioningModel(P) ;
4 update S^* by solving the SPP with a MIP solver calling ILS-RVND(NULL,S^*) each time a new best solution is found;
5 return (S^*) ;

The method was tested on 67 instances having up to 360 customers and obtained eight new improved solutions, while it recovered 54 best-known solutions.

5.2.3.3. *Granular variable neighborhood search for the team orienteering problem*

Recently, some attention has been devoted to the team orienteering problem with time windows (TOPTW), a problem in which it is not mandatory to service all customers but each time one is selected, it generates a positive score. In TOPTW, each visit must start within a given time window. Labadie *et al.* [LAB 12b] proposed a granular variable neighborhood search (GVNS) to solve the problem. More precisely, the algorithm uses information provided by the optimal solution of a related LP-problem relaxation to construct granular neighborhoods, instead of complete ones, which are then explored by a variable neighborhood search (VNS). In the following, the main ideas of this approach are given.

Consider the set of customers $N^* = \{1, 2, \cdots, n\}$ and the depot node indexed by 0. For the mathematical modeling purpose, a dummy copy of the depot, indexed by $n+1$, is created. $G = (N, A)$ is a directed complete graph with $N = N^* \cup \{0, n+1\}$ is the node set and A is the arc set. With each customer node $i \in N^*$ is associated a profit p_i, the scores of the depots are such that $p_0 = p_{n+1} = 0$. $[e_i, l_i]$ is the time window related to customer $i \in N^*$, while e_0 and l_0 indicate, respectively, the earliest leaving time and the latest arrival time of each vehicle to the depot. Let T_{max} be the maximum total travel time allowed to complete a tour. W.l.o.g. we assume that $e_0 = 0$ and $l_0 = T_{max}$. Let t_{ij} be the non-negative travel time associated with each arc $(i, j) \in A$. We assume that the service time at node i is included in the time value t_{ij} for all $i \in N \cup \{0\}$. If, for some $i \in N$ and $j \in N \cup \{0\}$, $i \neq j$, $e_i + t_{ij} > l_j$ we assume $t_{ij} = \infty$.

The objective is to build m tours with maximum total profit. Each tour starts at time e_0 at the origin node depot 0, visits a subset of nodes exactly once within their time windows and ends to the depot before the time limit l_0 (i.e. total travel time of each tour does not exceed T_{max}).

The variables used to model the TOPTW are: binary variables $y_i{}^v$, $i \in N$, equal to 1 if and only if i is visited in tour v, variables $x_{ij}{}^v$ that take the value 1 if and only if arc (i, j) is selected in tour v, and a_i^v, $i \in N$, which give the starting time of service at node i scheduled in route v. The variable a_{n+1}^v thus corresponds to the arrival time back to the depot of the vehicle v. The TOPTW can be modeled by the following MILP model:

$$(TOPTW) \quad \max \sum_{v=1}^{m} \sum_{i \in N^*} p_i y_i{}^v \qquad\qquad [5.21]$$

$$\sum_{j \in N \setminus \{0\}} x_{ij}^v = y_i^v \qquad i \in N^*, v = 1, ..., m$$

$$[5.22]$$

$$\sum_{i \in N \setminus \{n+1\}} x_{ij}^v - \sum_{i \in N \setminus \{0\}} x_{ji}^v = 0 \qquad j \in N^*, v = 1, ..., m$$

$$[5.23]$$

$$\sum_{v=1}^{m} \sum_{j \in N^*} x_{0j}^v = \sum_{v=1}^{m} \sum_{j \in N^*} x_{j,n+1}^v = \sum_{v=1}^{m} y_0^v = m \qquad\qquad [5.24]$$

$$\sum_{v=1}^{m} y_i^v \leq 1 \qquad i \in N^*,$$

$$[5.25]$$

$$a_i^v + t_{ij} - a_j^v \leq M(1 - x_{ij}^v) \qquad (i, j) \in A, v = 1, ..., m$$

$$[5.26]$$

$$e_i y_i^v \leq a_{i.}^v \leq l_i y_i^v \qquad i \in N, v = 1, ..., m$$

$$[5.27]$$

$$x_{ij}^v \in \{0, 1\} \qquad (i, j) \in A, v = 1, ..., m$$

$$[5.28]$$

$$y_i^v \in \{0, 1\} \qquad i \in N, v = 1, ..., m$$

$$[5.29]$$

$$a_i^v \in I\!R^+ \qquad i \in N, v = 1, ..., m$$

$$[5.30]$$

Denoting $P = \sum_{i \in N} p_i$ and introducing variables $x_{ii}^v = 1 - y_i^v$, $i \in N$, $v = 1, ..., m$, for each arc (i, i), the objective function and constraints [5.22]–[5.23] in formulation (TOPTW) can be rewritten as an assignment problem as shown in the following model denoted by (TOPTW1). Note that in this model, if the loop arc (i, i) is selected, then node i is not visited in the optimal solution.:

$$(TOPTW1) \quad \max \quad (P - \sum_{v=1}^{m} \sum_{i \in N} p_i x_{ii}^v) \qquad [5.31]$$

$$\sum_{j \in N \cup \{0\}} x_{ij}^v = 1 \qquad i \in N, v = 1, ..., m \qquad [5.32]$$

$$\sum_{i \in N \cup \{0\}} x_{ij}^v = 1 \qquad j \in N, v = 1, ..., m \qquad [5.33]$$

In the GVNS, first an initial solution is built thanks to a constructive heuristic (H). At each iteration, the method evaluates all feasible insertions of unvisited nodes and selects the node corresponding to the best insertion. An insertion is evaluated with the following criterion.

Let i be some node in a tour and let r be a node candidate for the insertion. S_r and g_r are, respectively, the set of nodes reachable from node r (i.e. the set of nodes s such that $a_r + t_{rs} \leq l_s$) and its cardinality. The best insertion is determined by the pair (i, r) for which ρ_{ir} is maximum:

$$\rho_{ir} = g_r \cdot \frac{p_r}{\Delta_{ir}} \qquad [5.34]$$

where p_r is the profit of node r and $\Delta_{ir} = t_{ir} + w_r + t_{rj} - t_{ij}$ measures the possible delay if node r is inserted between node i and its successor j in the tour, with w_r denoting the waiting time at r.

The GVNS considers a sequence of k_{max} neighborhoods $N_k(\cdot)$, $k = 1, ..., k_{max}$. Given a current solution x^*, its k-neighborhood $N_k(x^*)$ consists of all the solutions which can be obtained by randomly removing k consecutive nodes from x^*. The procedure starts by setting $k = 1$. A solution $x' \in N_k(x^*)$ is then obtained using the procedure $Random(x^*, k)$ which removes a random sequence of k consecutive nodes from solution x^* and replaces it by a sequence of unvisited nodes. The new sequence of nodes is determined using a simple heuristic. Let i and j denote the nodes between which the sequence should be inserted and u the current predecessor of the node that will be inserted in the tour. First, the procedure initializes $u = i$. In the next step, it searches for a node v (among all unrouted nodes), for which the insertion between u and j is feasible and the ratio

$\rho' = g_v p_v / (w_v + t_{u,v})$ is maximum. Recall that g_v denotes the number of nodes reachable from v, p_v is the profit of v, $t_{u,v}$ is the travel time from u to v and w_v denotes the waiting time in v when traveling from u. The node v is inserted into the sequence and the search starts again with $u = v$. The search continues until the sequence cannot be extended further.

A local search $LocalSearch$ is then applied to x'. If the resulting solution x'' is better than x^*, it becomes the new incumbent solution and the search is restarted with $k = 1$. Otherwise, the value of k is increased and a different neighborhood is analyzed.

The GVNS approach stops as soon as the number of iterations meets a predefined value $MaxIter$ or no solution value improvement has been obtained after $ItImp$ iterations (external while loop in algorithm 5.6).

The local search procedure explores two different neighborhoods. The first neighborhood is defined by classical routing moves which only modify the routes' time-duration:

1) 2-opt move: which removes and replaces two arcs in a tour and reorders nodes;

2) Or-opt move: relocating one node;

3) 2-opt* move: which interchanges two subpaths between two tours;

4) swap: which swaps two nodes.

The moves are considered subsequently and the first feasible move is performed. The search stops when no improving move can be found. Time window constraints require a feasibility check before a move is performed. This feasibility check can be done in $O(1)$ time (see Chapter 2). The aim behind the exploration of this neighborhood is to reduce the total travel time in order to get some slack for the insertion of other nodes.

The second neighborhood is defined by removing q consecutive nodes from a tour and replacing them by unvisited nodes. The determination of the optimal entering sequence is done exactly using dynamic programming. The problem of finding such an optimal sequence is NP-hard since it returns to solve a single tour orienteering problem with time windows (OPTW). Fortunately, the time window constraints reduce the number of feasible sequences so that the exact evaluation of the entering sequence can be implemented in an acceptable amount of time. The exploration of the second neighborhood begins with $q = 1$, the procedure considers all sequences X_{Out} of q consecutive nodes and determines a sequence X_{In} of entering nodes that fits the available time slot. If the sum of profits in X_{In} is greater than the sum of profits in X_{Out}, the move is admissible. Finally, the move with largest difference between the inserted and the removed profit is performed. The procedure stops when no admissible move can be found. To reduce the computational time, the number q of removed nodes is limited to a maximum value q_{max}.

Given a starting solution x', the procedure $LocalSearch$ first tries to reduce the total travel time of each tour in x' using the first neighborhood. Then, it searches for moves increasing the total collected profit by exploring the second neighborhood. If an improvement is found, it switches to the first neighborhood again. The procedure stops when no improving move can be found.

The second neighborhood is exponential and the determination of the entering sequence may be too time-consuming. The granular variant aims at reducing the size of the analyzed neighborhoods excluding non-promising arcs during the node sequences construction in the local search procedure.

In a preliminary step, the algorithm builds and optimally solves an assignment problem on graph $G(N \cup \{0\}, A)$ using an *ad-hoc* objective function (see model TOPTW1). Then, dual information (reduced costs) is used to identify more promising arcs. More precisely, the cost for each arc $(i, j) \in A$ in the assignment problem is set to $(t_{ij} + w_{ij}^U)/(p_i + p_j)$, where w_{ij}^U is the maximum possible waiting time at node j when the service at node i is assumed to start at time e_i.

Since arc costs take into account traveling and waiting times as well as profits, each reduced cost value can be seen as a measure of the likelihood that the corresponding arc will belong to high-quality solutions: the larger the reduced cost of the variable associated with an arc, the lower the likelihood that the insertion of such an arc in the tour will provide a high profit requiring a low traveling time. Note that arcs selected by the optimal assignment solution have null reduced costs, and thus they are among the most promising arcs considered by the GVNS for the construction of a solution. Given a solution x' and a parameter l_{max}, a set of neighborhoods $H_l(x')$, $l = 1, ..., l_{max}$ is introduced, where l is the granularity parameter defining the subset of arcs which can be taken into account when constructing the entering sequence of nodes in the local search procedure.

After optimally solving the assignment problem, the arcs are sorted in non-decreasing order of reduced cost value (set $\bar{A}$). Intervals of granularity are then created by partitioning $\bar{A}$ into l_{max} buckets. The first bucket $\bar{A}_1$ contains all arcs with null reduced cost. The remaining buckets, denoted by $\bar{A}_2, \bar{A}_3, ..., \bar{A}_{l_{max}}$, are obtained dividing set $\bar{A} \setminus \bar{A}_1$ into $l_{max} - 1$ subsets with the same cardinality (except possibly the last one).

Starting with $l = 1$, GVNS allows the procedure $LocalSearch$ to consider only arcs whose reduced costs are lower than or equal to the worst reduced cost in the subset $\bar{A}_l$ (i.e. for $l > 1$, only arcs contained in the union of buckets $\bar{A}_1, \bar{A}_2, ..., \bar{A}_l$ are considered). If an improved solution is found, l is set to 1, otherwise l is incremented and a larger subset of arcs is made available for the search. This allows the GVNS to diversify the search if a local optimum within the current neighborhood is reached, and to intensify the search considering only the most promising arcs when a potentially good region is explored. The GVNS pseudo-code is outlined in algorithm 5.6.

Algorithm 5.6: *LP-based GVNS* for the *TOPTW*

---

1 build an initial solution x_I with value $z(x_I)$;
2 $x^* := x_I$, $z(x^*) := z(x_I)$;
3 $it = imp := 0$;
4 $l := 1$;
5 $k := 1$;
6 **while** *(it < ItMAX and imp < ItIMP)* **do**
7     $x' := Random(x^*, k)$;
8     $x'' := LocalSearch(x', q_{max}, l)$;
9   **if** $z(x'') > z(x^*)$ **then**
10         $x^* := x''$ and $z(x^*) := z(x'')$;
11         $imp := 0$ and $k := 1$ and $l := 1$;
12   **else**
13         $k := \min(k + 1, k_{max} + 1)$;
14   **if** $k > k_{max}$ **then**
15             $l := \min(l + 1, l_{max})$;
16             $k := 1$;
17         $imp := imp + 1$
18     $it := it + 1$;
19 return x^* with value $z(x^*)$;

The GVNS was tested on two OPTW and TOPTW benchmarks which are derived from the two well-known sets of VRPTW instances (Solomon and Derosiers's [SOL 98], and Cordeau *et al*'s [COR 97]). To deal with TOPTW/OPTW, demands are considered as profits. In order to build more difficult instances, Vansteenwegen *et al.* proposed new data sets based on Solomon's instances and the first 10 of Cordeau's instances where the number of tours is set equal to the number of vehicles needed to visit all customers.

The standard setting of parameters was determined performing several experiments on a small subset of instances composed of six Solomon data files and four Cordeau instances. All the possible values $m = 1, ..., 4$ of fleet size are considered and five runs are executed for each instance. Based on results obtained on this sample, the maximum size k_{max} of the neighborhood explored is set to 7, whereas the parameter q_{max} of the local search procedure is fixed to 3. For the creation of granular neighborhoods, the sorted set is partitioned into $l_{max} = 10$

buckets. As stopping rule, the maximum number of iterations $ItMAX$ and the maximum number of iterations without improvement $ItIMP$ equal, respectively, 500 and 100.

The GVNS was compared to state-of-the-art methods and also to a pure VNS obtained without including the granularity. The algorithm performs, on average, quite well; it was able to improve 25 best-known solutions. Concerning the effect of the granularity, the results show that it contributes to improving the algorithm's efficiency while maintaining its effectiveness.

5.3. Conclusion

This chapter illustrates the main approaches that can be used to design hybrid metaheuristics either by combining only heuristics methods or by associating exact and heuristic paradigms. Some references are given on the vehicle routing problem, and six successful hybrids are detailed.

Research into hybrid metaheuristics is rather recent, and we believe that this kind of resolution approach will continue to receive more and more attention in the future. Even if it seems easy to combine two or more metaheuristic approaches or exact and heuristic paradigms, it does not mean that it can be performed blindly. Significant understanding of the problem structure is required before each successful implementation. This remark is already true for stand-alone methods and still valid for hybrid forms.

We think that too many articles on hybrid metaheuristics make a comparison with other published metaheuristics but forget to prove that the additional components really improve the original metaheuristic. Furthermore, when dealing with NP-hard problems we cannot prove that solving some subproblems optimally really improves the overall results. This is especially true when the comparison is made by fixing the computational time to a given value. An important question we might ask is if it would be better to look toward parallel metaheuristics?

The success of a hybrid method is not only to combine components from different exact and/or approximate methods. Future research direction should focus on the development of more theoretical than experimental-based designs of effective hybrid metaheuristics/matheuristics. Indeed, when dealing with hybridization, the number of possibilities to design hybrids can be very important which can result in an increase of parameters to be set. So, an important issue is, for instance, to use a fair and sound design of experiments and statistical tools in order to choose the best configurations.

Conclusion

This book is an introduction to the development of metaheuristics dedicated to the family of vehicle routing problems (VRPs), one of the most important and studied categories of combinatorial optimization problems. The interest about VRPs is motivated by both a high practical relevance and a challenging motivation to solve them given their considerable difficulty. The aim of the basic version also called capacitated VRP (CVRP) is to determine the optimal set of routes to be performed by a fleet of capacitated vehicles to serve the demand of a given customer set. Behind this classical formulation, historically designed to manage supply of goods, VRPs can model a large range of topics, particularly in services. In real-life context, the related integer programs are computationally intractable; heuristic approaches are thus suitable to get solutions quickly.

First, a general presentation of the fields of logistics, combinatorial optimization and VRPs is given (Introduction and Chapter 1). This preamble is completed in Chapter 2 with a description of significant heuristic methods usually employed to build quickly feasible solutions. The most used local improvement moves are detailed and some tricks are provided to deal with complex moves and to gain in terms of algorithmic complexity. The overview of these fundamentals aims to provide to young researchers on vehicle routing, the essential skills and background necessary to design metaheuristics. These methods are exposed next, according to their feature of working either on a sequence of single solutions (Chapter 3), or on a set of solutions (Chapter 4), or even by hybridizing various components (Chapter 5). A brief survey on implementations of each type of metaheuristics on vehicle routing problems (VRP) is given. Furthermore, for each one of these categories, three illustrative examples are detailed and the key factors which contributed to their success are discussed.

Looking closer to the current state-of-the art, we can attest that intensification and diversification remain the two important factors in the design of metaheuristics whose effectiveness tightly depends upon the balance made between these two components. All metaheuristics working well actually on vehicle routing variants contain both local improvement procedures and mechanisms that allow us to control diversity. These last ones depend on the metaheuristic and can be, for instance, mutations, perturbations, penalty functions, restarts, etc.

We must also note that currently, many effective metaheuristics are so problem-specific, that generalizing them to more complex variants can quickly become a rather hard task, if not impossible. This drawback prevents incorporation into commercial software which have to deal with complex real-world applications, involving several constraints and dealing with huge problem sizes. Designing generic methods able to solve many variants with a same algorithm still remains a challenging issue and a few attempts have been made to bridge that gap.

Indeed, through the overview of the methods, the main trends of approaches developed to solve the VRPs can be browsed. It appears that tabu search has been the dominant kind of metaheuristics applied to these problems until the 2000s, like the universal tabu search algorithm UTSA from Cordeau *et al.* [COR 01a]. At that time, the route-first cluster-second algorithms have been pitched up as a promising option within a metaheuristic. In fact, computing traveling salesman problem (TSP) tours covering all customers allows us to search in a smaller solution space. In addition, the second phase, which decomposes the so-called giant tour into feasible vehicle routes, can be solved exactly as a shortest path problem in an auxiliary graph. Prins [PRI 04a] proposed a compact version, denoted as Split, where the auxiliary graph is not generated explicitly. He embedded this concept in a genetic algorithm, with a chromosome being a giant tour. State-of-the art metaheuristics based on this approach have been available for many vehicle routing problems, due to its flexibility (many additional constraints can be handled) and efficiency: after genetic-based algorithms, other methods appeared, like iterated local search (ILS) or evolutionary local search (ELS), sometimes in hybrid versions like with a greedy randomized adaptive search procedure (GRASP) [PRI 09c, DUH 12].

Around the 2010s, another wave emerged with the large neighborhood search from Pisinger and Röpke [PIS 07]. Matheuristics, combining heuristic and exact approaches, are also a trend that brings interesting results when taking advantage of the structure of the problem [PRI 07], or the neighborhood [LAB 12b], for instance. However, genetic algorithms with Split are still on the front. Good examples are the memetic algorithm proposed by Vidal *et al.* for the capacitated vehicle routing problem (CVRP), the multi-depot VRP (MDVRP) and the periodic VRP [VID 12a], and another GA by the same authors for various problems with time windows [VID 14, VID 13b]. The last contribution, detailed in this book in Chapter 4, is due to Vidal *et al.* [VID 13b]. It is able to solve up to 26 VRP variants.

As mentioned throughout, a large number of metaheuristics applications are developed for solving vehicle routing problems. Recent contributions clearly illustrate the growing interest for hybrid approaches, obtained either by combining metaheuristics or by mixing exact and heuristic algorithms. However, few attempts have been made in the current state-of-the art to prove the real contribution of hybridization on the performance of such methods. It is hence very important in future studies to prove whether the additional complexity and sophistication introduced by hybridization is worthwhile in light of the obtained results. Indeed, many hybrid heuristics are so complicated that they become irreproducible.

Parallel metaheuristics also open interesting and challenging perspectives, especially with the multiplication of multi-core processors, powerful graphics cards (GPUs) and grid computing. We believe that they will gain even more attention, and that many metaheuristics such as tabu search and multi-population genetic algorithms would be up-to-date in their parallel versions in the near future.

Finally, we believe that research on vehicle routing and metaheuristic design will attract extensive interest in the future and we hope that this book will encourage and give the necessary guidelines for interested researchers.

Bibliography

[AGH 06] AGHEZZAF E.-H., RAA B., VAN LANDEGHEM H., "Modeling inventory routing problems in supply chains of high consumption products", *European Journal of Operational Research*, vol. 169, no. 3, pp. 1048–1063, 2006.

[AHU 01] AHUJA R., ORLIN J., SHARMA D., "Multi-exchange neighborhood search algorithms for the capacitated minimum spanning tree problem", *Mathematical Programming*, vol. 91, pp. 71–97, 2001.

[AI 07] AI T.J., KACHITVICHYANUKUL V., "A particle swarm optimization for the capacitated vehicle routing problem", *International Journal of Logistics and SCM Systems*, vol. 2, pp. 50–55, 2007.

[AI 09] AI T.J., KACHITVICHYANUKUL V., "A particle swarm optimization for the vehicle routing problem with simultaneous pickup and delivery", *Computers and OR*, vol. 36, pp. 1693–1702, 2009.

[AKS 14] AKSEN D., KAYA O., SALMAN F.S. *et al.*, "An adaptive large neighborhood search algorithm for a selective and periodic inventory routing problem", *European Journal of Operational Research*, vol. 239, no. 2, pp. 413–426, 2014.

[ARC 08] ARCHETTI C., SPERANZA M.G., SAVELSBERGH M.W., "An optimization-based heuristic for the split delivery vehicle routing problem", *Transportation Science*, vol. 42, no. 1, pp. 22–31, 2008.

[ARC 13] ARCHETTI C., DOERNER K.F., TRICOIRE F., "A heuristic algorithm for the free newspaper delivery problem", *European Journal of Operational Research*, vol. 230, no. 2, pp. 245–257, 2013.

[ARC 14] ARCHETTI C., SPERANZA M.G., "A survey on matheuristics for routing problems", *EURO Journal on Computational Optimization*, Springer, vol. 2, no. 4, pp. 223–246, 2014.

[ARC 15] ARCHETTI C., CORBERÁN Á., PLANA I. *et al.*, "A matheuristic for the team orienteering arc routing problem", *European Journal of Operational Research*, vol. 245, no. 2, pp. 392–401, 2015.

[ATA 07] ATASHPAZ-GARGARI E., LUCAS C., "Imperialist competitive algorithm: an algorithm for optimization inspired by imperialistic competition", *IEEE Congress on Evolutionary Computation*, pp. 4661–4667, 2007.

[BAK 03] BAKER B.M., AYECHEW M.A., "A genetic algorithm for the vehicle routing problem", *Computers & OR*, vol. 30, no. 5, pp. 787–800, 2003.

[BAL 64] BALINSKI M., QUANDT R., "On an integer program for a delivery program", *Operations Research*, vol. 12, pp. 300–304, 1964.

[BAL 07] BALDACCI R., TOTH P., VIGO D., "Recent advances in vehicle routing exact algorithms", *4OR*, Springer, vol. 5, no. 4, pp. 269–298, 2007.

[BAL 08a] BALDACCI R., CHRISTOFIDES N., MINGOZZI A., "An exact algorithm for the vehicle routing problem based on the set partitioning formulation with additional cuts", *Mathematical Programming*, vol. 115, pp. 351–385, 2008.

[BAL 08b] BALDACCI R., BATTARRA M., VIGO D., "Routing a heterogeneous fleet of vehicles", *The Vehicle Routing Problem: Latest Advances and New Challenges*, Springer, US, pp. 3–27, 2008.

[BAL 12] BALDACCI R., MINGOZZI A., ROBERTI R., "Recent exact algorithms for solving the vehicle routing problem under capacity and time window constraints", *European Journal of Operational Research*, Elsevier, vol. 218, no. 1, pp. 1–6, 2012.

[BAR 99] BARBARASOGLU G., OZGUR D., "A tabu search algorithm for the vehicle routing problem", *Computers & Operations Research*, vol. 26, pp. 255–279, 1999.

[BAU 86] BAUM E., Iterated descent: a better algorithm for local search in combinatorial optimization, Report, CALTECH, Pasadena, CA, 1986.

[BEA 83] BEASLEY J., "Route-first cluster-second methods for vehicle routing", *Omega*, vol. 11, pp. 403–408, 1983.

[BEL 04] BELL J., MULLEN P.M., "An improved ant system algorithm for the vehicle routing problem", *Advanced Engineering Informatics*, vol. 18, no. 1, pp. 41–48, 2004.

[BEL 09] BELFIORE P., YOSHIZAKI H.Y., "Scatter search for a real-life heterogeneous fleet vehicle routing problem with time windows and split deliveries in Brazil", *European Journal of Operational Research*, vol. 199, pp. 750–758, 2009.

[BEN 92] BENTLEY J.L., "Fast algorithms for geometric TSP", *ORSA Journal on Computing*, vol. 4, pp. 387–411, 1992.

[BER 03] BERGER J., BARKAOUI M., "A new hybrid genetic algorithm for the capacitated vehicle routing problem", *Journal of the Operational Research Society*, vol. 54, pp. 1254–1262, 2003.

[BEU 03] BEULLENS P., MUYLDERMANS L., CATTRYSSE D. *et al.*, "A guided local search heuristic for the capacitated arc routing problem", *European Journal of Operational Research*, vol. 147, pp. 629–643, 2003.

[BLU 11] BLUM C., PUCHINGER J., RAIDL G.R. *et al.*, "Hybrid metaheuristics in combinatorial optimization: a survey", *Applied Soft Computing*, vol. 11, no. 6, pp. 4135–4151, 2011.

[BOS 09] BOSCHETTI M.A., MANIEZZO V., ROFFILLI M. *et al.*, "Matheuristics: optimization, simulation and control", *Hybrid Metaheuristics*, Springer, pp. 171–177, 2009.

[BOU 07] BOUDIA M., LOULY M., PRINS C., "A reactive GRASP and path relinking for a combined production-distribution problem", *Computers & Operations Research*, vol. 34, pp. 3402–3419, 2007.

[BOU 09] BOUDIA M., PRINS C., OULD-LOULY A., "A memetic algorithm with dynamic population management for an integrated production-distribution problem", *European Journal of Operational Research*, vol. 195, pp. 703–715, 2009.

[BRA 97] BRANDÃO J., MERCER A., "A tabu search algorithm for the multi-trip vehicle routing and scheduling problem", *European Journal of Operational Research*, vol. 100, no. 1, pp. 180–191, 1997.

[BRA 98] BRAMEL J., SIMCHI-LEVI D., *The Logic of Logistic: Theory, Algorithms and Applications for Logistics Management*, Springer, 1998.

[BRA 04] BRANDÃO J., "A tabu search algorithm for the open vehicle routing problem", *European Journal of Operational Research*, vol. 157, no. 3, pp. 552–564, 2004.

[BRA 06] BRANDÃO J., "A new tabu search algorithm for the vehicle routing problem with backhauls", *European Journal of Operational Research*, vol. 173, no. 2, pp. 540–555, 2006.

[BRA 09] BRANDÃO J., "A deterministic tabu search algorithm for the fleet size and mix vehicle routing problem", *European Journal of Operational Research*, vol. 195, no. 3, pp. 716–728, 2009.

[BRA 11] BRANDÃO J., "A tabu search algorithm for the heterogeneous fixed fleet vehicle routing problem", *Computers & Operations Research*, vol. 38, no. 1, pp. 140–151, 2011.

[BUL 99] BULLNHEIMER B., HARTL R., STRAUSS C., "An improved ant system algorithm for the vehicle routing problem", *Annals of Operations Research*, vol. 89, pp. 319–328, 1999.

[CAM 04] CAMPBELL A.M., SAVELSBERGH M.W., "A decomposition approach for the inventory-routing problem", *Transportation Science*, vol. 38, no. 4, pp. 488–502, 2004.

[CAM 05] CAMPOS V., LAGUNA M., MARTI R., "Context-independent scatter and tabu search for permutation problems", *INFORMS Journal on Computing*, vol. 17, no. 1, pp. 111–122, 2005.

[CHA 94] CHANDRA P., FISHER M.L., "Coordination of production and distribution planning", *European Journal of Operational Research*, vol. 72, no. 3, pp. 503–517, 1994.

[CHE 06] CHEN A.L., YANG G.K., WU Z.M., "Hybrid discrete particle swarm optimization algorithm for capacitated vehicle routing problem", *Journal of Zhejiang University Science A*, Springer, vol. 7, no. 4, pp. 607–614, 2006.

[CHE 10] CHEN P., HUANG H., DONG X., "Iterated variable neighborhood descent algorithm for the capacitated vehicle routing problem", *Expert Systems with Applications*, vol. 37, pp. 1620–1627, 2010.

[CHR 79] CHRISTOFIDES N., MINGOZZI A., TOTH P., "The vehicle routing problem", in CHRISTOFIDES N., MINGOZZI A., TOTH *et al.* (eds), *Combinatorial Optimization*, Wiley, Chichester, vol. 27. pp. 315–338, 1979.

[CHU 06] CHU F., LABADI N., PRINS C., "A scatter search for the periodic capacitated arc routing problem", *European Journal of Operational Research*, vol. 169, pp. 586–605, 2006.

[CLA 64] CLARKE G., WRIGHT J., "Scheduling of vehicles from a central depot to a number of delivery points", *Operations Research*, vol. 12, pp. 568–581, 1964.

[COE 12] COELHO L.C., CORDEAU J.-F., LAPORTE G., "The inventory-routing problem with transshipment", *Computers & Operations Research*, vol. 39, no. 11, pp. 2537–2548, 2012.

[COR 97] CORDEAU J.-F., GENDREAU M., LAPORTE G., "A tabu search heuristic for periodic and multi-depot problems", *Networks*, vol. 30, pp. 105–119, 1997.

[COR 01a] CORDEAU J.-F., LAPORTE G., MERCIER A., "A unified tabu search heuristic for vehicle routing problems with time windows", *Journal of the Operational Research Society*, vol. 52, pp. 928–936, 2001.

[COR 01b] CORDEAU J.-F., STOJKOVI G., SOUMIS F. *et al.*, "Benders decomposition for simultaneous aircraft routing and crew scheduling", *Transportation Science*, vol. 35, no. 4, pp. 375–388, 2001.

[COR 02] CORDEAU J.-F., LAPORTE G., Tabu search heuristics for the vehicle routing problem, Report no. G-2002-15, GERAD, March 2002.

[COR 12] CORDEAU J.-F., MAISCHBERGER M., "A parallel iterated tabu search heuristic for vehicle routing problems", *Computers & Operations Research*, vol. 39, no. 9, pp. 2033–2050, 2012.

[CUD 15] CUDA R., GUASTAROBA G., SPERANZA M., "A survey on two-echelon routing problems", *Computers & Operations Research*, vol. 55, pp. 185–199, 2015.

[DAN 59] DANTZIG G.B., RAMSER J.H., "The truck dispatching problem", *Management Science*, vol. 6, no. 1, pp. 80–91, 1959.

[DEF 06] DE FRANCESCHI R., FISCHETTI M., TOTH P., "A new ILP-based refinement heuristic for vehicle routing problems", *Mathematical Programming*, vol. 105, nos. 2–3, pp. 471–499, 2006.

[DEM 12] DEMIR E., BEKTA T., LAPORTE G., "An adaptive large neighborhood search heuristic for the pollution-routing problem", *European Journal of Operational Research*, vol. 223, no. 2, pp. 346–359, 2012.

[DER 02] DEROUSSI L., Heuristiques, algorithmes stochastiques et modèles d'évaluation pour l'optimisation combinatoire, PhD dissertation, University Blaise Pascal, Clermont-Ferrand, France, 2002.

[DOE 04] DOERNER K.F., HARTL R., KIECHLE G. *et al.*, "Parallel ant systems for the capacitated vehicle routing problem", *Evolutionary Computation in Combinatorial Optimization*, Springer Berlin Heidelberg, vol. 3004, pp. 72–83, 2004.

[DOE 10] DOERNER K.F., SCHMID V., "Survey: matheuristics for rich vehicle routing problems", in BLESA M.J., BLUM C., RAIDL G. *et al.* (eds.), *Hybrid Metaheuristics*, Springer, vol. 6373, pp. 206–221, 2010.

[DOR 04] DORIGO M., STUTZLE T., *Ant Colony Optimization*, MIT Press, Cambridge, 2004.

[DRÉ 03] DRÉO J., PÉTROWSKI A., TAILLARD É.D. *et al.*, *Métaheuristiques pour l'optimisation difficile*, Eyrolles, 2003.

[DUH 11] DUHAMEL C., LACOMME P., QUILLIOT A. *et al.*, "A multi-start evolutionary local search for the two-dimensional loading capacitated vehicle routing problem", *Computers & Operations Research*, vol. 38, no. 3, pp. 617– 640, 2011.

[DUH 12] DUHAMEL C., LACOMME P., PRODHON C., "A hybrid evolutionary local search with depth first search split procedure for the heterogeneous vehicle routing problems", *Engineering Applications of Artificial Intelligence*, vol. 25, no. 2, pp. 345–358, 2012.

[ELF 08] EL FALLAHI A., PRINS C., WOLFLER CALVO R., "A memetic algorithm and a tabu search for the multi-compartment vehicle routing problem", *Computers & Operations Research*, vol. 35, no. 5, pp. 1725–1741, 2008.

[ERG 02] ERGUN Ö., ORLIN J., STEELE-FELDMAN A., Creating very large scale neighborhoods out of smaller ones by compounding moves: a study on the vehicle routing problem, Working Paper no. 4393-02, MIT Sloan School of Management, Cambridge, MA, 2002.

[ERG 06] ERGUN Ö., ORLIN J.B., STEELE-FELDMAN A., "Creating very large scale neighborhoods out of smaller ones by compounding moves", *Journal of Heuristics*, Springer, vol. 12, nos. 1–2, pp. 115–140, 2006.

[ESC 14] ESCOBAR J.W., LINFATI R., BALDOQUIN M.G. *et al.*, "A granular variable tabu neighborhood search for the capacitated location-routing problem", *Transportation Research Part B: Methodological*, vol. 67, pp. 344–356, 2014.

[EUC 12] EUCHI J., *Metaheuristics to Solve Some Variants of Vehicle Routing Problems: Metaheuristics Algorithms for the Optimization of Some Variants of Logistics and Transport Problems*, LAP LAMBERT Academic Publishing, 2012.

[FEO 89] FEO T., RESENDE M., "A probabilistic heuristic for a computationally difficult set covering problem", *Operations Research Letters*, vol. 8, pp. 67–71, 1989.

[FEO 94] FEO T., RESENDE M., SMITH S., "A greedy randomized adaptive search procedure for maximum independent set", *Operations Research*, vol. 42, pp. 860–878, 1994.

[FIS 81] FISHER M., JAIKUMAR R., "A generalized assignment heuristic for vehicle routing", *Networks*, vol. 11, pp. 109–124, 1981.

[FIS 94] FISHER M., "Optimal solution of vehicle routing problems using minimum k-trees", *Operations Research*, vol. 42, pp. 626–642, 1994.

[FIS 03] FISCHETTI M., LODI A., "Local branching", *Mathematical Programming*, vol. 98, no. 1–3, pp. 23–47, 2003.

[FLE 09] FLESZAR K., OSMAN I., INDI K., "A variable neighborhood search algorithm for the open vehicle routing problem", *European Journal of Operational Research*, vol. 195, pp. 803–809, 2009.

[FOS 76] FOSTER B.A., RYAN D.M., "An integer programming approach to the vehicle scheduling problem", *Operational Research Quarterly*, vol. 27, pp. 367–384, 1976.

[FUE 09] FUELLERER G., DOERNER K.F., HARTL et al., "Ant colony optimization for the two-dimensional loading vehicle routing problem", *Computers & Operations Research*, vol. 36, no. 3, pp. 655–673, 2009.

[FUN 05] FUNKE B., GRÜNERT T., IRNICH S., "Local search for vehicle routing and scheduling problems: review and conceptual integration", *Journal of Heuristics*, vol. 11, pp. 267–306, 2005.

[GEE 05a] GEEM Z., "School bus routing using harmony search", *Genetic and Evolutionary Computation Conference (GECCO 2005)*, Washington DC, USA, June 25–29, 2005.

[GEE 05b] GEEM Z., TSENG C., PARK Y., "Harmony search for generalized orienteering problem: best touring in China", *Lecture Notes in Computer Science*, vol. 3612, pp. 741–750, 2005.

[GEN 92] GENDREAU M., HERTZ A., LAPORTE G., "New insertion and post-optimization procedures for the traveling salesman problem", *Operations Research*, vol. 40, pp. 1086–1094, 1992.

[GEN 94] GENDREAU M., HERTZ A., LAPORTE G., "A tabu search heuristic for the vehicle routing problem", *Management Science*, vol. 40, pp. 1276–1290, 1994.

[GEN 06] GENDREAU M., IORI M., LAPORTE G. et al., "A tabu search algorithm for a routing and container loading problem", *Transportation Science*, vol. 40, no. 3, pp. 342–350, 2006.

[GEN 15] GENDREAU M., GHIANI G., GUERRIERO E., "Time-dependent routing problems: a review", *Computers & Operations Research*, vol. 64, pp. 189–197, 2015.

[GIL 74] GILLETT B., MILLER L., "A heuristic algorithm for the vehicle dispatch problem", *Operation Research*, vol. 22, pp. 340–349, 1974.

[GLO 77] GLOVER F., "Heuristics for integer programming using surrogate constraints", *Decision Sciences*, vol. 8, pp. 156–166, 1977.

[GLO 86] GLOVER F., "Future paths for integer programming and links to artificial intelligence", *Computers and Operations Research*, vol. 5, pp. 533–549, 1986.

[GLO 89] GLOVER F., "Tabu search. Part I", *ORSA Journal on Computing*, vol. 1, pp. 190–206, 1989.

[GLO 90] GLOVER F., "Tabu search. Part II", *ORSA Journal on Computing*, vol. 2, pp. 4–32, 1990.

[GLO 97a] GLOVER F., "Tabu search and adaptive memory programing – advances, applications and challenges", in BARR R., HELGASON R., KENNINGTON J. (eds.), *Interfaces in Computer Science and Operations Research*, Kluwer, pp. 1–75, 1997.

[GLO 97b] GLOVER F., LAGUNA M., *Tabu Search*, Kluwer Academic Publishers, Boston, 1997.

[GLO 00] GLOVER F., LAGUNA M., MARTÍ R., "Fundamentals of scatter search and path relinking", *Control and Cybernetics*, vol. 39, pp. 653–684, 2000.

[GOL 89] GOLDBERG D., *Genetic Algorithms in Search, Optimization, and Machine Learning*, Addison-Wesley Longman, 1989.

[GOL 08] GOLDEN B., RAGHAVAN S., WASIL E., *The Vehicle Routing Problem, Latest Advances and New Challenges*, Springer, New York, 2008.

[GRO 11] GROËR C., GOLDEN B., WASIL E., "A parallel algorithm for the vehicle routing problem", *INFORMS Journal on Computing*, vol. 23, pp. 315–330, 2011.

[GUE 13] GUERRERO W.J., PRODHON C., VELASCO N. *et al.*, "Hybrid heuristic for the inventory location-routing problem with deterministic demand", *International Journal of Production Economics*, vol. 146, no. 1, pp. 359–370, 2013.

[HAN 99] HANSEN P., MLADENOVI N., *An Introduction to Variable Neighborhood Search*, Springer, 1999.

[HAN 10] HANSEN P., MLADENOVI N., BRIMBERG J. *et al.*, *Variable Neighborhood Search*, Springer, 2010.

[HAR 87] HART J., SHOGAN A.W., "Semi-greedy heuristics: an empirical study", *Operations Research Letters*, vol. 6, no. 3, pp. 107–114, 1987.

[HAR 06] HARTL R.F., HASLE G., JANSSENS G.K., "Special issue on rich vehicle routing problems", *Central European Journal of Operations Research*, vol. 14, no. 2, pp. 103–104, 2006.

[HAS 07] HASLE G., KLOSTER O., "Industrial vehicle routing", *Geometric Modelling, Numerical Simulation, and Optimization*, Springer, pp. 397–435, 2007.

[HEM 12] HEMMELMAYR V.C., CORDEAU J.-F., CRAINIC T.G., "An adaptive large neighborhood search heuristic for two-echelon vehicle routing problems arising in city logistics", *Computers & Operations Research*, vol. 39, no. 12, pp. 3215–3228, 2012.

[HER 01] HERTZ A., MITTAZ M., "A variable neighborhood descent algorithm for the undirected capacitated arc routing problem", *Transportation Science*, vol. 35, pp. 425–434, 2001.

[HO 06] HO S., GENDREAU M., "Path relinking for the vehicle routing problem", *Journal of Heuristics*, vol. 12, pp. 55–72, 2006.

[HOL 75] HOLLAND J., *Adaptation in Natural and Artificial Systems*, University of Michigan Press, Ann Arbor, MI, 1975.

[HON 12] HONG L., "An improved LNS algorithm for real-time vehicle routing problem with time windows", *Computers & Operations Research*, vol. 39, no. 2, pp. 151–163, 2012.

[IRN 06] IRNICH S., FUNKE B., GRÜNERT T., "Sequential search and its application to vehicle-routing problems", *Computers & Operations Research*, vol. 33, pp. 2405–2429, 2006.

[JIN 08] JIN M., LIU K., EKSIOGLU B., "A column generation approach for the split delivery vehicle routing problem", *Operations Research Letters*, vol. 36, no. 2, pp. 265–270, 2008.

[KAR 05] KARABOGA D., An idea based on honey bee swarm for numerical optimization, Report no. TR06, Erciyes University, 2005.

[KEL 99] KELLY J.P., XU J., "A set-partitioning-based heuristic for the vehicle routing problem", *INFORMS Journal on Computing*, vol. 11, no. 2, pp. 161–172, 1999.

[KEN 95] KENNEDY J., EBERHART R.C., "Particle swarm optimization", *Proceedings of IEEE International Conference on Neural Networks*, pp. 1942–1948, 1995.

[KEN 97] KENNEDY J., EBERHART R.C., "A discrete binary version of the particle swarm algorithm", *Systems, Man, and Cybernetics. Computational Cybernetics and Simulation, IEEE International Conference*, vol. 4105, pp. 4104–4108, 1997.

[KIL 99] KILBY P., PROSSER P., SHAW P., "Guided local search for the vehicle routing problem", in VOSS S., MARTELLO S., OSMAN I. *et al.* (eds.), *Metaheuristics: Advances and Trends in Local Search Paradigms for Optimization*, Kluwer, pp. 473–486, 1999.

[KIN 97] KINDERVATER G.A.P., SAVELSBERGH M.W.P., "Vehicle routing: handling edge exchanges", in AARTS E.H.L., LENSTRA J.K. (eds.), *Local Search in Combinatorial Optimization*, John Wiley & Sons, pp. 337–360, 1997.

[KIR 83] KIRKPATRICK S., GELATT C.D., VECCHI M.P. *et al.*, "Optimization by simulated annealing", *Science*, vol. 220, no. 4598, pp. 671–680, 1983.

[KUO 12] KUO Y., WANG C.-C., "A variable neighborhood search for the multi-depot vehicle routing problem with loading cost", *Expert Systems with Applications*, vol. 39, no. 8, pp. 6949–6954, 2012.

[KYT 07] KYTÖJOKI J., NUORTIO T., BRÄYSY O. *et al.*, "An efficient variable neighborhood search heuristic for very large scale vehicle routing problems", *Computers & Operations Research*, vol. 34, no. 9, pp. 2743–2757, 2007.

[LAB 08a] LABADI N., PRINS C., REGHIOUI M., "GRASP with path relinking for the capacitated arc routing problem with time windows", in FINK A., ROTHLAUF F. (eds.), *Advances in Computational Intelligence in Transport, Logistics, and Supply Chain Management*, Springer, vol. 144, pp. 111–135, 2008.

[LAB 08b] LABADIE N., PRINS C., REGHIOUI M., "A memetic algorithm for the vehicle routing problem with time windows", *RAIRO-Operations Research*, vol. 42, no. 3, pp. 415–431, 2008.

[LAB 11] LABADIE N., MELECHOVSK J., CALVO R.W., "Hybridized evolutionary local search algorithm for the team orienteering problem with time windows", *Journal of Heuristics*, vol. 17, pp. 729–753, 2011.

[LAB 12a] LABADIE N., PRODHON C., "Vehicle routing nowadays: compact review and emerging problems," *Production Systems and Supply Chain Management in Emerging Countries: Best Practices*, Springer, pp. 141–166, 2012.

[LAB 12b] LABADIE N., MANSINI R., MELECHOVSK J. *et al.*, "The team orienteering problem with time windows: an LP-based granular variable neighborhood search", *European Journal of Operational Research*, vol. 220, no. 1, pp. 15–27, 2012.

[LAB 14] LABADIE N., PRODHON C., Chapter A survey on multi-criteria analysis in logistics: focus on vehicle routing problems, *Applications of Multi-Criteria and Game Theory Approaches*, Springer, pp. 3–29, 2014.

[LAC 01] LACOMME P., PRINS C., RAMDANE-CHERIF W., *Competitive Genetic Algorithms for the Capacitated Arc Routing Problem and its Extensions*, Springer, pp. 473–483, 2001.

[LAC 04] LACOMME P., PRINS C., RAMDANE-CHERIF W., "Competitive memetic algorithms for arc routing problems", *Annals of Operations Research*, vol. 131, pp. 159–185, 2004.

[LAG 95] LAGUNA M., MARTÍ R., "GRASP and path relinking for 2-layer straight line crossing minimization", *INFORMS Journal on Computing*, vol. 11, no. 1, pp. 44–52, 1995.

[LAP 02] LAPORTE G., SEMET F., Chapter Classical heuristics for the capacitated VRP, *"The Vehicle Routing Problem"*, Society for Industrial and Applied Mathematics, Philadelphia, PA, pp. 109–128, 2002.

[LAP 09] LAPORTE G., "Fifty years of vehicle routing", *Transportation Science*, vol. 43, no. 4, pp. 408–416, 2009.

[LEN 81] LENSTRA J.K., KAN A., "Complexity of vehicle routing and scheduling problems", *Networks*, Wiley Online Library, vol. 11, no. 2, pp. 221–227, 1981.

[LEU 11] LEUNG S.C., ZHOU X., ZHANG D. *et al.*, "Extended guided tabu search and a new packing algorithm for the two-dimensional loading vehicle routing problem", *Computers & Operations Research*, vol. 38, no. 1, pp. 205–215, 2011.

[LEU 13] LEUNG S.C., ZHANG Z., ZHANG D. *et al.*, "A meta-heuristic algorithm for heterogeneous fleet vehicle routing problems with two-dimensional loading constraints", *European Journal of Operational Research*, vol. 225, no. 2, pp. 199–210, 2013.

[LI 05] LI F., GOLDEN B., WASIL E., "Very large-scale vehicle routing: new test problems, algorithms, and results", *Computers & Operations Research*, vol. 32, no. 5, pp. 1165–1179, 2005.

[LI 07] LI F., GOLDEN B., WASIL E., "The open vehicle routing problem: algorithms,large-scale test problems, and computational results", *Computers & Operations Research*, vol. 34, pp. 2918–2930, 2007.

[LI 12] LI X., LEUNG S.C., TIAN P., "A multistart adaptive memory-based tabu search algorithm for the heterogeneous fixed fleet open vehicle routing problem", *Expert Systems with Applications*, vol. 39, no. 1, pp. 365–374, 2012.

[LIN 73] LIN S., KERNIGHAN B., "An effective heuristic algorithm for the traveling salesman problem", *Operations Research*, vol. 21, pp. 498–516, 1973.

[LIN 09] LIN S.-W., YU V.F., CHOU S.-Y., "Solving the truck and trailer routing problem based on a simulated annealing heuristic", *Computers & Operations Research*, vol. 36, no. 5, pp. 1683–1692, 2009.

[LIN 11] LIN S.-W., YU V.F., LU C.-C., "A simulated annealing heuristic for the truck and trailer routing problem with time windows", *Expert Systems with Applications*, vol. 38, no. 12, pp. 15244–15252, 2011.

[LIN 12] LIN S.-W., YU V.F., "A simulated annealing heuristic for the team orienteering problem with time windows", *European Journal of Operational Research*, vol. 217, no. 1, pp. 94–107, 2012.

[LIN 13] LIN S.-W., "Solving the team orienteering problem using effective multi-start simulated annealing", *Applied Soft Computing*, vol. 13, no. 2, pp. 1064–1073, 2013.

[LOU 10] LOURENÇO H.R., MARTIN O.C., STÜTZLE T., "Iterated local search", in GENDREAU M., POTVIN J. (eds.), *Handbook of Metaheuristics (second edition)*, Springer, vol. 146, pp. 363–397, 2010.

[LOZ 10] LOZANO M., GARCÍA-MARTÍNEZ C., "Hybrid metaheuristics with evolutionary algorithms specializing in intensification and diversification: overview and progress report", *Computers & Operations Research*, vol. 37, no. 3, pp. 481–497, 2010.

[MAR 05] MARTÍ R., LAGUNA M., CAMPOS V., "Scatter search vs genetic algorithms: an experimental evaluation with permutation problems", *Metaheuristic Optimization via Memory and Evolution: Tabu Search and Scatter Search*, Kluwer Academic Publishers, pp. 263–283, 2005.

[MAR 10a] MARINAKIS Y., MARINAKI M., "A hybrid genetic particle swarm optimization algorithm for the vehicle routing problem", *Expert Systems with Applications*, vol. 37, no. 2, pp. 1446–1455, 2010.

[MAR 10b] MARINAKIS Y., MARINAKI M., "A hybrid multi-swarm particle swarm optimization algorithm for the probabilistic traveling salesman problem", *Computers & Operations Research*, Elsevier, vol. 37, no. 3, pp. 432–442, 2010.

[MAR 11] MARINAKIS Y., MARINAKI M., "Bumble bees mating optimization algorithm for the vehicle routing problem", *Handbook of Swarm Intelligence*, Kluwer Academic Publishers, pp. 347–369, 2011.

[MAR 12] MARINAKIS Y., "Multiple phase neighborhood search-GRASP for the capacitated vehicle routing problem", *Expert Systems with Applications*, vol. 39, no. 8, pp. 6807–6815, 2012.

[MAR 13] MARINAKIS Y., IORDANIDOU G.-R., MARINAKI M., "Particle swarm optimization for the vehicle routing problem with stochastic demands", *Applied Soft Computing*, vol. 13, no. 4, pp. 1693–1704, 2013.

[MEI 11] MEI Y., TANG K., YAO X., "A memetic algorithm for periodic capacitated arc routing problem", *IEEE Transactions on Systems, Man, and Cybernetics, PART B: Cybernetics*, vol. 41, no. 6, pp. 1654–1667, 2011.

[MEN 13] MENDOZA J.E., VILLEGAS J.G., "A multi-space sampling heuristic for the vehicle routing problem with stochastic demands", *Optimization Letters*, vol. 7, no. 7, pp. 1503–1516, 2013.

[MIC 96] MICHALEWICZ Z., *Genetic Algorithms + Data Structures = Evolution Programs*, Springer, 1996.

[MIC 14] MICHALLET J., PRINS C., AMODEO L. *et al.*, "Multi-start iterated local search for the periodic vehicle routing problem with time windows and time spread constraints on services", *Computers & Operations Research*, vol. 41, pp. 196–207, 2014.

[MLA 97] MLADENOVI N., HANSEN P., "Variable neighborhood search", *Computers & Operations Research*, vol. 24, no. 11, pp. 1097–1100, 1997.

[MOG 12] MOGHADDAM B.F., RUIZ R., SADJADI S.J., "Vehicle routing problem with uncertain demands: an advanced particle swarm algorithm", *Computers & Industrial Engineering*, vol. 62, no. 1, pp. 306–317, 2012.

[MOL 76] MOLE R.H., JAMESON S.R., "A sequential route-building algorithm employing a generalized savings criterion", *Operational Research Quaterly*, vol. 27, p. 5036511, 1976.

[MON 15] MONTOYA-TORRES J.R., FRANCO J.L., ISAZA S.N. *et al.*, "A literature review on the vehicle routing problem with multiple depots", *Computers & Industrial Engineering*, vol. 79, pp. 115–129, 2015.

[MOS 89] MOSCATO P., "On evolution, search, optimization, genetic algorithms, martial arts: towards memetic algorithms", *Caltech Concurrent Computation Program c3p* Report 826, 1989.

[MOS 99] MOSCATO P., "Memetic algorithms: ashort introduction", *New Ideas in Optimization*, McGraw-Hill, UK, pp. 219–234, 1999.

[MUY 03] MUYLDERMANS L., Routing, districting and location for arc traversal problems, PhD Dissertation, Catholic University of Leuven, Belgium, 2003.

[NAG 09] NAGATA Y., BRÄYSY O., "Edge assembly-based memetic algorithm for the capacitated vehicle routing problem", *Networks*, vol. 54, pp. 205–215, 2009.

[NAG 10] NAGATA Y., BRÄYSY O., DULLAERT W., "A penalty based edge assembly memetic algorithm for the vehicle routing problem with time windows", *Computers & Operations Research*, vol. 37, pp. 724–737, 2010.

[NGU 10a] NGUEVEU S.U., PRINS C., CALVO R.W., "A hybrid tabu search for the m-peripatetic vehicle routing problem", *Matheuristics*, Springer, pp. 253–266, 2010.

[NGU 10b] NGUEVEU S., PRINS C., WOLFLER CALVO R., "An effective memetic algorithm for the cumulative capacitated vehicle routing problem", *Computers & Operations Research*, vol. 37, pp. 1877-1885, 2010.

[NGU 12a] NGUYEN V.-P., PRINS C., PRODHON C., "A multi-start iterated local search with tabu list and path relinking for the two-echelon location-routing problem", *Engineering Applications of Artificial Intelligence*, vol. 25, no. 1, pp. 56–71, 2012.

[NGU 12b] NGUYEN V.-P., PRINS C., PRODHON C., "Solving the two-echelon location routing problem by a GRASP reinforced by a learning process and path relinking", *European Journal of Operational Research*, vol. 216, no. 1, pp. 113–126, 2012.

[NOR 15] NOROUZI N., SADEGH-AMALNICK M., ALINAGHIYAN M., "Evaluating of the particle swarm optimization in a periodic vehicle routing problem", *Measurement*, vol. 62, pp. 162–169, 2015.

[NOV 99] NOVÃES A., GRACIOLLI O., "Designing multi-vehicle delivery tours in a grid-cell format", *European Journal of Operational Research*, vol. 119, pp. 613–634, 1999.

[OR 76] OR I., Traveling salesman-type combinatorial optimization problems and their relation to the logistics of regional blood banking, PhD dissertation, Northwestern University, Evanston, IL, 1976.

[OSM 93] OSMAN I., "Metastrategy simulated annealing and tabu search algorithms for the vehicle routing problem", *Annals of Operations Research*, vol. 41, pp. 421–451, 1993.

[PAL 14] PALHAZI CUERVO D., GOOS P., SÖRENSEN K. *et al.*, "An iterated local search algorithm for the vehicle routing problem with backhauls", *European Journal of Operational Research*, vol. 237, no. 2, pp. 454– 464, 2014.

[PAR 12] PARRAGH S.N., CORDEAU J.-F., DOERNER K.F. *et al.*, "Models and algorithms for the heterogeneous dial-a-ride problem with driver-related constraints", *OR Spectrum*, vol. 34, no. 3, pp. 593–633, 2012.

[PAR 13] PARRAGH S.N., SCHMID V., "Hybrid column generation and large neighborhood search for the dial-a-ride problem", *Computers & Operations Research*, vol. 40, no. 1, pp. 490–497, 2013.

[PEN 13] PENNA P.H.V., SUBRAMANIAN A., OCHI L.S., "An iterated local search heuristic for the heterogeneous fleet vehicle routing problem", *Journal of Heuristics*, vol. 19, no. 2, pp. 201–232, 2013.

[PER 08] PERBOLI G., PEZZELLA F., TADEI R., "EVE-OPT: a hybrid algorithm for the capacitated vehicle routing problem", *Mathematical Methods of Operations Research*, vol. 68, no. 2, pp. 361–382, 2008.

[PI 04] PIÑANA E., PLANA I., CAMPOS V. *et al.*, "GRASP and path relinking for the matrix bandwidth minimization", *Discrete Optimization*, vol. 153, no. 1, pp. 200–210, 2004.

[PIS 07] PISINGER D., RÖPKE S., "A general heuristic for vehicle routing problems", *Computers & Operations Research*, vol. 34, pp. 2403–2435, 2007.

[PIS 10] PISINGER D., RÖPKE S., "Large neighborhood search", *Handbook of Metaheuristics*, Springer, pp. 399–419, 2010.

[POL 08] POLACEK M., DOERNER K., HARTL R. *et al.*, "A variable neighborhood search for the capacitated arc routing problem with intermediate facilities", *Journal of Heuristics*, vol. 14, no. 5, pp. 405–423, 2008.

[POP 12] POPOVI D., VIDOVI M., RADIVOJEVI G., "Variable neighborhood search heuristic for the inventory routing problem in fuel delivery", *Expert Systems with Applications*, vol. 39, no. 18, pp. 13390–13398, 2012.

[POT 96] POTVIN J.-Y., BENGIO S., "The vehicle routing problem with time windows - Part II: genetic search", *INFORMS Journal on Computing*, vol. 8, pp. 165–172, 1996.

[PRA 00] PRAIS M., RIBEIRO C., "Reactive GRASP: an application to a matrix decomposition problem in TDMA traffic assignment", *INFORMS Journal on Computing*, vol. 12, no. 3, pp. 164–176, 2000.

[PRI 01] PRINS C., "A simple and effective evolutionary algorithm for the vehicle routing problem", in *MIC 2001 (4th Metaheuristics International Conference)*, Porto, Portugal, pp. 143–148, 16–20 July 2001.

[PRI 04a] PRINS C., "A simple and effective evolutionary algorithm for the vehicle routing problem", *Computers & Operations Research*, vol. 31, pp. 1985–2002, 2004.

[PRI 04b] PRINS C., SEVAUX M., SÖRENSEN K., "A genetic algorithm with population management $(GA \mid PM)$ for the CARP", *Tristan V (5th Triennal Symposium on Transportation Analysis)*, Le Gosier, Guadeloupe, 13–18 June 2004.

[PRI 05] PRINS C., WOLFLER CALVO R., "A fast GRASP with path relinking for the capacitated arc routing problem", in GOUVEIA L., MOURÃO C. (eds.), *3rd International Network Optimization Conference (INOC)*, University of Lisbon, pp. 289–295, 2005.

[PRI 06] PRINS C., PRODHON C., WOLFLER-CALVO R., "Solving the capacitated location-routing problem by a GRASP complemented by a learning process and a path relinking", *4OR - A Quarterly Journal of Operations Research*, vol. 4, pp. 221–238, 2006.

[PRI 07] PRINS C., PRODHON C., RUIZ A. *et al.*, "Solving the capacitated location-routing problem by a cooperative Lagrangean relaxation - granular tabu search heuristic", *Transportation Science*, vol. 41, no. 4, pp. 470–483, 2007.

[PRI 09a] PRINS C., "Two memetic algorithms for heterogeneous fleet vehicle routing problems", *Engineering Applications of Artificial Intelligence*, vol. 22, pp. 916–928, 2009.

[PRI 09b] PRINS C., LABADIE N., REGHIOUI M., "Tour splitting algorithms for vehicle routing problems", *International Journal of Production Research*, vol. 47, pp. 507–535, 2009.

[PRI 09c] PRINS C., "A GRASP× evolutionary local search hybrid for the vehicle routing problem", *Bio-inspired Algorithms for the Vehicle Routing Problem*, Springer, pp. 35–53, 2009.

[PRI 14] PRINS C., LACOMME P., PRODHON C., "Order-first split-second methods for vehicle routing problems: a review", *Transportation Research Part C*, vol. 40, pp. 179–200, 2014.

[PRO 14] PRODHON C., PRINS C., "A survey of recent research on location-routing problems", *European Journal of Operational Research*, vol. 238, no. 1, pp. 1–17, 2014.

[RAH 13] RAHIMI-VAHED A., CRAINIC T.G., GENDREAU M. *et al.*, "A path relinking algorithm for a multi-depot periodic vehicle routing problem", *Journal of Heuristics*, vol. 19, no. 3, pp. 497–524, 2013.

[RAK 11] RAKKE J.G., STÅLHANE M., MOE C.R. *et al.*, "A rolling horizon heuristic for creating a liquefied natural gas annual delivery program", *Transportation Research Part C: Emerging Technologies*, vol. 19, no. 5, pp. 896–911, 2011.

[REG 96] REGO C., ROUCAIROL C., "A parallel tabu search algorithm using ejection chains for the vehicle routing problem", *Meta-Heuristics: Theory and Applications*, Kluwer, Boston, pp. 661–675, 1996.

[REG 98] REGO C., "A subpath ejection method for the vehicle routing problem", *Management Science*, vol. 44, no. 10, pp. 1447–1459, 1998.

[REI 04] REIMANN M., DOERNER K., HARTL R., "D-Ants: savings based ants divide and conquer the vehicle routing problem", *Computers & Operations Research*, vol. 31, no. 4, pp. 563–591, 2004.

[REP 10] REPOUSSIS P.P., TARANTILIS C.D., BRÄYSY O. *et al.*, "A hybrid evolution strategy for the open vehicle routing problem", *Computers & Operations Research*, vol. 37, pp. 443–455, 2010.

[RES 03] RESENDE M., RIBEIRO C., "Greedy randomized adaptive search procedures", in GLOVER F., KOCHENBERGER G. (eds.), *Handbook of Metaheuristics*, Kluwer Academic Publishers, pp. 219–249, 2003.

[RES 05] RESENDE M., RIBEIRO C., "GRASP with path relinking: recent advances and applications", in IBARAKI T., NONOBE K., YAGIURA M. (eds.), *Metaheuristics: Progress as Real Problem Solvers*, Kluwer Academic Publishers, pp. 29–63, 2005.

[RIB 12] RIBEIRO G.M., LAPORTE G., "An adaptive large neighborhood search heuristic for the cumulative capacitated vehicle routing problem", *Computers & Operations Research*, vol. 39, no. 3, pp. 728–735, 2012.

[ROC 95] ROCHAT Y., TAILLARD E., "Probabilistic diversification and intensification in local search for vehicle routing", *Journal of Heuristics*, vol. 1, no. 1, pp. 147–167, 1995.

[ROP 06] RÖPKE S., PISINGER D., "An adaptive large neighborhood search heuristic for the pickup and delivery problem with time windows", *Transportation Science*, vol. 40, no. 4, pp. 455–472, 2006.

[RUS 06] RUSSELL R., CHIANG W., "Scatter search for the vehicle routing problem with time windows", *European Journal of Operational Research*, vol. 169, pp. 606–622, 2006.

[SAL 99] SALHI S., NAGY G., "A cluster insertion heuristic for single and multiple depot vehicle routing problems with backhauling", *European Journal of Operational Research*, vol. 50, pp. 1034–1042, 1999.

[SAL 10] SALARI M., TOTH P., TRAMONTANI A., "An ILP improvement procedure for the open vehicle routing problem", *Computers & Operations Research*, vol. 37, no. 12, pp. 2106–2120, 2010.

[SAN 10] SANTOS L., COUTINHO-RODRIGUES J., CURRENT J., "An improved ant colony optimisation based algorithm for the capacitated arc routing problem", *Transportation Research Part B: Methodological*, vol. 44, no. 2, pp. 246–266, 2010.

[SAV 08] SAVELSBERGH M., SONG J.-H., "An optimization algorithm for the inventory routing problem with continuous moves", *Computers & Operations Research*, vol. 35, no. 7, pp. 2266–2282, 2008.

[SCH 00] SCHRIMPF G., SCHNEIDER J., STAMM-WILBRANDT H. *et al.*, "Record breaking optimization results using the ruin and recreate principle", *Journal of Computational Physics*, vol. 159, no. 2, pp. 139–171, 2000.

[SHA 98] SHAW P., "Using constraint programming and local search methods to solve vehicle routing problems", *Principles and Practice of Constraint Programming-CP98*, Springer, pp. 417–431, 1998.

[SIA 14] SIARRY P., *Métaheuristiques*, Eyrolles, 2014.

[SIE 98] SIERKSMA G., TIJSSEN G.A., "Routing helicopters for crew exchanges on off-shore locations", *Annals of Operations Research*, vol. 76, pp. 261–286, 1998.

[SIL 12] SILVA M.M., SUBRAMANIAN A., VIDAL T. *et al.*, "A simple and effective metaheuristic for the minimum latency problem", *European Journal of Operational Research*, vol. 221, pp. 513–520, 2012.

[SIL 15] SILVA M.M., SUBRAMANIAN A., OCHI L.S., "An iterated local search heuristic for the split delivery vehicle routing problem", *Computers & Operations Research*, vol. 53, no. 0, pp. 234 –249, 2015.

[SOL 98] SOLOMON M., DESROSIERS J., "Time windows constrained routing and scheduling problems", *Transportation Science*, vol. 22, pp. 1–22, 1998.

[SOR 06] SÖRENSEN K., SEVAUX M., "*GA | PM*: memetic algorithms with population management", *Computers & Operations Research*, vol. 33, no. 5, pp. 1214–1225, 2006.

[SOU 10] SOUFFRIAU W., VANSTEENWEGEN P., VANDEN BERGHE G. *et al.*, "A path relinking approach for the team orienteering problem", *Computers & Operations Research*, vol. 37, no. 11, pp. 1853–1859, 2010.

[SUB 12] SUBRAMANIAN A., PENNA P.H.V., UCHOA E. *et al.*, "A hybrid algorithm for the heterogeneous fleet vehicle routing problem", *European Journal of Operational Research*, vol. 221, no. 2, pp. 285–295, 2012.

[SZE 11] SZETO W., WUB Y., HO S.C., "An artificial bee colony algorithm for the capacitated vehicle routing problem", *European Journal of Operational Research*, vol. 215, pp. 126–135, 2011.

[TAI 93] TAILLARD E., "Parallel iterative search methods for vehicle routing problem", *Networks*, vol. 23, pp. 661–673, 1993.

[TAR 02] TARANTILIS C., KIRANOUDIS C., "Bone route: an adaptive memory-based method for effective fleet management", *Annals of Operations Research*, vol. 115, pp. 227–241, 2002.

[TAR 05] TARANTILIS C., "Solving the vehicle routing problem with adaptive memory programming methodology", *Computers & Operations Research*, vol. 32, pp. 2309–2327, 2005.

[TAR 08] TARANTILIS C.D., ZACHARIADIS E.E., KIRANOUDIS C.T., "A hybrid guided local search for the vehicle-routing problem with intermediate replenishment facilities", *INFORMS Journal on Computing*, vol. 20, no. 1, pp. 154–168, 2008.

[TAY 07] TAYLOR G.D., *Logistics Engineering Handbook*, CRC Press, Taylor & Francis Group, 2007.

[THA 95] THANGIAH S., "Vehicle routing with time windows using genetic algorithms", in CHAMBERS L. (ed.), *Application Handbook of Genetic Algorithms: New Frontiers*, CRC Press, pp. 253–277, 1995.

[THO 93] THOMPSON P., PSARAFTIS H., "Cyclic transfer algorithms for the multi-vehicle routing and scheduling problems", *Operations Research*, vol. 41, pp. 935–946, 1993.

[TIN 13] TING C.-J., CHEN C.-H., "A multiple ant colony optimization algorithm for the capacitated location routing problem", *International Journal of Production Economics*, vol. 141, no. 1, pp. 34–44, 2013.

[TOL 30] TOLSTOI A., "Metody nakhozhdeniya naimen'shego summovogo kilometrazha pri planirovanii perevozok v prostranstve [Methods of finding the minimal total kilometrage in cargo-transportation planning in space]", *Planirovanie Perevozok, Sbornik pervy [Transportation Planning, Volume I], Transpechat'NKPS [TransPress of the National Commissariat of Transportation]*, Moscow, pp. 23–55, 1930.

[TOT 02] TOTH P., VIGO D., (eds.), *The Vehicle Routing Problem*, Society for Industrial and Applied Mathematics, Philadelphia, PA, 2002.

[TOT 03] TOTH P., VIGO D., "The granular tabu search (and its application to the vehicle routing problems", *INFORMS Journal on Computing*, vol. 15, no. 4, pp. 333–346, 2003.

[TOT 14] TOTH P., VIGO D., *Vehicle Routing: Problems, Methods and Applications*, 2nd ed., SIAM, Philadelphia, 2014.

[USB 13] USBERTI F.L., FRANÇA P.M., FRANÇA A.L.M., "GRASP with evolutionary path-relinking for the capacitated arc routing problem", *Computers & Operations Research*, vol. 40, no. 12, pp. 3206–3217, 2013.

[VAN 87] VAN LAARHOVEN P.J., AARTS E.H., *Simulated Annealing: Theory and Applications*, Springer Science & Business Media, vol. 37, 1987.

[VAN 06] VANDERBECK F., SAVELSBERGH M.W., "A generic view of Dantzig-Wolfe decomposition in mixed integer programming", *Operations Research Letters*, vol. 34, no. 3, pp. 296–306, 2006.

[VAN 09a] VANSTEENWEGEN P., SOUFFRIAU W., BERGHE G.V. *et al.*, "A guided local search metaheuristic for the team orienteering problem", *European Journal of Operational Research*, vol. 196, no. 1, pp. 118–127, 2009.

[VAN 09b] VANSTEENWEGEN P., SOUFFRIAU W., BERGHE G.V. *et al.*, "Iterated local search for the team orienteering problem with time windows", *Computers & Operations Research*, vol. 36, no. 12, pp. 3281 –3290, 2009.

[VID 12a] VIDAL T., CRAINIC T.G., GENDREAU M. *et al.*, "A hybrid genetic algorithm for multidepot and periodic vehicle routing problems", *Operations Research*, INFORMS, vol. 60, no. 3, pp. 611–624, 2012.

[VID 12b] VIDAL T., CRAINIC T.G., GENDREAU M. *et al.*, A unifying view on timing problems and algorithms, Report no. 2012-59, CIRRELT, Montreal, Canada, 2012.

[VID 13a] VIDAL T., CRAINIC T.G., GENDREAU M. *et al.*, "Heuristics for multi-attribute vehicle routing problems: a survey and synthesis", *European Journal of Operational Research*, vol. 231, no. 1, pp. 1–21, 2013.

[VID 13b] VIDAL T., CRAINIC T.G., GENDREAU M. *et al.*, "A hybrid genetic algorithm with adaptive diversity management for a large class of vehicle routing problems with time-windows", *Computers & Operations Research*, vol. 40, no. 1, pp. 475–489, 2013.

[VID 14] VIDAL T., CRAINIC T.G., GENDREAU M. *et al.*, "A unified solution framework for multi-attribute vehicle routing problems", *European Journal of Operational Research*, vol. 234, pp. 658–673, 2014.

[VID 15] VIDAL T., CRAINIC T.G., GENDREAU M. *et al.*, "Timing problems and algorithms: time decisions for sequences of activities", *Networks*, vol. 65, no. 2, pp. 102–128, 2015.

[VIL 11] VILLEGAS J.G., PRINS C., PRODHON C. *et al.*, "A GRASP with evolutionary path relinking for the truck and trailer routing problem", *Computers & Operations Research*, vol. 38, no. 9, pp. 1319–1334, 2011.

[VIL 13] VILLEGAS J.G., PRINS C., PRODHON C. *et al.*, "A matheuristic for the truck and trailer routing problem", *European Journal of Operational Research*, vol. 230, no. 2, pp. 231–244, 2013.

[VOL 83] VOLGENANT A., JONKER R., "The symmetric traveling salesman problem and edges exchanges in Minimal 1-Tree", *European Journal of Operational Research*, vol. 12, pp. 394–403, 1983.

[VOU 96] VOUDOURIS C., TSANG E., "Partial constraint satisfaction problems and guided local search", *Proceedings, Practical Application of Constraint Technology (PACT'96)*, London, pp. 337–356, 1996.

[VOU 99] VOUDOURIS C., TSANG E., "Guided local search and its application to the traveling salesman problem", *European Journal of Operational Research*, vol. 113, no. 2, pp. 469–499, 1999.

[WAN 15] WANG C., MU D., ZHAO F. *et al.*, "A parallel simulated annealing method for the vehicle routing problem with simultaneous pickup–delivery and time windows", *Computers & Industrial Engineering*, vol. 83, pp. 111–122, 2015.

[WEI 15] WEI L., ZHANG Z., ZHANG D. *et al.*, "A variable neighborhood search for the capacitated vehicle routing problem with two-dimensional loading constraints", *European Journal of Operational Research*, vol. 243, no. 3, pp. 798–814, 2015.

[WOL 07] WOLF S., MERZ P., "Evolutionary local search for the super-peer selection problem and the p-hub median problem", in BARTZ-BEIELSTEIN T., BLESA AGUILERA M., BLUM C. *et al.* (eds.), *Hybrid Metaheuristics*, Springer, vol. 4771 pp. 1–15, 2007.

[WOL 11] WOLFLER CALVO R., TOUATI-MOUNGLA N., "A matheuristic for the dial-a-ride problem", *Network Optimization*, Springer, pp. 450–463, 2011.

[YAS 15] YASSEN E.T., AYOB M., NAZRIA M.Z.A. *et al.*, "Meta-harmony search algorithm for the vehicle routing problem with time windows", *Information Sciences*, vol. 325, pp. 140–158, 2015.

[YI 07] YI W., ÖZDAMAR L., "A dynamic logistics coordination model for evacuation and support in disaster response activities", *European Journal of Operational Research*, vol. 179, no. 3, pp. 1177–1193, 2007.

[YIL 14] YLDRM U.M., ÇATAY B., "A parallel matheuristic for solving the vehicle routing problems", *Computer-based Modelling and Optimization in Transportation*, Springer, pp. 477–489, 2014.

[YOU 14] YOUSEFIKHOSHBAKHT M., SEDIGHPOUR M., "A new imperialist competitive algorithm to solve the traveling salesman problem", *International Journal of Computer Mathematics*, vol. 90, no. 7, pp. 1495–1505, 2014.

[YU 08] YU Y., CHEN H., CHU F., "A new model and hybrid approach for large scale inventory routing problems", *European Journal of Operational Research*, vol. 189, no. 3, pp. 1022–1040, 2008.

[YU 09] YU B., YANG Z.Z., YAO B., "An improved ant colony optimization for vehicle routing problem", *Journal of Operational Research*, vol. 196, no. 1, pp. 171–176, 2009.

[YU 10] YU V.F., LIN S.-W., LEE W. *et al.*, "A simulated annealing heuristic for the capacitated location routing problem", *Computers & Industrial Engineering*, vol. 58, no. 2, pp. 288–299, 2010.

[YU 11a] YU B., YANG Z.Z., "An ant colony optimization model: the period vehicle routing problem with time windows", *Transportation Research Part E: Logistics and Transportation Review*, vol. 47, no. 2, pp. 166–181, 2011.

[YU 11b] YU B., YANG Z.Z., XIE J.X., "A parallel improved ant colony optimization for multi-depot vehicle routing problem", *Journal of the Operational Research Society*, vol. 62, no. 1, pp. 183–188, 2011.

[YU 14] YU V.F., LIN S.-W., "Multi-start simulated annealing heuristic for the location routing problem with simultaneous pickup and delivery", *Applied Soft Computing*, vol. 24, pp. 284–290, 2014.

[YU 15] YU V.F., LIN S.-Y., "A simulated annealing heuristic for the open location-routing problem", *Computers & Operations Research*, vol. 62, no. 0, pp. 184–196, 2015.

[ZAC 09] ZACHARIADIS E.E., TARANTILIS C.D., KIRANOUDIS C.T., "A hybrid metaheuristic algorithm for the vehicle routing problem with simultaneous delivery and pick-up service", *Expert Systems with Applications*, vol. 36, pp. 1070–1081, 2009.

[ZHA 12] ZHANG T., CHAOVALITWONGSE W., ZHANG Y., "Scatter search for the stochastic travel-time vehicle routing problem with simultaneous pick-ups and deliveries", *Computers & Operations Research*, vol. 39, no. 10, pp. 2277–2290, 2012.

[ZHO 05] ZHONG Y., COLE M.H., "A vehicle routing problem with backhauls and time windows: a guided local search solution", *Transportation Research Part E: Logistics and Transportation Review*, vol. 41, no. 2, pp. 131–144, 2005.

Index

A, C, D

adaptive large neighborhood search (ALNS), 36, 57–59, 69, 72–74, 125
destroy operator, 36
repair operator, 36, 57
ant colony optimization (ACO), 77, 86–89, 91, 106, 127
artificial bee colony (ABC), 91
capacitated vehicle routing problem (CVRP), 1, 6, 10, 11, 12, 16, 20, 24, 29–30, 33–36, 41, 43, 45–47, 57, 59, 65, 80, 81, 85, 89, 91, 105, 111, 112, 114, 115–118, 125, 145, 146
capacitated arc routing problem (CARP), 21, 35, 43, 55, 80–82, 85, 89, 92–96, 104
combinatorial optimization, 1, 5–7, 13, 14, 39, 79, 83, 86, 92, 106, 109, 145,
cumulative capacitated vehicle routing problem (CCVRP), 11, 28–30
decision level, 12, 125
operational level, 5
strategic level, 5
tactical level, 5

dial-a-ride problem (DARP), 10, 127
distance measure
broken pairs, 80, 104
Hamming, 80, 98–100, 104
diversification, 46, 53, 54, 61, 64, 82, 83, 90, 112, 143

E, G, H

evolutionary local search (ELS), 59–61, 75, 110–112, 114–118, 146
genetic algorithm (GA), 77–80, 82, 84, 86, 88, 101, 110, 111, 146
order crossover (OX), 81, 96, 104
greedy randomized adaptive search procedure (GRASP)
reactive GRASP, 54–56, 74, 110, 113, 114, 121,
guided tabu search (GTS), 44, 65–67, 112–114, 119, 121, 122, 129–134
harmony search (HS), 92
heterogeneous fleet vehicle routing problem (HFVRP), 9, 46, 134, 137, 138
heuristics, 15–37, 125, 126, 144, 147
Clarke and Wright, 17, 18, 23, 61, 66, 115, 119, 121
cluster-first route-second, 19, 20, 80, 124

constructive, 14, 16, 22, 33, 61, 64,
  80, 112, 113, 121, 132, 135,
  140
Gillett and Miller, 19
route-first cluster-second, 20, 122,
  124, 146
simple, 12, 15–37, 44, 47, 52, 74,
  75, 104, 109, 114, 117, 125,
  140
sweep, 19
hybrid genetic search with adaptive
  diversity control (HGSADC), 101,
  102, 104, 105

I, L

imperialist competitive algorithm
  (ICA), 91, 92
integrative cooperative search, (ICS),
  97
intensification, 15, 46, 61, 64, 79, 85,
  90, 106, 112, 113, 116, 145
inventory routing problem (IRP), 10,
  125–127
iterated local search (ILS), 50–54, 59,
  60, 74, 75, 110, 111, 127, 134, 135,
  137, 138, 146
large neighborhood search (LNS), 36,
  56–58, 69, 123, 127
last mile problem, 3, 4, 13
local search, 15–37, 41, 42, 44, 46–
  48, 50, 55, 59, 61, 77, 83, 110, 112,
  118
location-routing problem (LRP), 9,
  10, 41, 43, 53, 58, 61, 64, 65,69,
  74, 89, 125, 128, 131, 133
logistics, 1–6, 8, 9, 11, 13, 29, 125,
  126, 145
city, 4
reverse, 3
LP-based neighborhood reduction
  techniques, 123, 128

M

mathematical programming, 7, 122,
mathheuristics,109, 122–124, 144, 146
memetic algorithm (MA), 77, 79–81,
  106
memetic algorithm with population
integer, 1, 12, 14, 22, 56, 123–127,
  134, 145
linear, 12, 83, 123, 124, 126, 130,
  137
management (MA|PM), 77, 79
mixed integer, 56, 123, 126, 127,
  134
moves (in a local search), 23–36
acceleration techniques, 23, 33–36
classical, 23–25
complex, 23, 36
feasibility testing of
multi-depot periodic vehicle routing
  problem (MDPVRP), 92, 97, 98
multi-depot vehicle routing problem
  (MDVRP), 9, 101, 129, 146

O, P, R

open vehicle routing problem
  (OVRP), 46, 118, 119
particle swarm optimization (PSO),
  77, 89–91, 106, 111
path relinking (PR), 43, 77, 83–86,
  91, 92, 97–101, 111
penalty, 46, 54, 55, 66, 97, 100–105,
  110, 115, 121, 146
periodic capacitated arc routing
  problem (PCARP), 92–96
periodic vehicle routing problem
  (PVRP), 10, 101
pick up and delivery vehicle routing
  problem with time windows
  (PDPTW), 69, 70, 73, 74
reactive guided tabu search (ReGTS),
  119, 121, 122

record-to-record travel (RRT), 41
reduced variable neighborhood
  search (RVNS), 48, 74
resource-constrained project
  scheduling problem (RCPSP), 115,
  117, 118
restricted savings list (RSL), 119, 120
rich vehicle routing problems, 10

S, T

scatter search (SS), 77, 82–84, 92, 93,
  95, 96
  branching approaches, 127
  column generation, 123, 126, 127
  Dantzig–Wolfe decomposition,
    123, 126
  master problem, 102, 126, 127
  pricing problem, 126, 127
  referenceset (RefSet), 82–85
set partitioning problem (SPP), 126,
  127, 134, 135, 137, 138
simulated annealing (SA), 39–41, 43,
  44, 49, 51, 58, 69, 71, 75, 111
splitting procedure, 20, 21, 60, 93–
  95, 104, 117
supply chain, 2, 4, 5, 9
structural decomposition
  hierarchical decomposition, 124–
    126, 128
tabu search (TS), 44–47, 55, 61, 65,
  74, 111, 114, 121
  aspiration criteria, 44, 45
  long-term memory, 44–46
  mid-term memory, 45
  tabu lists, 44
  tabu tenure, 44, 45, 66, 133

team orienteering problem (TOP), 41,
  128, 138–140, 142, 143
time warp, 103
traveling salesman problem (TSP), 7,
  16, 17, 19, 20, 24, 29, 31, 34–36,
  46, 47, 55, 56, 59, 60, 80, 86, 90,
  92, 105, 124, 146
truck and trailer routing problem
  (TTRP), 9, 41, 59, 61
two-dimensional loading capacitated
  vehicle routing problem
  (2L-CVRP), 114–116, 118, 125
two-echelon location-routing problem
  (LRP-2E), 83, 61
two-echelon vehicle routing problem
  (VRP-2E), 9, 58

V

variable neighborhood descent
  (VND), 47–49, 74, 111, 136
variable neighborhood search, 47–52,
  57, 74, 110, 127, 128, 138, 144
  shaking, 48–50, 52
vehicle routing problem with
  simultaneous pickups and
  deliveries (VRPSPD), 91, 112, 114,
vehicle routing problem with split
  deliveries (SDVRP), 10, 104, 105,
  127
vehicle routing problem with time
  windows (VRPTW), 9, 13, 26, 28,
  33, 34, 46, 55, 58, 101, 102, 104,
  105, 125, 143,
very large scale neighborhood search
  (VLSN), 36, 58, 59

Other titles from

in

Computer Engineering

2015

BARBIER Franck, RECOUSSINE Jean-Luc
COBOL Software Modernization: From Principles to Implementation with the BLU AGE® Method

CHEN Ken
Performance Evaluation by Simulation and Analysis with Applications to Computer Networks

CLERC Maurice
Guided Randomness in Optimization (Metaheuristics Set - Volume 1)

DURAND Nicolas, GIANAZZA David, GOTTELAND Jean-Baptiste, ALLIOT Jean-Marc
Metaheuristics for Air Traffic Management (Metaheuristics Set - Volume 2)

MAGOULÈS Frédéric, ROUX François-Xavier, HOUZEAUX Guillaume
Parallel Scientific Computing

MAGOULÈS Frédéric, ZHAO Hai-Xiang
Data Mining and Machine Learning in Building Energy Analysis

MUNEESAWANG Paisarn, YAMMEN Suchart
Visual Inspection Technology in the Hard Disk Drive Industry

2014

BOULANGER Jean-Louis
Formal Methods Applied to Industrial Complex Systems

BOULANGER Jean-Louis
Formal Methods Applied to Complex Systems: Implementation of the B Method

GARDI Frédéric, BENOIST Thierry, DARLAY Julien, ESTELLON Bertrand, MEGEL Romain
Mathematical Programming Solver based on Local Search

KRICHEN Saoussen, CHAOUACHI Jouhaina
Graph-related Optimization and Decision Support Systems

LARRIEU Nicolas, VARET Antoine
Rapid Prototyping of Software for Avionics Systems: Model-oriented Approaches for Complex Systems Certification

OUSSALAH Mourad Chabane
Software Architecture 1
Software Architecture 2

QUESNEL Flavien
Scheduling of Large-scale Virtualized Infrastructures: Toward Cooperative Management

RIGO Michel
Formal Languages, Automata and Numeration Systems 1: Introduction to Combinatorics on Words
Formal Languages, Automata and Numeration Systems 2: Applications to Recognizability and Decidability

SAINT-DIZIER Patrick
Musical Rhetoric: Foundations and Annotation Schemes

TOUATI Sid, DE DINECHIN Benoit
Advanced Backend Optimization

2013

ANDRÉ Etienne, SOULAT Romain
The Inverse Method: Parametric Verification of Real-time Embedded Systems

BOULANGER Jean-Louis
Safety Management for Software-based Equipment

DELAHAYE Daniel, PUECHMOREL Stéphane
Modeling and Optimization of Air Traffic

FRANCOPOULO Gil
LMF — Lexical Markup Framework

GHÉDIRA Khaled
Constraint Satisfaction Problems

ROCHANGE Christine, UHRIG Sascha, SAINRAT Pascal
Time-Predictable Architectures

WAHBI Mohamed
Algorithms and Ordering Heuristics for Distributed Constraint Satisfaction Problems

ZELM Martin *et al.*
Enterprise Interoperability

2012

ARBOLEDA Hugo, ROYER Jean-Claude
Model-Driven and Software Product Line Engineering

BLANCHET Gérard, DUPOUY Bertrand
Computer Architecture

BOULANGER Jean-Louis
Industrial Use of Formal Methods: Formal Verification

BOULANGER Jean-Louis
Formal Method: Industrial Use from Model to the Code

CALVARY Gaëlle, DELOT Thierry, SÈDES Florence, TIGLI Jean-Yves
Computer Science and Ambient Intelligence

MAHOUT Vincent
Assembly Language Programming: ARM Cortex-M3 2.0: Organization, Innovation and Territory

MARLET Renaud
Program Specialization

SOTO Maria, SEVAUX Marc, ROSSI André, LAURENT Johann
Memory Allocation Problems in Embedded Systems: Optimization Methods

2011

BICHOT Charles-Edmond, SIARRY Patrick
Graph Partitioning

BOULANGER Jean-Louis
Static Analysis of Software: The Abstract Interpretation

CAFERRA Ricardo
Logic for Computer Science and Artificial Intelligence

HOMES Bernard
Fundamentals of Software Testing

KORDON Fabrice, HADDAD Serge, PAUTET Laurent, PETRUCCI Laure
Distributed Systems: Design and Algorithms

KORDON Fabrice, HADDAD Serge, PAUTET Laurent, PETRUCCI Laure
Models and Analysis in Distributed Systems

LORCA Xavier
Tree-based Graph Partitioning Constraint

TRUCHET Charlotte, ASSAYAG Gerard
Constraint Programming in Music

VICAT-BLANC PRIMET Pascale *et al.*
Computing Networks: From Cluster to Cloud Computing

2010

AUDIBERT Pierre
Mathematics for Informatics and Computer Science

BABAU Jean-Philippe *et al.*
*Model Driven Engineering for Distributed Real-Time Embedded Systems
2009*

BOULANGER Jean-Louis
Safety of Computer Architectures

MONMARCHE Nicolas *et al.*
Artificial Ants

PANETTO Hervé, BOUDJLIDA Nacer
Interoperability for Enterprise Software and Applications 2010

PASCHOS Vangelis Th
Combinatorial Optimization – 3-volume series
Concepts of Combinatorial Optimization – Volume 1
Problems and New Approaches – Volume 2
Applications of Combinatorial Optimization – Volume 3

SIGAUD Olivier *et al.*
Markov Decision Processes in Artificial Intelligence

SOLNON Christine
Ant Colony Optimization and Constraint Programming

AUBRUN Christophe, SIMON Daniel, SONG Ye-Qiong *et al.*
Co-design Approaches for Dependable Networked Control Systems

2009

FOURNIER Jean-Claude
Graph Theory and Applications

GUEDON Jeanpierre
The Mojette Transform / Theory and Applications

JARD Claude, ROUX Olivier
Communicating Embedded Systems / Software and Design

LECOUTRE Christophe
Constraint Networks / Targeting Simplicity for Techniques and Algorithms

2008

BANÂTRE Michel, MARRÓN Pedro José, OLLERO Hannibal, WOLITZ Adam
Cooperating Embedded Systems and Wireless Sensor Networks

MERZ Stephan, NAVET Nicolas
Modeling and Verification of Real-time Systems

PASCHOS Vangelis Th
Combinatorial Optimization and Theoretical Computer Science: Interfaces and Perspectives

WALDNER Jean-Baptiste
Nanocomputers and Swarm Intelligence

2007

BENHAMOU Frédéric, JUSSIEN Narendra, O'SULLIVAN Barry
Trends in Constraint Programming

JUSSIEN Narendra
A to Z of Sudoku

2006

BABAU Jean-Philippe *et al.*
From MDD Concepts to Experiments and Illustrations – DRES 2006

HABRIAS Henri, FRAPPIER Marc
Software Specification Methods

MURAT Cecile, PASCHOS Vangelis Th
Probabilistic Combinatorial Optimization on Graphs

PANETTO Hervé, BOUDJLIDA Nacer
Interoperability for Enterprise Software and Applications 2006 / IFAC-IFIP I-ESA'2006

2005

GÉRARD Sébastien *et al.*
Model Driven Engineering for Distributed Real Time Embedded Systems

PANETTO Hervé
Interoperability of Enterprise Software and Applications 2005

Lightning Source UK Ltd.
Milton Keynes UK
UKOW06n1942160316

270298UK00007B/29/P